CW00799140

SOUL EXERCISES

SOLUTIONS

SOUL EXERCISES

Word and Symbol Meditations

1904 – 1924

TRANSLATED BY MATTHEW BARTON
INTRODUCTION BY HELLA WIESBERGER

RUDOLF STEINER

SteinerBooks

CW 267

Copyright © 2014 by SteinerBooks

SteinerBooks
Anthroposophic Press

610 Main Street
Great Barrington, Massachusetts 01230
www.steinerbooks.org

Translated from the German by Matthew Barton.

This book is volume 267 in the Collected Works (CW) of Rudolf Steiner, published by SteinerBooks, 2014. It is a translation of *Seelenübungen I, Übungen mit Wort- und Sinnbild-Meditationen zur methodischen Entwicklung höherer Erkenntniskräfte, 1904–1924*, published by Rudolf Steiner Verlag, Dornach, Switzerland,1997.

Library of Congress Cataloging-in-Publication Data is available.

ISBN: 978-0-88010-628-3 (print)
ISBN: 978-0-88010-665-8 (eBook)

All rights reserved.
No part of this book may be reproduced in any form without written permission from the publisher, except for brief quotations embodied in critical articles for review.

CONTENTS

PART ONE
GENERAL RULES

PART TWO
MAIN EXERCISES
FOR MORNING AND EVENING

A

Nine groups of exercises – each group using one meditative verse
(1904 to about 1914)

B

Exercises with individually composed meditative verses

C

Further meditations without indication of "morning / evening"

PART THREE

EXPLANATIONS RELATING
TO THE EXERCISES

APPENDIX

EDITOR'S COMMENTARIES

TRANSLATOR'S FOREWORD

Human language only approximates the realities it seeks to embody. The more abstract and intellectual it becomes, the further removed it can often be from its source in living realities. In a passage quoted in this volume (p. xxxv), Rudolf Steiner wonderfully conveys how he has wrestled with earthly language to make it a vessel for subtle insights:

> Those who gain this type of vision remove themselves from what can be expressed in language. Their vision initially does not find its way to their lips. If they reach for words, they immediately sense that the content of their vision changes. If they wish to communicate their visions, their battle with language begins. They try everything possible within the realm of language to form a picture of what their vision shows them. From sound qualities to turns of phrase and syntax they search the field of language. They fight a tough, inner battle. They have to acknowledge that language has its own idiosyncratic willfulness. It can express all sorts of things as it likes, and we have to submit to its willfulness so that it incorporates what we perceive. In trying to pour spiritual vision into words, we do not, in fact, encounter an indeterminate, malleable element that we can form as we like, but instead a living spirit, the spirit of language. If we battle honestly in this way, the best, the loveliest outcome can emerge. A moment arrives when we feel that the spirit of language takes up what we have seen in vision.[1]

The translator of meditations such as those gathered here faces the same task, in a sense, all over again. Translation, too, is only an approximation of the spirit that the author originally invested in his "sound qualities...turns of phrase and syntax," his formulations and rhythms.

---

1. In *Das Goetheanum*, July 23, 1922.

Auden famously said that "poetry is what is lost in translation." To recreate the spirit of prose in a new language is hard enough; but to convey something of the living organism of a poem or meditation is sometimes nearly impossible. Steiner certainly claimed a special status for such meditations:

> One would have to write a great many books to fully exhaust the meaning of these verses, for besides the fact that every word in them is meaningful, there is meaning in the symmetry of their words, the way they are arranged, the intensifications at work in them, and much more; and therefore only long, patient devotion to them can fully fathom what they contain.[2]

In other words, poetry and meditative verses are already several steps away from mundane language; they are heading back (or forward) into the deep, complex and often ineffable springs of reality. This is the essential nature of "mantric verse."

One of the dangers in translating such verses is that the translator subtly interposes himself, his own interpretations, into his "versions," unwittingly directing the reader toward a particular sense of them and thus narrowing their original scope. I have tried my utmost to render them "faithfully"; but the reader should be aware that this faithfulness inevitably passes through my own limited capacities, and is colored by them and by the intrinsic difficulties of "re-conjuring" the original lines in a new form.

Even in the realm of something as apparently mundane as punctuation, a problem immediately emerges. Steiner's own punctuation of the verses is often either non-existent or erratic. Frequently he did not even place a period at the end of the verse, thus seemingly leaving it "open." In pondering this, I came to two conclusions: first, that he regarded punctuation as being of very secondary importance to the process of

---

2. *Bilder okkulter Siegel und Säulen. Der Münchener Kongress Pfingsten 1907 und seine Aus-wirkungen*, CW 284, 1993 edition, p. 40. Published in English as: *Rosicrucianism Renewed The Unity of Art, Science, & Religion: The Theosophical Congress of Whitsun 1907*, 13 lectures, various cities, 1907–1924, SteinerBooks 2007.

receiving intuitions and wrestling with language to convey them; but second, also, that punctuation itself, of such eminent value in prose, is a means to guide, govern, and at times abruptly halt the living flow of language, and thus comes from a more analytic and intellectual side of the psyche. It points up specific meaning, shows how a phrase is to be understood. Steiner says, however, that the character of mantric verses is "such that it sometimes renders grammatical structure difficult."[3] In other words, lack of punctuation in many of the original verses may be at least partly intentional. It often seems to ask the readers to make an effort of insight instead of doing this for them; to ponder more deeply on how exactly each line relates to another; and, in fact, to allow that ambiguities and multiple meanings may sometimes be intrinsic to the verses.

In the end I decided to follow Steiner in largely avoiding punctuation except where he himself emphatically punctuates a verse. Although its absence may strike the reader as odd, there are good precedents for this in modern poetry, such as that of M.S. Merwin. And it does seem to me that the greater effort needed to read without punctuation's guiding hand is inherent in the meditative process. However, I did not follow Steiner in capitalizing the initial letter of each line, which had been common in all verse until the second half of the twentieth century, since this now seems a somewhat outmoded convention.

Rhythm is another whole realm of vital importance in the original versions and their translation. Each verse is, as I have suggested, an organism that lives in its own subtle rhythms, which often cannot simply be brought over wholesale from the original, but must be discovered afresh in the new language.

Finally there is the realm of musical sound so vital in mantric verse; of vowels and consonants and their relationships, and the deep qualities they convey below (or above) the level of rational "meaning." In a passage quoted at the end of this volume (see page 421), Steiner explored the vowel qualities of the verse that occurs most frequently of all in this book, and his account implicitly highlights some of the problems—in fact the impossibilities—of translation. The German original is as follows:

---

3. Berlin, January 19, 1915, in CW 157.

In den reinen Strahlen des Lichts
Erglänzt die Gottheit der Welt
In der reinen Liebe zu allen Wesen
Erstrahlt die Göttlichkeit meiner Seele
Ich ruhe in der Gottheit der Welt
Ich werde mich selbst finden
In der Gottheit der Welt.

Like so many other verses in this book it contains seven lines; and the reason for that could be the subject of a further set of reflections. In living with this verse over many months, repeatedly speaking it aloud and silently both in German and in my own changing English versions, I gradually arrived at a translation that I think "will do," although inevitably it remains only an attempt.

In the pure rays of the light
gleams out the godhood of the world
in pure love for every being
shines out the godliness of my soul
I rest in the godhood of the world
I will find myself
in the godhood of the world.

This "final" version has sacrificed a great deal in returning, I hope, to something like the clarity and economy, and thus the power of vision, of the original. I repeatedly had to weigh up and make choices about sound, rhythm, and coloring. At one point I had "gleams forth" and "shines forth"; but though I liked the fire sound of the "f," the "orth" seemed to darken and weigh down the verse, whereas "out" retained its original brightness.

I would also, however, like to offer another "attempt" here, which some readers may prefer because it stays closer to the original mantric vowel sounds:

In the pure shafts of the light
gently gleams the godhood of the world
in pure love for every being
shines out the godliness of my soul
I am rooted in the godhood of the world
I will find myself
in the godhood of the world.

In comparing these two versions and their subtle differences, readers may perhaps get insight into the problems of translating meditations such as these. Any version will always be only provisional. And greater "faithfulness" to mantric sounds may be (as I believe to be the case here) at the expense of some shade of meaning intimately interwoven with those sounds in German. Although "rooted" echoes *ruhe* more closely, for instance (though it brings the "oo" vowel up short in an abrupt "t" sound), the idea of rest and repose in the ground of the world has been altered, if not lost. It was for such reasons that I often ultimately went for deeper underlying meaning, as I experienced it, than for mantric sound, despite inevitable regret at this loss.

Matthew Barton, January 6, 2013

PREFACE TO THIS EDITION

This volume forms part of the Collected Works of Rudolf Steiner, which are divided into three major sections comprising his writings, lectures, and artistic works.

From 1900 until his death, Rudolf Steiner (1861–1925) presented his anthroposophic science of the spirit in publications, numerous lectures, and lecture courses. Following a request from German theosophists, he embarked on his spiritual-scientific work in association with the Theosophical Society, which was founded in 1875 by, among others, the Russian seer Helena Petrovna Blavatsky. In 1902 the German section of this society was founded with Steiner as its general secretary, and was developed by him in association with Marie Steiner-von Sivers. When the German section was expelled ten years later (1912–13) because of profound differences with the organization's governing body in India, it formed a separate, independent entity as the Anthroposophical Society.

Between 1904 and 1914, alongside his work as writer and lecturer, Rudolf Steiner taught in his Esoteric School. This work was interrupted by World War I (1914–1918) and the post-war years; it was re-established in 1923–24 when all anthroposophic activity was reorganized and given a new impetus at the Christmas Foundation Meeting. In line with his lifelong efforts to anchor anthroposophy in the public domain as a modern science of initiation, he then began to develop the "School for Spiritual Science at the Goetheanum" with three esoteric classes and various scientific and artistic "sections." But succumbing to grave illness in the fall of 1924, which led to his death in 1925, he was unable to do more than establish the first resources of the School (see GA volumes 260, 260a and 270).

Documentary compilations relating to Rudolf Steiner's esoteric teaching activity (as yet not published in their entirety in English) include the present volume, which collects so-called "main exercises" for morning and evening practice with meditative verses. These also include exercises given in written correspondence, published in the first volume of the series.[4]

All these exercises and meditative verses originated between 1904 and 1924. Despite closing the Esoteric School in the summer of 1914, after the outbreak of World War I, Rudolf Steiner continued to give such exercises to people during private conversations, right up to the time when he fell ill at the end of September 1924. Apart from a few exceptions, he always wrote these out by hand. A great many of them (probably most) were collected by Marie Steiner either as original, photocopy, or written or verbal communication. After her death they passed to the Rudolf Steiner Estate and also to the Goetheanum executive. We are grateful that they have been made available for the present publication. It must be remembered, however, that because of World War II some material has been lost over the decades. Nor can we entirely exclude the possibility that relevant documents, still unknown to us, may exist in private bequests.

For the purposes of publication, the material was divided into groups as they appear in the Contents. In Group A, especially, a selection had to be made because many of the exercises are almost identical. Subject to this proviso, the aim here has been to offer as complete a compilation as possible.

A purely chronological order was not possible since less than half of all exercises can be dated. Overall, though, the chronological sequence is apparent. All exercises of the nine groups with identical meditation verses were composed between 1904 and around 1908, but continued to be given to pupils of the Esoteric School until 1914. The exercises consisting of single meditative verses originated largely in the years between 1910 and 1924. The dates given in the index were compiled from various archive documents, and are also noted at the top left corner of the individual pages. Exercises with the Rose Cross symbol date from 1907 onward, and those which refer to the book *Esoteric*

---

4. See CW 264, *From the History and Contents of the First Section of the Esoteric School 1904–1914. Letters, Documents, and Lectures.* SteinerBooks 2007.

Science were composed after 1910. Any exercises containing the word "theosophy" were given before 1913.

The exercises not based on original manuscripts but only communicated verbally were included only if they were clearly fully authentic. These are marked with an "A" preceding an archive number.

Dorothea and Julius Zoll-Weyrather compiled the index, and I would like to thank them for their help in extensive initial work on this volume and its overall shape.

For more in relation to the original texts see the editorial and reference notes in the Appendix at the end of the volume beginning on page 455.

* * *

Can exercises given to specific individuals be of general use?

It is worth pointing out that Rudolf Steiner himself clearly believed this important question can be answered in the affirmative. Connected with a certain incident in the early summer of 1917 (see page xxxviii) he said in a personal conversation[5] that his intention was for all exercises "to be printed for the widest possible public." He would scarcely have proposed this if he had regarded them as worthless for others. Although he himself did not undertake publication of this material, Marie Steiner, his close collaborator for many years and the beneficiary of his will, did initiate it in the final years of her life.

Furthermore, the exercises themselves reveal that the same initial conditions applied to all pupils on the spiritual-scientific path of schooling. They all, in fact, show the same basic structure; likewise, they accord with exercises described in published works. In numerous exercises, too, meditative verses appear with the same wording.

All this indicates the general applicability of these meditative exercises originally given to particular individuals.

H.W.

5. According to a written communication from Professor Hans Wohlbold to the Rudolf Steiner Estate, dated May 12, 1949.

INTRODUCTION

Accounts of the anthroposophic path of schooling in Rudolf Steiner's works

HELLA WIESBERGER

This volume contains texts originating in a personal relationship between teacher and pupil. Since this is a very distinct part of the spiritual schooling taught by Rudolf Steiner, in what follows I will try to show, albeit in outline only, how this part of his work relates to his whole *oeuvre*.

———

One cannot separate Rudolf Steiner's works from his biography. Everything he taught was personally accomplished and developed by him, in the same way that, by his own testimony, his major philosophical work, *The Philosophy of Freedom*, contained "personal experience in every line."[6] He developed the book's philosophical outlook in relation to the nature of pure thinking, as his own personal point of departure. Twenty years later, he proposed it as the necessary starting point for those "who wish to undergo their own esoteric development," formulating this in the following simple yet vivid terms:

> A great figure of the Enlightenment was held to have expressed something of great importance when he said in the eighteenth century: "Man, dare to use your faculty of reason!" Today, a still greater phrase needs to resound in our souls: "Man, dare to see your concepts and ideas as the beginnings of your clairvoyant faculties!"

———

6. Letter dated November 4, 1894, to Rosa Mayreder, in *Briefe* ["Letters"] vol. II, 1891–1924, CW 39.

Real seership could not develop if one did not already have a "grain" of clairvoyance in one's soul (initially in one's concepts and ideas), which can be developed to an increasing and unlimited extent. This is why it is important to understand that clairvoyance really starts with very mundane things. "We need only grasp the suprasensory nature of our concepts and ideas," becoming clear that these enter our soul not from the sensory world, but from worlds of spirit.[7]

Steiner himself developed his scientific outlook and ethics of freedom from this grasp of the suprasensory nature of concepts and ideas; and he was able to realize ethical individualism, also in the realm of esoteric research, through the resulting "emancipation of *higher* human consciousness from the chains of all authority."[8] He regarded it as his special task to make individual research the sole basis of his work. From the beginning of his spiritual-scientific endeavors, he stressed that what he developed in this field would be oriented to "the starting point initiated in *The Philosophy of Freedom*."[9] This remark accords with the statement at the same period about pure thinking as the core idea of *The Philosophy of Freedom*: "I regard this pure thinking as the first still shadowy revelation of spiritual stages of knowledge."[10]

Until Rudolf Steiner embarked on his work, secrecy and strict personal tutelage governed all serious paths into suprasensory worlds. He was the first to initiate a modern path to spiritual knowledge without dependence on authority. In order to make this path available to humanity as a whole, the results of his spiritual research were always reported alongside an account of the method by which he had gained them. He once referred to this as follows:

We can distinguish two aspects of what is now called anthroposophy. The one is the type of thinking used, the mode of enquiry

7. Helsingfors [Helsinki], May 29, 1913, CW 146.
8. Letter of December 14, 1983, to Rosa Mayreder, op. cit.
9. Dornach, October 27, 1918, CW 185.
10. Essay, "Spiritual science as anthroposophy and the contemporary theory of knowledge," 1917, in: *Philosophy and Anthroposophy*, CW 35.

and research involved. The other is the content, the results of this spiritual research, insofar as it has been possible to elaborate these.[11]

Development of these two aspects occurred, naturally, as a gradual process.

I

The epistemological foundation

A capacity to meet the reality of the conceptual realm is something I have presented as primary philosophical experience, saying also that such an experience allows us to stand in the world as a confluence of the human "I" and the content of the spiritual world. I have tried to show that this experience is just as real as sensory experience. The spiritual content of anthroposophy has grown out of this primary experience of spiritual insight.[12]

In his *Autobiography*, Rudolf Steiner related how, as a child he already experienced the world as dual reality: "I had two notions which, although somewhat vague, played a great part in my inner life before I was eight. I distinguished between things and entities 'one sees' and those 'one does not see'." And although the world of spirit was as self-evident for him as the world of the senses, he felt the need for a "kind of justification" of this other realm of experience: "I wanted to be able to tell myself that my experience of the spiritual world was not illusory but as real as that of the sensory world." The eight-year-old then had an experience that helped orient him. He discovered a book on geometry in his village schoolmaster's classroom; and entirely on his own, he began

---

11. Dornach, June 5, 1920 (not yet included in the CW [complete works]).
12. Review: "Alois Mager's book *Theosophy and Christianity*. My experience in reading this book," November 1924 in *Der Goetheanumgedanke inmitten der Kulturkrise der Gegenwart*, CW 36.

to explore mathematical ideas enthusiastically. He felt an inner joy at "being able to grasp something purely in the mind." And it struck him that, as in geometry, when the soul "experiences things through its own powers alone" then inevitably one gains inner knowledge of the spiritual world. Looking back to his relationship with geometry he saw "the first surfacing of an outlook" that gradually developed and assumed a "fully conscious form" when he was about twenty.[13]

Following this experience of geometry he sought increasingly to develop his powers of thinking. He tried to delineate every thought clearly, to avoid its being pulled in some uncontrolled direction by any vague, passing feeling. He also wished to form a clear view about how "human thinking relates to the creative life of nature."[14] Thus his striving for knowledge focused tirelessly on the scientific outlook of the time, and on philosophical views of the nature of knowledge, that informed the intellectual life of the second half of the nineteenth century.

In the scientific domain, Darwin and Haeckel's theories of the natural evolution of living creatures and the human being were having a revolutionary impact, and had radically undermined traditional views of divine creation. Rudolf Steiner witnessed how a great many people began to question past ideals and religious convictions, being compelled to believe that if scientific views were correct, then human beings must be the product of natural necessity. In this case, all ideals and religious persuasions would be illusory, and freedom would be impossible.[15] In philosophy, the prevailing view was that we come up against certain limits to knowledge, which human consciousness cannot move beyond. Thus it must accept these limits and forego any knowledge of what lies as true reality beyond the world it creates within itself.

Rudolf Steiner was unable to embrace contemporary evolutionary theory wholeheartedly because it failed to take any account of the

---

13. *Autobiography*, CW 28, chapter 1. All quotations from works already published in English have been translated anew for this volume.
14. *Autobiography*, CW 28, chapter 2.
15. Public lecture in Stuttgart on May 25, 1921, in *Beiträge zur Rudolf Steiner Gesamtausgabe*, no. 116, 1996.

autonomous existence and activity of the spirit. Nor could he accept the postulate of limits to knowledge. His own experience of cognition told him that when sensory reality is "properly known," it shows itself to be a manifestation of spirit; and that when we develop and deepen our thinking sufficiently, we live "within world reality as a spiritual realm."[16]

He became ever more convinced, therefore, that a new worldview was needed to do full justice to both halves of reality—nature and spirit. He was clear from the outset that the scientific value of this new outlook would depend on the soundness of its epistemological basis. Only when a theory of knowledge, as a foundational science of the diverse sciences, was able to show that they are all predicated on the very nature of cognition itself, would it be possible to clarify the relationship of each scientific domain to the world, and thus arrive at a true worldview. In contrast to previous theories of knowledge (none of which, he found, had dispensed with underlying assumptions) this required proof through "analysis of the act of cognition delving back into its ultimate elements" that "our thinking can attain everything necessary for explaining and fathoming the world."[17] This fundamental idea was already present in his very first written attempt to reformulate Fichte's *Science of Knowledge* in 1879, written during the period between his completion of secondary education and the start of his studies at Vienna's technical college.[18]

At the beginning of the 1880s, Steiner was commissioned to edit and write commentaries on Goethe's scientific writings for Kuerschner's German National Literature series; and in doing so, he explored Goethe's epistemological approach to diverse fields of research. It became ever clearer to him that his own outlook was in harmony with Goethe's worldview. He therefore wrote his first epistemological work as a supplement to Goethe's scientific writings—*Goethe's Theory of Knowledge: An Outline of the Epistemology of His Worldview* (1886).

---

16. *Goethe's Theory of Knowledge: An Outline of the Epistemology of His Worldview*, CW 2, Preface to the New Edition 1924.
17. *Truth and Science*, CW 3, Preface.
18. In *Beiträge...* No. 30, summer 1970.

Nearly forty years later, when he reissued this text in 1923, Steiner wrote in the preface to the new edition that this text still seemed to him to be the "basis and justification of all he had subsequently stated and published," since it speaks of the nature of cognition as releasing us from the sensory world and pursuing a path into a world of spirit.

Looking back to his initial basic research at various later points, he always stressed that his principal question at the time concerned the extent to which one can prove the reality of spirit at work in human thinking. To solve this question, he set himself the task of comprehending the nature of human thinking itself. To do so, he first set aside all visions of a spiritual world available to him. In his words,

> ... however convincing subjective visions might be, however intensely they rise before the soul, one is not justified in concluding objective validity from their subjective emergence, unless one is also able to span a bridge from sure scientific foundations to the world of spirit.

By every means possible he tried to discover the real nature of human thinking, until he realized that we can properly understand this thinking only if we see in its highest expressions something that is accomplished "independently of corporeal organization." This meant that already in the "most mundane daily life" there is a "suprasensory" element, if we can only raise ourselves to pure thinking, where we are not governed or determined by anything other than the contents of thinking itself; rather than what proceeds from bodily processes as the natural necessity of instincts, will impulses, and so forth.[19]

He had therefore gained the certainty required to span a bridge between science and spirit knowledge:

> I tried to build this bridge already in my introductions to Goethe's scientific writings [1883–1897]. Then I pursued this particularly in my little book *Truth and Science* [1892] and my longer book *The*

---

19. Public lecture, Stuttgart May 25, 1921, in *Beiträge...*, no. 116, 1996.

Philosophy of Freedom [1894].... And I believe that this *Philosophy of Freedom* confirmed for me nothing less than the suprasensory nature of human thinking.[20]

In Steiner's view, he had therefore found proof that our capacity to penetrate the reality of the spiritual realm can be epistemologically substantiated just as fully as the way we penetrate sensory reality. And for him this justified the claim of exact scientific procedure in developing, in accordance with the "model of pure thinking," stages of higher knowledge passing through imagination, inspiration, and intuition.

In my spiritual-scientific writings I present processes of cognition that lead, through spiritual experience and observation, to concepts of the spiritual world in just the same way as our senses and the rationality associated with them lead to concepts of the sensory world, and the human life unfolding in it. In my view this can be justified as truly scientific only if there exists proof that the process of pure thinking itself is already the first stage in processes by means of which suprasensory knowledge can be attained. I believe that I have given such proof in my earlier writings.[21]

After developing anthroposophy (at that time still called "theosophy") over a ten-year period, Steiner was asked to give a lecture on theosophy at the fourth international philosophy conference in Bologna (April 1911). The title of his lecture was "Theosophy's Psychological Foundations and Epistemological Stance."[22] He concluded his observations with the following words:

The soul disposition of the spiritual researcher can only be understood as a state in which the illusion of ordinary consciousness is overcome, giving rise in the soul to an incipient experience of the

---

20. Op. cit.
21. Essay, "Spiritual science as anthroposophy and the contemporary theory of knowledge," 1917, in *Philosophy and Anthroposophy*, CW 35.
22. Quoted in *Philosophy and Anthroposophy*, CW 35.

core and essence of the human being in free release from the corporeal organism. Everything else that can then be achieved through practice is only a deeper delving into the transcendent, in which the "I" of ordinary consciousness really resides, although it may be unaware that it does. Spiritual research is therefore proven to be epistemologically conceivable. This conceivability, of course, will be acknowledged only by those who can accept that our so-called critical theory of knowledge maintains the impossibility of a leap in consciousness solely by failing to penetrate the illusion that the core human entity is imprisoned in the body and can receive only sensory impressions. I am aware that my epistemological comments here offer only rough indications. However, it may be possible to see from these suggestions that they are not isolated instances; but, in fact, arise from a fully developed underlying epistemological outlook.

II

Public (exoteric) accounts of spiritual schooling

> I wish to build on the power that enables me to help spiritual pupils embark on self-development. That must be the whole import of my inaugurating deed.[23]

Toward the end of the nineteenth century, Rudolf Steiner became ever more certain that if suprasensory knowledge (which he saw as essential for the flourishing of further human development) were to become common currency in a form fully appropriate to modern consciousness, then it would have to be conveyed other than in purely scientific and philosophical ways. He therefore wondered how to "express the inner truths of my vision in a way that could be understood

---

23. Letter of August 16, 1902, to Wilhelm Hübbe-Schleiden. Published so far only in the first edition of "Letters II," Dornach 1955.

by the modern age."[24] Having wrestled with this question, he resolved to go public with detailed accounts of the world of spirit.

To really get a sense of the gravity of this decision, we should recall that at that period suprasensory knowledge was known as something to be cultivated only within strictly closed circles, in the form of ancient traditions and symbols. An initial breach had been made in this tradition of secrecy by H.P. Blavatsky's publications; but among the general public there was greater interest in sensational phenomena such as somnambulism, mediumism and spiritualism. Rudolf Steiner inevitably rejected such things, because of his view of higher human powers of cognition. His spiritual insight showed him that "supposed perception," which fails to acknowledge pure thinking as a kind of model, and moves in the realm of spirit without the same degree of careful reflection and inner clarity as sharply delineated thinking, "cannot lead us into a real world of spirit."[25] At the time therefore, since prevailing scientific circles repudiated anything suprasensory as wholly suspect, great courage was needed for a well-known writer in the fields of science and philosophy to publicize his detailed perceptions of suprasensory realities and to claim scientific respectability for them.

When, in the final year of the nineteenth century, he began to act on this decision, he took his point of departure from a cultural legacy that he had long regarded as one of the "most profound texts in world literature. This was Goethe's mysterious fairytale, *The Green Snake and Beautiful Lily*.[26] He saw this tale as an expression of the fact that Goethe had always regarded the human faculty of knowledge as capable of development, and that this indicated nothing other than the principle of initiation: "Initiation therefore means nothing other than enhancing human capacities to ever-higher levels of knowledge and perception; and thus achieving deeper insights into the true nature of the world."[27]

---

24. *Autobiography*, CW 28, chapter 23.
25. Essay, "Spiritual science as anthroposophy and the contemporary theory of knowledge," 1917, in *Philosophy and Anthroposophy*, CW 35.
26. Munich, May 22, 1907, CW 99.
27. Berlin, October 24, 1908, CW 57.

In his essay, "Goethe's secret revelation. In celebration of the 150th anniversary of Goethe's birth. August 1899," Steiner began by transposing the content of the fairytale's images into modern concepts. He showed that the fairytale is concerned with the great question of how to develop the powers of our psyche in a new era in which we seek to rise from an earthly realm to a spiritual realm. The solution to this riddle, he said, is hinted at in the story. Previously there were only two states of soul that enabled people to reach suprasensory realms, both involuntary.

One was through creative imagination, which is a reflection of suprasensory experience; and the other arises when conscious perception is darkened and weakened, in the form of superstition, visions, and mediumistic states. The time had arrived, said Steiner, for a new state of awareness that could be *consciously and intentionally* created. This, however, required "the snake," representing sensory forms of knowledge, to gain the insight that the highest can be achieved only through selfless devotion and sacrifice. As soon as the snake is willing to give up her own, self-referential existence, her body forms itself into a bridge over the great river, uniting the two realms of sensory and spiritual reality, and allowing *all* to pass over it.[28]

No one is likely to have noticed at the time that this transposition of Goethean images into modern conceptual language was also a significant step in cultural history, although this became ever more apparent as time passed. Just one year later, in the fall of 1900, Rudolf Steiner was invited to give lectures to a group of people who, although not scientists, were profoundly interested in real spiritual knowledge. This was the Berlin group of the Theosophical Society, which H.P. Blavatsky and others had founded in America in 1875, and which relocated its headquarters to India shortly afterward. In this group of Berlin theosophists, who were open to detailed accounts of spiritual insight, Steiner was now able to speak "very esoterically" of things he had only hinted at in his essay on Goethe's fairytale. "For me it was

---

28. The essay of 1899 is contained in CW 30, "Methodical Foundations of Anthroposophy." A new edition was published in 1918 (see CW 22, "Goethe's Spirit as Revealed in His Faust and the Fairytale of the Snake and the Lily").

an important experience to be able to speak in words informed by the world of spirit, having previously been compelled by circumstances ... to allow the spiritual realm to shine through what I had to say in only a veiled way."[29]

This lecture on the fairytale became the "germ" of the anthroposophic movement. The first, decisive phrase in the tale, "The time has come!" is uttered in a mighty voice by the "old man with the lamp," a figure who guides and directs all that occurs. That phrase gained added force from the growing realization of the tale's second phrase: "One person alone does not help, but rather he who unites with many at the right time." Teacher and pupils have a mutually enhancing effect. With this in mind, after being invited in the spring of 1902 to take on the role of general secretary of the new German section of the society, and just before accepting it, Rudolf Steiner described how he saw his task in a letter to a representative of the German theosophists. "I wish to build on the power which enables me to help spiritual pupils embark on self-development. That must be the whole import of my inaugurating deed."[30] From then on, with increasing intensity, he elaborated his spiritual science, at the same time developing an association geared to cultivating this work and representing it publicly.

Whereas his essay on Goethe's fairytale (1899) could only hint at the new initiation principle, this was now clearly documented in the first two series of lectures he gave to the theosophists in Berlin, published as *Mystics after Modernism* (CW 7, 1901) and *Christianity as Mystical Fact* (CW 8, 1902). In the foreword to *Mystics after Modernism*, he expressed his conviction that the modern achievements of science need enhancing into true mysticism, stating that it is perfectly possible to be both a "faithful adherent of the scientific worldview" and yet at the same time also seek "the paths of the soul" that lead to an appropriate mysticism. Indeed, one can gain a full understanding of natural phenomena only if one acknowledges the spirit as true mysticism does. Likewise in his foreword to *Christianity as Mystical Fact*, which examines Christianity in

---

29. *Autobiography*, CW 28, chapter 30.
30. See note 23.

the context of the Mysteries, and thus in terms of initiation, he wrote: "I hope I have written no single line that I could not justify in terms of a truly self-comprehending examination of nature, nor one that agrees with the crassly materialistic view of many modern scientific thinkers."

As his work continued, his insight into the nature of Christianity, its "mystical fact," became ever more profound and was accentuated in relation to the path of schooling. The death of Christ at Golgotha enabled the power of Christ, previously found only in spiritual heights, to unite with earthly evolution. Since then, there lives within the soul of each of us the strength to find the path into the world of spirit by our own resources. By contrast, before that event, this was possible only by adhering to the authority and instructions dispensed by teachers in the Mystery schools.

It is therefore due to the Golgotha event that we can attain higher knowledge through spiritual self-education. This can happen, though, only if we make ourselves into appropriate instruments. Just as no one can see that water contains hydrogen and oxygen (which have quite different properties from water), by mere external observation, and without chemical analysis, so we cannot recognize the true reality of the soul and spirit without using methods of spiritual-scientific research to release soul and spirit from external corporeality. This, however, is a different kind of process, one that takes place within the soul and must be prepared in its most profound depths.[31] Guidance and instruction necessary for this could not, however, be taught publicly until the required forces of the consciousness soul developed, as they did increasingly from the fifteenth and sixteenth centuries. Only in consequence of this did it become possible for a scientist with spiritual vision to elaborate the methodology of the path of knowledge and teach this methodology in public. For a modern spiritual researcher who works in this way, the time of the old prophets is now past. As a "sober investigator," the researcher desires only to draw attention to what is needed in order to pursue studies of the human soul's profundities. The spiritual researcher says: "I have found this; and if you search for it, you too

---

31. Norrköping, July 13, 1914, CW 155.

will find it!" In Steiner's view the time would soon come when people would regard a spiritual researcher, like a chemist or biologist, as a "sober investigator." The only difference is that the spiritual researcher inquires into a realm that closely concerns every human soul.[32]

As we move on into the future, the importance of Rudolf Steiner's work will inevitably be seen primarily in the methodology he developed for all of us, as a pioneer in his field. Prior to this, no such method existed for independent and reproducible verification of the reality of the world of spirit.

Theosophy (1904) was Steiner's first written introduction to the suprasensory foundations of the world and humanity. It has a final chapter entitled "The Path of Knowledge" in which he first publicly described the conditions necessary for pursuing a spiritual-scientific methodology. In this first account, he stressed, above all, that higher faculties of cognition can proceed only from thinking, since this is the highest capacity that we possess within the sensory world. Immediately after this, in ongoing essays, he began to describe specific stages on this path, later published in *How to Know Higher Worlds*. Its first sentence states: "In each of us slumber capacities by means of which we can acquire knowledge of higher worlds." In further publications, in particular the major work *Esoteric Science* (1910), and in many lectures, besides publicizing ongoing new research findings, he also kept adding new aspects of the path of spiritual schooling.

We can see the importance Rudolf Steiner himself ascribed to these public accounts of the path of schooling from statements such as the following:

In our time the principle of initiation has undergone a mighty change insofar as it can be achieved, to a certain degree, a certain level, without direct personal instruction, by virtue of the fact that today one can present the principles of initiation in the public domain; I did this in my book *How to Know Higher Worlds*. Anyone who makes earnest efforts to follow and experience what

---

32. Berlin, February 3, 1913, CW 144).

is described there can make a great deal of progress in relation to the principle of initiation.[33]

It would be a misunderstanding, however, to conclude from these words that anyone interested in spiritual science must embark on spiritual schooling. Steiner expressed his view about this in a personal letter as follows: "Theosophy is necessary today.... However, it would be undesirable for every theosophist to decide to become an esoteric pupil. This would be rather as if everyone thought they had to become tailors because *everybody* needs clothes."[34] He also stated this in public: "I would expressly point out that there is no need for every person to become a spiritual researcher in order to gain the proper soul benefit from spiritual science or anthroposophy."[35] Although he was very concerned to help spiritual pupils embark on self-development, the primary need, as he saw it, was for a knowledge of the reality of the spiritual world to increasingly inform humanity in general through the publicizing of spiritual-scientific research results. However, he considered it essential that this should occur in a way appropriate to the nature of such knowledge, and not in some diluted or popularized form. For this reason, he said, he had intentionally given his writings a character that required real efforts of thinking to engage with their content. He was clear that such activation of thinking already contained the seeds of spiritual schooling.[36] In another context one even finds the following remark: "I do not lecture on theosophy for any external reason but because this is the first stage of Rosicrucian initiation."[37] By "Rosicrucian," however, he did not mean the return to some historical body of knowledge, but rather a further evolving and living Rosicrucianism. For this reason too, what is presented in *How to Know Higher Worlds* as "the most suitable

---

33. Berlin, February 3, 1913, CW 144.

34. Letter dated Sept. 20, 1907, in CW 264, *From the History and Contents of the First Section of the Esoteric School 1904–1914. Letters, Documents, and Lectures.* SteinerBooks 2007.

35. "Human life from the perspective of spiritual science (anthroposophy)" in *Philosophy and Anthroposophy*, CW 35.

36. *Esoteric Science*, CW 13, preface to the 16th–20th editions.

37. Munich, June 6, 1907, CW 99.

path" into the spiritual spheres should not be confused with what can be called the Rosicrucian path. "Our stream," which encompasses a far broader field than that of the Rosicrucians, should be designated simply as "modern spiritual science," or as "anthroposophically-oriented spiritual science of the twentieth century."[38]

After years of tireless lecturing throughout Europe, and thus developing more widespread understanding for spiritual science, Steiner was then able to start presenting his research method in the more precise thought-forms of a science of cognition. *Esoteric Science*, published in 1910, has two main sections, "World Evolution and the Human Being" and "Knowledge of Higher Worlds," in which he proposed that study of spiritual-scientific communications is a sure path leading to sense-free thinking. He stated that there is also another way "that is still more sure and above all more focused, yet at the same time harder for many people"; that is, the path he outlined in his epistemological writings, especially in *The Philosophy of Freedom*. Although these texts made no reference to spiritual science, they showed, he said, that pure thinking, working on its own terms, can give us insight into the world, life, and human nature.

> These texts stand at a very important intermediate stage between knowledge of the sense world and that of the spiritual world. They offer what thinking can achieve if it raises itself above sensory observation without as yet engaging in spiritual research. Those who allow these writings to work upon their whole soul already stand within the world of spirit, except that this world reveals itself to them as a thought world. Those who feel able to let this intermediate stage work upon them are pursuing a sure path; and through it they can achieve a sense of higher worlds that will subsequently bear the finest fruits for them.[39]

One can say that this reference to the epistemological writings as intermediate stage between perception of the sensory world and of

---

38. Karlsruhe, October 6, 1911, CW 131.
39. Op. cit., in the chapter "Knowledge of Higher Worlds."

the spiritual world is a bridge leading to the account that Steiner next elaborated, of the three-level cognitive method of imagination, inspiration, and intuition. In April 1911, at the philosophers' conference at Bologna mentioned earlier, he gave a lecture on "Theosophy's Psychological Foundations and Epistemological Stance."[40] In his subsequent books, *The Riddles of Philosophy* (with its final chapter entitled "From Philosophy to Anthroposophy" [1914]), *The Riddle of Humanity* (1916), and *Riddles of the Soul* (1917), he further elaborated the epistemological and philosophical foundations of his anthroposophic spiritual research. These writings include several key essays published between 1916 and 1918 (all in CW 35), as well as his reflections published in 1922 in the weekly *Das Goetheanum* on a cycle of ten lectures, containing a particularly incisive, concentrated formulation of the spiritual research method and the knowledge of the world and the human being gained through it.[41] In 1923, four further essays followed in *On the Life of the Soul.*[42] There he stressed repeatedly that there was an entirely organic train of development starting from basic epistemological views expressed in *Truth and Science* and *The Philosophy of Freedom* through to the content of spiritual science or "anthroposophy."

Not only in publications but also in public events (conferences, School for Spiritual Science courses, and so forth), he described the method used for gaining spiritual-scientific insights, showing how these can make the diverse sciences more fruitful. At the first School course at the Goetheanum,[43] he once again pointed out, as he had done in 1910 in *Esoteric Science*, that there are two different means to describe the path of knowledge. "In my book *How to Know Higher Worlds*, the path described for entering suprasensory realms is a safe and sure one; and it is described in a way that makes it suitable for those without any real scientific training or experience." But someone who wishes to

---

40. Quoted in *Philosophy and Anthroposophy*, CW 35.
41. *Cosmology, Religion and Philosophy*, CW 25.
42. Anthroposophic Press 1985, from CW 36.
43. Lecture in Dornach October 3, 1920, in *The Boundaries of Natural Science*, CW 322, AP 1983.

pursue the path of knowledge as a scientist should engage with what is presented as pure thinking in his *Philosophy of Thinking*, proceeding from this via the other pole of knowledge, perception, toward imagination. Steiner regarded this path as more appropriate for western culture. The exercises for cultivating this path are, however, the same in nature as those in *How to Know Higher Worlds* and in this present volume. They are all based on meditative engagement with symbolic images, metaphors, and ideas, as also described in the lecture at the philosophy conference in Bologna in 1911 (see p. 403 of this volume).

It was clear to Rudolf Steiner from the very outset that true spirit knowledge must be incorporated into mainstream science for the sake of all cultural progress. In the difficult years after World War I, this moved him and his colleagues to establish courses that could awaken interest and understanding of the science of the spirit and its methodology in people with a scientific background. In words that can move us today because they still largely apply, he spoke of his efforts in this direction, looking back at the ways he had been trying, for more than twenty years, to explain to the world how spiritual researchers arrive at their findings.

> If I have not had greater success in eliciting a general response to this anthroposophically-oriented spiritual science; if it has repeatedly been necessary instead to speak to those without scientific training, who are therefore not so used to attending to details; and if it has not really been possible to speak to those with a science background, then in my experience this is due largely to these scientists themselves. Up until now they have shown very little inclination to listen to what spiritual researchers have to say about their paths to knowledge. Let us hope that this may change in future. You see, it really is essential to find an upward path by accessing deeper powers than those which are clearly incapable of helping us progress because, basically, they have led us into cultural decline.[44]

---

44. Stuttgart, March 18, 1921, CW 324.

III
Internal (esoteric) accounts

> My sole endeavor is this: to communicate what I am able to
> investigate in suprasensory worlds to contemporary human-
> ity, in a form of knowledge aware of its due responsibility
> toward modern science. I present what, as I see it, is either
> entirely appropriate to modern humanity at its current stage
> of intellectual maturity, or other things for which certain
> groups of people are in the process of acquiring maturity
> through (esoteric) preparation.[45]

It was not at all because Rudolf Steiner, an exotericist *par excel-
lence*, wished to withhold certain spiritual truths from the public that
he also worked as an esoteric teacher. The esoteric, as he presented
it, was for him, rather, a specific form of expression of what, as true
esoteric life, ultimately cannot be uttered in words at all, but can only
be experienced. If it is necessary to reach for words in order to chart
the paths that lead to such experiential capacity, this depends a great
deal on the teacher's ability to formulate such things. "One says it first
exoterically, then esoterically, and in speaking in both an exoteric and
esoteric way, one is, as it were, resorting to two different dialects of an
inexpressible language."[46] This means that "there is no absolute boundary between exoteric and esoteric, but one flows into the other."[47] And
this is because "at the moment we find a form of expression for the
inner nature of something, we have rendered the esoteric as exoteric.
The esoteric, therefore, can never be communicated in any other way
than exoterically."[48]

---

45. October 1924: "Aphoristic notes on the book *Reformation or Anthroposophy*" (by
Edmund Ernst) in CW 36.
46. Dornach, October 18, 1915, CW 254.
47. Stuttgart, June 12, 1921, CW 342.
48. See *Beiträge...* No.51/52, Michaelmas 1975, p. 35.

Often over the years Steiner spoke of the objective difficulty involved in transposing what he saw in spiritual vision into the conceptual language of modern times.

If we approach language with the great treasures of wisdom that are unveiled in our souls and try to pour into words what is inwardly revealed to us, a battle arises with this really very weak instrument of language, which in certain respects is hugely inadequate.[49]

The reason why such a "fierce inner battle" is involved in this process becomes clear in his short essay "Language and the Spirit of Language."[50] It is due to the fact that, in working our way through from merely conceptual thinking to revelatory vision, the soul discovers the living power of the spirit of language.

Those who gain this type of vision remove themselves from what can be expressed in language. Their vision initially does not find its way to their lips. If they reach for words, they immediately sense that the content of their vision changes. If they wish to communicate their visions, their battle with language begins. They try everything possible within the realm of language to form a picture of what their vision shows them. From sound qualities to turns of phrase and syntax they search the field of language. They fight a tough inner battle. They have to acknowledge that language has its own idiosyncratic willfulness. It can express all sorts of things as it likes, and we have to submit to its willfulness so that it incorporates what we perceive. In trying to pour spiritual vision into words, we do not, in fact, encounter an indeterminate, malleable element that we can form as we like, but instead a living spirit, the spirit of language. If we battle honestly in this way, the best, the loveliest outcome can emerge. A moment arrives when we feel that the spirit of language takes up what we have seen in vision. The words

___

49. Bern, September 2, 1910, CW 123.
50. Contained in CW 36.

and phrases we arrive at themselves assume something of a spiritual quality. They cease "meaning" what they usually mean and slip into the content of vision. Then something like a living dialog with the spirit of language unfolds. Language assumes a personal character and we engage with it as with another human being.[51]

If we consider the wealth of research findings that Steiner communicated during more than two decades, we can get a sense, in regard to what he said above, of the spiritual achievement necessary to transpose the suprasensory realities he perceived into the language of modern thought. This was essential for speaking of them in public; for only in that form could modern awareness accept them, or cast doubt on, or reject them, in full freedom. By contrast, there were other conditions governing the representation of spiritual realities that cannot yet "be revealed in the form of ideas," either at all, or only at certain times.[52] Such communications required a group of people who wish to pass from the exoteric to the esoteric. In other words, people who were prepared to undertake to engage with such truths with the degree of responsibility appropriate to their nature. This is indicated in the note stating that certain communications depend on "particular groups of people" who "are in the process of acquiring maturity through (esoteric) preparation."[53]

We can see from the history of such groups taught by Rudolf Steiner, that he met with some disappointment in this respect; and that here too, in consequence, the trend toward the exoteric became ever stronger over time.

The first group for such esoteric preparation was called the Esoteric School.[54] It was established at the same time as accounts of the path

---

51. In *Das Goetheanum*, July 23, 1922.
52. Essay, "The Free School for Spiritual Science, I." (Dornach, January 20, 1924) in CW 260a.
53. See note 45 above.
54. This school existed from 1904 until the outbreak of World War I in the summer of 1914. Initially it was administered as a department of the Theosophical Society's Esoteric School of Theosophy directed by Annie Besant. When Annie Besant sought appointment as the president of the T.S. in 1907, and used esoteric matters for her campaign, Rudolf Steiner, in agreement with her, dissolved this administrative connection at the Munich Congress. For more on this, see CW 264.

of schooling were published in the book *Theosophy*, in the essays comprising *How to Know Higher Worlds*, and in *The Stages of Higher Knowledge* in 1904/05. The aim of the Esoteric School was to help "spiritual pupils embark on the path of self-development" through specific instruction. Such a school was also necessary because the whole cultural situation at the beginning of the century showed clearly that spiritual-scientific teachings would fall on "half-deaf ears" without a foundation of people who wished to make spiritual development a key aspect of their lives.[55]

Initially there was a very small number of esoteric pupils; this made it possible for them to receive personal instruction. This was in line with Rudolf Steiner's principle that only individual developmental processes exist, rather than development in general: "There is only development of one or the other person, or of a third, a fourth or a thousandth."[56] Schooling instructions in published texts, by contrast, have to be general in character. Between 1910 and 1913, in his four Mystery Dramas, he resolved in exemplary artistic form the problem of how individual developmental processes could be represented. After the initial performance of the first of these plays, *The Portal of Initiation: A Rosicrucian Mystery*, based on images contained in Goethe's fairytale, he referred as follows to the two ways of representing the path of schooling: "Whereas the book *How to Know Higher Worlds* contains, as it were, the starting point and the secret of every person's self-development, the *Portal of Initiation* relates the secret of the development of a single person, that of Johannes Thomasius." Accounts in the books *How to Know Higher Worlds* and *Esoteric Science* inevitably "have an abstract, a semi-theoretical character despite their specificity" because they are applicable to every human individual. By contrast, the play was able to offer "a really much more intense, lifelike, and real" representation, because it was "much more individual." He was convinced, in fact, that he would no longer need to speak of many things "in the realm of the

---

55. Letter dated April 16, 1903, to Marie von Sivers in *Correspondence and Documents 1901–1925*, CW 262, Anthroposophic Press 1988.
56. Berlin, October 31, 1910, CW 125.

esoteric, the occult," if all that was contained in the Rosicrucian play "took effect in the souls of our dear friends and diverse other people."[57]

After the outbreak of the World War I in the summer of 1914, it seemed better to close the Esoteric School because under war conditions closed meetings might have seemed suspicious. Nevertheless, people continued to ask him for personal esoteric instruction. He complied with such requests in many personal conversations, although he already considered that personal instruction was no longer needed, since there was now enough published schooling material available. In the preface to the fifth edition of *How to Know Higher Worlds*, dated September 7, 1914, he stressed the following:

> At the time [1904/05 when the essays comprising the book were written] it seemed clear to me that much which the book did not contain could be received by "personal communication." Today, *a great deal* has now been published that I referred to in this way. Such references may not have entirely excluded possible misconceptions in readers, however. For instance, some may have attributed much greater importance than necessary to the personal relationship which a person seeking spiritual schooling has with a particular teacher. I hope that I have succeeded in this new edition in emphasizing more clearly that, under the spiritual conditions prevailing today, it is much more important to gain a full, direct relationship with the objective world of spirit than with the personality of a teacher. In spiritual schooling such a teacher will increasingly exercise the function of a guide or helper, as is the case, in line with modern views, in any other field of study.

Steiner was compelled to stress this again within the Anthroposophical Society in the spring of 1917, when former members of the society accused him in a public journal of giving people harmful exercises.[58] At the time he categorically refused to continue to give esoteric advice in private conversations. In future, everything must be done in full

---

57. Berlin, October 31, 1910, CW 125.
58. In "Psychische Studien" XLIV, Leipzig 1917.

transparency in the public domain. He stated that there was sufficient schooling material available (one should just read *How to Know Higher Worlds*) and that he would soon show that private conversations of this kind were no longer in the least necessary for esoteric practice: "They will soon be entirely replaced."[59] In fact this happened seven years later, when the esoteric school was re-founded in an entirely new form as the "School for Spiritual Science at the Goetheanum."

Steiner's intention, as voiced within the Anthroposophical Society at this time, to bring the mode of esoteric tuition fully into line with contemporary ideas, clearly led to his repeated emphasis in a public lecture of that year[60] that anthroposophy aimed to live entirely in accordance with the transparency demanded by the *zeitgeist*. He continued by saying that although much still seemed like "the old institutions" (in 1917), this was only insofar as certain preparations were necessary in order to understand subsequent developments. The eighth edition of *How to Know Higher Worlds*, published soon after this (May 1918) was consistent with this stated aim. As previously in the preface to the 1914 edition, it made clear that "statements regarding the need for an esoteric pupil to receive personal instruction should be understood to mean that the book itself offers personal instruction." And the article entitled "Former Secrecy and Modern Disclosure," published two months later, in July 1918, concludes with the words:

> We live in an age in which suprasensory knowledge can no longer remain a secret possession of the few. It must instead become the common possession of all who sense in their souls a need to fathom the meaning of life. This need is already far more active and widespread in unconscious depths of soul than many are aware. This will increasingly manifest as a need for greater worth to be accorded to suprasensory cognition, giving it equal status with scientific inquiry.

---

59. Lectures in Stuttgart on May 11 and 13, 1917, in CW 174b; Munich, May 19, 1917, in CW 174a; Leipzig, June 10, 1917 (not yet published in the CW).
60. Berlin, October 19, 1917, CW 72.

In 1923/24, when Rudolf Steiner set about reconfiguring the whole anthroposophic movement in line with necessary public transparency, and released for publication typescripts of lectures previously available only to members, he sought also to re-establish the esoteric school in accordance with this principle. The "School for Spiritual Science at the Goetheanum" was to be the first public esoteric school, for "secret societies are no longer possible today; our modern era requires something different," and "steps would be taken" to insure "'that what they do will be known as widely as possible."[61] The only reservation, self-evident, was (as applies equally in the public school system) that no one will be admitted to a higher level of study before being conversant with lower ones. Accordingly, spiritual science was to be cultivated within the Anthroposophical Society in the form of ideas, because it is appropriate for people today to encounter the spiritual world through ideas initially. In the three classes of the School for Spiritual Science, students were also to be led upward by degrees into realms of the spiritual world that "cannot be revealed in the form of ideas... Here we encounter the need to find the means of expressing imaginations, inspirations, and intuitions."[62]

In fact, because of the death of Rudolf Steiner one and a half years later, only the first of the planned three esoteric classes could be established; and only "the first section of this first class," as he noted in the last of the Dornach class lessons, the nineteenth. In these class lessons, esoteric instruction was no longer divided (as it had been in the former Esoteric School) into personal exercises and lectures for all; but was given in the form of meditative verses, and their exegesis, in wording that was the same for all who attended.[63] Rudolf Steiner's comments on these two different modes of instruction can be found on page 442 of this present volume.

61. Dornach, January 30, 1924, CW 260a.
62. Essay, "The School for Spiritual Science...I," (Dornach January 20, 1924) in CW 260a.
63. CW 270/ I–IV.

IV

The esoteric exercises

> The aim of contemplation (meditation) of symbolic pictures
> and feelings is, specifically, to develop higher organs of
> perception within the human being's astral body. These
> organs are initially created from the substance of this astral
> body. (*Esoteric Science*)

In order to perceive in higher worlds we need healthy organs of perception, just as we do in the physical world. The prime concern of every esoteric schooling has therefore always been to carefully develop such organs. All the exercises that Rudolf Steiner gave are also focused on achieving this; and there are many accounts of how to do so in his works, most fundamentally in *How to Know Higher Worlds*. That book also explains the effect of the exercises, for "the principles of true esoteric science include being fully aware of what we are doing when we devote ourselves to it. We should undertake nothing, practice nothing without knowing what effect it has. An esoteric teacher giving someone advice or instruction will always also say what effect it will have on the body, soul and spirit of the person seeking higher knowledge."

The extent to which we can fulfill the first requirement of the spiritual-scientific schooling method (development of the astral body's organs of perception) is repeatedly described as follows. During daily life we are entirely given up to external impressions acting on our senses and reason. The astral body participates in this, since it is fully immersed in the physical body while we are awake. Even when it leaves the physical body as we fall asleep, it is still subject to the after-effect of these forces. It adheres to the elasticity of the physical body rather than to its own laws, and is therefore prevented from developing its own organs. If this is to change, something "very specific" must be accomplished with the physical body while we are awake, in order for this to be imprinted in the astral body and subsequently resonate during the night. For this change to happen, we must take our inner life in hand through a methodical schooling: "This is called meditation, concentration, or contemplation. These are exercises governed by instructions that are as strict in the schools where they are taught as, say, the regulations governing how to examine objects under a microscope in laboratories." The nature of the exercises is based on teachers applying "all knowledge" about the effects of the exercises that has been gathered over millennia of human experience. Such teachers know that these exercises work intensively to cause the astral body, on emergence from the physical body during sleep, to liberate itself from the after-effects of the latter and acquire its own intrinsic form; or in other words, gradually unfold the organs necessary for higher perception. If the wrong exercises are done, however, then "forms contrary to nature" are built into the astral body; perverted forms in disharmony with the greater context of the world. This is why those who decide to undertake such exercises also take on a great responsibility.[64]

This is no doubt one of the key reasons why Steiner repeatedly stressed that the spiritual-scientific method is the most appropriate one for westerners. Although the human significance of such exercises is the same in all schools of initiation, they were focused more on schooling the powers of thinking in pre-Christian times, and more on schooling forces of heart and soul in the time since Christ. Since the fourteenth century, however, because of the changed nature of the times, a "special kind of will culture, of will exercises" were introduced in the so-called Rosicrucian schools.[65]

The three main types of initiation method that have developed through the post-Atlantean period are characterized as having these differences, along with the changing nature of the teacher-pupil relationship. Thus we have the ancient eastern yoga method, the Christian-Gnostic method, and the Christian-Rosicrucian method, or its continuation as the spiritual-scientific method. Before Steiner gave these accounts, however, he first clarified that there are other methods besides that of ancient Indian schooling, which at that time was the only path discussed in the Theosophical Society. This clarification was

---

64. Hamburg, May 30 and 31, 1908, CW 103; Nuremberg, June 18 and 19, 1908, CW 104; Munich, August 24, 1909, CW 113.
65. Nuremberg, June 19, 1908, CW 104.

also immediately published. In the journal *Lucifer-Gnosis* (May 1905), in a very positive review of the recently published German translation of Annie Besant's lectures, *Path of Discipleship*, Steiner went on to stress that the path outlined there is right for people of Indian ancestry, and that this fact should not go unmentioned. While there is but "one truth," he said, and the highest summit of knowledge and life for all times and all people is also a "single" one, it would be wrong to think that the path of discipleship can be the same for people in modern Europe as for the people of India:

> While intrinsic nature remains the same, the forms alter in this realm. For this reason it must be seen as quite natural that various things are presented differently in the articles in this journal entitled *How to Know Higher Worlds* from the way they appear in lectures that Annie Besant gave for the people of India. The path described in this journal has developed in the esoteric schools of Europe since the fourteenth century as rightful adaptation to western life and the stage of development of Europeans. And Europeans can be successful in such endeavors only if they pursue this path as directed by their own esoteric teacher.

This does not mean there is no point in Europeans' becoming acquainted with what is appropriate for the people of India:

> The current stage of development for Europeans requires them to acquaint themselves with everything through their rational faculties. To progress, reason must compare and contrast, measuring what it possesses against what is more distant from it. It must hearken to the beneficial guidance given to our brothers in the Far East. This is why books such as this one should be gladly welcomed, and not because the same can be done in Europe.[66]

Shortly after this, in essays in the same journal entitled *The Stages*

66. CW 34.

of Higher Knowledge (CW 12), Steiner began to describe the three possible modes and methods of initiation embodied in ancient eastern yoga, Christian-Gnostic, and Rosicrucian initiations. He stated that he would soon give a "precise account" of the differences between these three methods, and under what circumstances it might be possible for an esoteric pupil "even in modern Europe, not to pursue the Rosicrucian, but the eastern path, or the older Christian path; although the Rosicrucian path is the most natural one for our times." This latter, he said, was not only just as Christian as the older Christian path, but could also be undertaken by people "who believe they stand at the summit of a modern, scientific worldview." This precise account was never forthcoming, however, because Rudolf Steiner's workload meant that the journal ceased publication. From then on, though, in lectures to theosophists, he repeatedly described the stages involved in each of these three methods.[67]

V

The meditative verses —
the heart of the esoteric exercises

One would have to write a great many books to fully exhaust the meaning of these verses, for besides there being meaning in every word, there is meaning in the symmetry of their words, the way they are arranged, the intensifications at work in them, and much more; and therefore, only long, patient devotion to them can fully fathom what they contain.[68]

---

67. See for example the Stuttgart lecture cycle of August 1906, published as *Founding a Science of the Spirit*, CW 95, Rudolf Steiner Press 1999.

68. *Bilder okkulter Siegel und Säulen. Der Münchener Kongress Pfingsten 1907 und seine Auswirkungen*, CW 284, 1993 edition, p. 40. Published in English as: *Rosicrucianism Renewed – The Unity of Art, Science, & Religion: The Theosophical Congress of Whitsun 1907*, Steiner-Books 2007.

Since the spiritual-scientific method for developing astral organs of perception starts with imagination, this requires us to open ourselves to as many symbolic and pictorial ideas as possible. These do not have to be only inwardly visualized images, however; they can also be words that embody profound cosmic truths in compressed form.[69]

The real heart of Rudolf Steiner's esoteric teachings consisted in such cosmic truths repeatedly formed anew into meditative verses. As yet we still cannot fully assess the significance of this accomplishment for modern spiritual life; it would require comprehensive evaluation of his whole creative *oeuvre* in the realm of language. He himself once said that anthroposophy presented him not only with "formal tasks of knowledge," but also with "historically creative tasks"; and by this he meant forming language into an appropriate instrument for presenting spiritual perceptions.[70]

Many years before this statement, he had already spoken of the increasing trend to apply language grown abstract to merely material things, saying that this trend was one of the reasons that had led to an inauguration of the spiritual world stream at the end of the nineteenth and beginning of the twentieth centuries. If "one had waited another 100 years, our words could no longer have expressed what spiritual science has to say." And this had required "hearkening to the most favorable moment" for seizing the opportunity to "impress new words" on everything through spiritual science, giving all words a "new imprint"; and in fact "really renewing language itself" so that people could regain a sense that certain words refer not merely to tangible or visible things, but also to what leads us upward into higher worlds.[71] And in the public lecture "Spiritual Science and Language"[72] the following lofty aim was presented:

Spiritual science will be able to appropriate suprasensory worlds through thought; will develop the capacity to pour the thought

69. Vienna, March 28, 1910, CW 119.
70. Dornach, September 29, 1921, CW 343.
71. Berlin, October 19, 1907, CW 284.
72. Berlin, January 20, 1910, CW 59.

into the sound and pattern of speech, so that our language can also once again become a means to communicate what the soul perceives in the suprasensory realm.

Repeatedly, in the most varied contexts, Steiner suggested that understanding of how everything arose from the "Word" (an instinctive insight in ancient times) can be regained only by penetrating the sound-forming, creative powers of speech themselves. Until the time when idea and sound content in language fell asunder, all ancient wisdom and all scholarship had really only been a rewriting of the phrase that underpinned the secret of the whole cosmos—"In the beginning was the Word."[73] How essential it is that spiritual science rediscover this insight comes to succinct expression in this sentence: "Basically, all our spiritual science is a search for the lost Word."[74] This is a matter, ultimately, of becoming aware of the lofty developmental goal that is called the "Mystery of the creative Word"; or in other words, the knowledge that just as everything first arose from the divine Word, so in humanity's far-distant future the human word itself will become creative.

Once the earth has transformed into Jupiter, the Word will become creative in the mineral realm; in the Venus planetary embodiment, the larynx will bring forth plants; and so it will continue until we are capable of bringing forth our own kind.... In future evolutionary stages of the earth, we will be able to produce in an enduring way what today we are only able to utter.

He sought to show how this could be possible, using the following metaphor:

I am speaking to you here. You hear my words, my thoughts, which are first within my soul, and which I could also conceal from you if I did not transpose them into words. I transpose them

73. Dornach, April 9, 1921, CW 204.
74. Berlin, April 25, 1916, CW 167.

into tones. If the air were not spread out between us, you would be unable to hear my words. The moment I speak a word here, the air in the room moves. Every time I speak, my words make the whole air resonate in a certain way; the air vibrates in conformity with my words. Let us take this a little further. Imagine that you could make the air fluid and then solid. In fact, it is already possible today to make air solid; water can exist as steam or gas, can then cool and become fluid, and in turn become solid in the form of ice. Imagine now that I speak the word "God" out into the air. If, at the moment when the sound waves of this word were present, you could solidify the air, then a shape, such as a shell form, would fall down. With the word "world" a different wave-form would fall down. You would be able to pick up my words, and every word would correspond to a crystallized air form.[75]

Accordingly, everything originally arose from the Word, the "choral harmony and interplay" of divine spiritual beings, with the aim of creating the human being, the human form. "The human being [the origin of the human form] is a divine ideal and divine aim."[76] There are various pointers in Steiner's collected works to the connection of this human form with the most profound secrets of evolution. At one place he even said that realizing this human form is no less than "the meaning of all earthly evolution." It is, he says, the spiritual foundation of the earth, but not "in this or that form, as image of the human race, but as universal ideal of humanity."[77] One should remember, however, he continued, that a "huge difference" exists between this ideal form, as that of the I-evolving human being, and the physical body. "The physical body is what occurs within the human entity as physical and chemical processes. In the human being today this takes place within the human form, which is, however, something thoroughly and absolutely spiritual."[78]

---

75. Kassel, June 28, 1907, CW 100.
76. See "What is revealed when one looks back at our past life between death and a new birth?" (Reflections of January 18, 1925) in *Anthroposophical Leading Thoughts*, CW 26.
77. Leipzig, September 4, 1908, CW 106.
78. Op. cit.

It is our task today to collaborate in realizing this divine ideal. If this human form is eventually to become capable of being reproduced by the human word itself, we must start preparing this now by working on language to make the human word creative. "The word, language, is what we already bring forth from ourselves as preparation of the future nature of the human being." For what we speak remains in the Akashic Record. "It is the first foundation of the future human being."[79]

From this perspective, meditative phrases not only have the potential to offer help for our spiritual development; they can also enable us to participate consciously in preparing this goal of human evolution. This is because they are "spiritually articulated" words and can engender "word resonances" that accord with the resonances of thought in the Akashic material.[80]

This is because the words in such phrases conjure, and are imbued with, sound qualities, as something of intrinsic importance in esoteric life. "At the moment when a thought is reconfigured into a word, even if the word itself is only invoked in thought as in a word meditation, the word imprints itself in the world ether"; whereas the thought itself does not; "otherwise, we could never become free beings in pure thinking."[81] In meditation, therefore, when the sound qualities of words come alive inwardly, every letter, every turn of phrase can have an effect upon the soul; and, in consequence, the gateway to the world of spirit can open.[82] Similarly, many years later, he reiterated this; if one can become aware that there is "more than speaking" in the word, then the word can become something enabling us to perceive "the first connection, the first dialog with the divine." Thereby, he added, since "this is, as it were, a path from the subjectivity of thinking to objectivity," something "spiritually objective can flow into the word."[83] This points to the second stage of schooling, that of inspiration; "through inspiration it becomes

79. Berlin, October 2, 1905, CW 93a.
80. Berlin, December 28, 1905, CW 264; Munich, October 28, 1906, CW 94.
81. Dornach, March 13, 1921, CW 203.
82. Vienna, February 22, 1907, CW 97.
83. Dornach, September 27, 1921, morning lecture, CW 343.

possible to acquire awareness of an outer soul-spiritual world around us, a soul-spiritual objectivity."[84]

Although Rudolf Steiner often referred to the meditative phrases and verses he gave using the Indian term *mantras*[85] or "mantric verses," there are key differences between them and what are regarded as mantras in India. In Hinduism, the world's oldest religion, this term refers to sacred texts in Sanskrit; in particular, the part of the Vedas containing hymns relating to acts of worship and sacrifice; or to the Tantra (mantra yoga) formulae consisting of letters and syllables of the Sanskrit alphabet, whose meaning is found by combining them in particular ways with corresponding intonations. The content of Rudolf Steiner's meditative verses, by contrast, consists of meaningful thought configurations. He did, however, agree with the Indian view according to which illumination lies concealed within a mantra as a tree lies hidden in a seed, and that, as soon as illumination takes effect, the mantra is endowed with a wonderful power through which it develops the cosmic energy latent in it. [Hindu Swami Nikhilananda:] "Tantra believes that some of the chief mantras were not created by human brains but exist eternally, and that the seeker can attain perfection by reciting them."[86] This accords with Steiner's statement that meditative phrases are based on "centuries of experience of the masters of wisdom and of the harmony of feelings"; this is why not every thought content is suitable as meditation material, but only "if given by the masters of wisdom and of the harmony of feelings."[87] Tantric "recitation" here becomes an inner speaking and hearkening appropriate to our modern consciousness.

While the mantric tradition is certainly rooted in ancient Indian practice, other ancient cultures continuing through to the Christian

84. Stuttgart, September 3, 1921, CW 78.
85. The word *mantra* (plural: mantras, mantrams) is formed from the first syllable of *manana* ("to think," and also "human being"), and *tra* in *Trana* ("liberation from the chains of the world of maya"). Mantra therefore literally means "something that brings liberation when one thinks upon it." See Arthur Avalon (Sir John Woodroffe), *The Garland of Letters.* ISBN 81-85988-12-9.
86. See Swami Nikhilananda, *Hinduism: Its Meaning for the Liberation of the Spirit.* ISBN 0-911206-26-4.
87. Berlin, January 28, 1908, CW 96.

era knew of the occult power of speech sounds.[88] However, the real origins of this, according to spiritual-scientific research, lead back even long before ancient Indian culture to Atlantean times. At that period, in a great school of adepts, which flowered during the fourth of the so-called Turanian epochs, skills in "occult speech" had developed alongside reading of the "occult script," in a tradition that has continued through to the present day.[89] At this primal stage of mantric practice, said Steiner, it was possible to exert mighty influences through the great power contained in words in those times. Since Atlanteans had not yet developed rationality, the Mystery leaders had been able to use tone combinations, symbols, and phrases to put their pupils in a state in which the godhead could directly illumine them. This was no longer possible after the great Atlantean flood. Because of the great change in awareness that had arisen as a result of the flood, it was necessary to start transposing the primal, unified, Atlantean wisdom into rational thought mode, and to teach it in ways that were appropriate to diverse, evolving national cultures.[90]

This change also made it necessary to develop a new level of mantram practice. In order to attain higher knowledge, the breathing process had to be schooled in yoga, since at that time thought lived in deeper regions of human nature than did the word. Only gradually, said Steiner, did thought raise itself into language; and today it has elevated itself beyond the word.[91] This gradual rising of thought into the region of the word meant that experience of thought increasingly focused on words borne on the breath, rather than on the breathing process as

---

88. Primarily in Judaic esotericism (the Q'abbalah). For instance, see Gershom Scholem, *Kabbalah*, Meridian 1974, Plume Books 1987 reissue: ISBN 0-452-01007-1; and *Jewish Gnosticism, Merkabah Mysticism, and the Talmudic Tradition*, 1960. See also: Roelof van den Broek (ed): *Gnosis and Hermeticism from Antiquity to Modern Times*, University of New York Press 1997.

89. Something similar is described in Balavatsky's *Secret Doctrine* (vol. I.). She stated that priests of those times had succeeded in invoking their gods in the latter's own language, consisting not only of words, but of tones, numbers and figures. This, she said, is the language of invocation, otherwise known, in India, as mantras.

90. Leipzig, February 17, 1907, and Dusseldorf March 7, 1907, both in CW 97.

91. Vienna, June 3, 1922, CW 83.

such. And therefore what came to expression in words, raised up in this way by the breathing process, started to be formed into "simple, word-laden verses." At that point, efforts were made to live fully within the "word chime" or "word tone."[92]

It is in this sense that Arthur Avalon, a classic connoisseur of Indian mantram lore, refers to a mantra as "power in tonal form."[93] What is generally called a mantra, he says, "are the particular tones used in worship and sacred practice, consisting of certain letters, or letters arranged in a particular sequence of tones, whose representative symbols they are."[94]

The strong dominance of tonal and musical elements in eastern mantric practice is something that Blavatsky accentuated. She said that the "mystic language" lives in the mantra, or rather in its tones (the tones of the speech sounds); for, in her words,[95] the tone is the "first of the keys that open the gateway of intercourse between mortals and immortals."[96] In the West, she said, we have little idea, however, "of the powers that lie concealed in the tone, in the akashic resonances that can be invoked by those who know how to utter certain words." In relation to the best-known mantric formula, *AUM*, she stated:

> *Om* is of course *Aum*, which can be uttered in two, three, and seven syllables, and invokes a range of different vibrations.... The seven meanings and the seven effects depend on the intonation given to the whole formula and to each of its syllables.[97]

Rudolf Steiner devoted a whole lecture to this ancient eastern prayer, or knowledge utterance.[98] There he showed how, in ancient eastern

---

92. Dornach, October 2, 1920, evening lecture, CW 322.
93. Arthur Avalon (Sir John Woodroffe): *The Serpent Power*, ISBN 81-85988-05-6. This and the following quote are re-translated from the German.
94. Arthur Avalon (Sir John Woodroffe): *The Garland of Letters*. ISBN 81-85988-12-9.
95. This and further quotations re-translated from the German.
96. Blavatsky, *The Secret Doctrine*, vol. I.
97. Blavatsky, *The Secret Doctrine*, vol. III.
98. Dornach, April 1, 1922, CW 211.

yoga, people sensed the inner dome of the head by sounding on the inbreath the vowel tone lying between "ah" and "o," or between "ah" and "oo." In doing so, they could grasp the revelation of the cosmic Word; of what surges and weaves as dynamic creativity through the world, since the head is an image or reflection of the whole universe. Then, sounding the consonantal tone "m" on the outbreath, they exhaled an affirmation of the cosmic word in absolute devotion to the universe. And in this way they were able to perceive that "inhalation is revelation, exhalation is affirmation; and 'aum' is the merging of revelation and avowal or affirmation, the enlivening within oneself of the cosmic mystery, and affirmation of this cosmic mystery in oneself."

Steiner described how the path to this experience has changed in our current era:

> The tone has risen higher and comes to expression in real, tangible, and specific (as opposed to intellectual) thought. Thus we can say that inhalation becomes thought, while exhalation becomes will-enacted realization of a thought. In other words, we separate what was once inhalation-as-revelation and exhalation-as-avowal into thought exercise and will exercise. By this means, likewise, in thoughts (but in the kind we practice in meditation) we gain revelation; and in the will exercises that we also carry out, we avow or affirm what has been revealed to us. For people today, what was once experienced only in the breathing process and was formed as vowel tone in the inhalation process, and as consonantal tone in the exhalation process, now unfolds in a more inward way in the soul, in an inwardly contemplated thought; it then is permeated by the will in devotional dedication to the universe. The process is the same, but has been shifted into the soul realm, internalized. Nevertheless, the process still involves perceiving our inner experience of the universe and its mysteries, and affirming, avowing this universe and its spiritual foundations.

Whereas ancient eastern wisdom consisted in gaining the highest inspiration through breathing and mantra exercises, based on the intrinsic interplay between *melos* and inner experience of the breathing process,[99] when we seek inspiration today, "merely logical connections" must become a "musical connection within the thought itself" through exercises that are purely soul-spiritual in nature.[100] Regarding the difference between an eastern and western approach to mantras, Steiner stated clearly on one occasion that in eastern mantras "a music living in these verses is heard or uttered in the soul"; whereas in western culture this must happen in a soul-spiritual way, so that we "do not fall into this kind of chanting or reciting of mantric verses or repeated phrases."[101]

It is clear from all this that mantric practice has undergone changes determined by human evolution. During an esoteric class, Steiner once spoke of the fundamental effect of the Christ event on mantric practice, and a participant in the class recorded it in his notes as follows:

> Through the fact that the Word became flesh, the mode of instruction in the esoteric schools changed also. In the pre-Christian era, the Word was not yet active. Teachings were imparted in silence; and silently, in images, pupils received communications from the spiritual worlds in visions.... In responsible modern esoteric schools, centered on the Christ power, teaching can be given only through the Word. In former times, dialog with divine-spiritual worlds could come about only through mantras, through sound. Now, however, we can prepare to unite with the Christ power through the meaning-imbued word within us. Words should be winged messengers that bear us upward into worlds of spirit.[102]

In a lecture given soon after, this principle was exemplified in relation to the archetypal Christian prayer, the Lord's Prayer:

> [Sevenfold human nature] was explained to the Turanian initiation pupil by requiring him to listen to a tonal scale as metaphor for

99. Dornach, September 29 and December 2, 1922, CW 282, and Dornach October 2, 1920, evening lecture, CW 322.
100. Dornach, May 27, 1922, CW 212.
101. Berlin, February 28, 1918, CW 67.
102. Esoteric Class, Munich, December 5, 1909, CW 266/I.

the seven human bodies, in combination with an aroma scale and the picturing of certain colors. What lay in the sevenfold harmony scale rose up in him as inner experience invoked and mediated by what was outwardly present. The great religious founders poured this into certain phrases, and the greatest of them poured it into the Lord's Prayer. Each person who says the Lord's Prayer receives its effects. It is a prayer, which is not a mantra as such [in the sense of an exercise using speech sounds]. It will still retain its significance after thousands upon thousands of years have passed, for it is a thought mantra. The effect of the Lord's Prayer was poured into thoughts. The effect of the Lord's Prayer remains, for this effect lies in the mighty nature of the thoughts themselves.[103]

Everyone who prays the Lord's Prayer can receive its effects. It is not a mantra as such, although it can have mantric powers. It is a thought mantra. Naturally it had its greatest power in the original language (Aramaic). But since it is a thought mantra, its power will never fade, even if translated into a thousand languages.[104]

This formulation points to the fact that there must be a huge difference between eastern speech-sound mantras that cannot be translated and spiritual-scientific thought mantras.[105]

The extent to which the concept of a "thought mantra" corresponds to the current stage of language evolution, and must therefore also apply to the nature of Rudolf Steiner's mantric verses, becomes clear in his highly significant comments in the lecture in Dornach on April 13, 1923 (GA 224). There he described the evolutionary process of human speech from its origination in Atlantean times through to our own day: its advance from a "will language" in Atlantean times to a "feeling

---

103. Berlin, February 18, 1907, CW 96.
104. Leipzig, February 17, 1907, CW 96.
105. As Indian mantras are understood, a mantra ceases to be one when it is translated; "the words heard or spoken in the translation are not the tone of the Devata [divinity] and do not invoke the latter. We do not use the same tone [as in the Sanskrit mantra] but rather the translation into another language, with other tones and speech sounds." Arthur Avalon: *The Garland of Letters*. ISBN 81-85988-12-9 [here re-translated from the German]

language" in the post-Atlantean epoch up to the ancient Greek era and on to a "thought language" in our own times.

This great evolutionary trajectory ended with the loss, necessary for the development of human freedom, of an experience of the creative powers of speech sounds and the capacity to form language in a living way. A new impulse is needed. Since the Mystery of Golgotha, this can only be the Christ impulse, which is so decisive for earthly evolution. This impulse involves spiritualization; or in other words, an evolutionary return, or involution. Whereas the path progressed previously from the Word to thinking, as spiritualization begins we must start with thinking and find our way back to the real formative powers at work in words.

> We must seek the path from concept to Word. A quite different experience is involved when, without speaking outwardly, we have within us, not the content of a merely abstract concept, but a living experience of the speech sound, whichever language it happens to be.[106]

A quite different and quite particular kind of formative speech power will then come to the fore, Steiner said, so that the Christ impulse can itself become the creative power in language.[107]

Accordingly, a new mantric culture could be inaugurated only with thought mantras, in which the thought content conceived as meditation is poured into fitting speech sounds. If we look at all of Rudolf Steiner's work in this context, we can recognize his great efforts at reconfiguring and re-enlivening language in his writings and talks, his poems and mantras, and above all, in the movements of speech sounds rendered visible in the new movement art of eurythmy. We can recognize him not only as a great spiritual teacher and researcher, but also as a great artist who sought to shape the Word in a way that could once again mediate and convey the spirit.

---

106. Dornach, September 30, 1921, morning lecture, CW 343.
107. Dornach, April 13, 1923, CW 244 and Pforzheim, March 7, 1914, CW 152.

PART ONE

GENERAL RULES

All meditation, concentration and other such exercises are worthless, and may even be harmful in certain ways, if we do not regulate our lives in accordance with these conditions.

General Conditions

that one must require of oneself in order to undergo esoteric development *[sometimes called balancing, preparatory, or supplementary exercises]*

In what follows, the conditions will be described that must provide the foundation for esoteric development. No one should imagine that any inner or outer measures one takes in life will ensure progress if these conditions are not fulfilled. All meditation, concentration and other such exercises are worthless, and may even be harmful in certain ways, if we do not regulate our lives in accordance with these conditions. Powers cannot be conferred upon the human being. Only those powers can unfold and develop that a person already bears within. The powers do not develop by themselves because of outer and inner hindrances. The outer hindrances are addressed through the following rules, while inner hindrances can be overcome through detailed instructions regarding meditation, concentration, and so forth.

The first condition is to acquire completely clear thinking. To do this, we have to free ourselves from the usual flitting about of thoughts, even if only for a brief moment during the day, say five minutes (the longer, the better). We have to master our world of thoughts. We cannot do so if outward circumstances, profession, traditions of any kind, social relationships, and even our particular nationality, or the time of day, and so forth, dictate the thoughts we have and how we spin them out. During moments of quiet reflection we must intentionally free our souls from our usual daily trains of thought, and by our own initiative place a thought at the center of our attention. Don't imagine that this must be an outstanding or especially interesting thought; the esoteric effect will actually be better achieved by starting with a thought that is as uninteresting and unimportant as possible. This better stimulates the independent activity of thinking, whereas a thought of intrinsic interest itself urges our thinking forward. It is better to practice control of thoughts by focusing on a pin than on Napoleon. Do it like this: start from the chosen thought and, through nothing but your own inner initiative, sequentially add all that can objectively be connected with it. At the end of this period of reflection, the thought should still retain as much color and life in your soul as at the outset. Do this exercise day after day for at least a month. You can start with a new thought each day, or continue with the same one for several days. At the end of such an exercise, try to become fully aware of the inner sense of stability and security that you will soon notice if you pay subtle attention to it; and then end the exercise by thinking of your head and the middle of your back (brain and spinal cord) as if you would pour this sense of stability into those parts of the body.

After practicing for about a month in this way, add another task. Try to think of some action that you would otherwise certainly never undertake in the normal course of life. Now make this a self-imposed duty to be carried out each day. It will therefore be good if you choose an action that can be performed each day for as long a period as possible. Once again it is better to start with an unimportant action, one that you more or less have to force yourself to take; for instance, to water a flower at a certain time every day. After a while, a second such action should be added to the first, then later a third, and so on; as many as you can manage without neglecting your other daily tasks. This exercise should again last a month. But during this second month you should, as far as possible, continue with the first exercise as well, though no longer as the exclusive duty it was during the first month. Yet you should not overlook it, for otherwise you would soon notice the fruits of the first month fading, and the old roller-coaster of uncontrolled thoughts starting again. In general you need to take care that the fruits once gained are never lost again. Having accomplished this second exercise for self-initiated action, you will become subtly aware of a sense in the soul of inner motivation; and you should, as it were, pour this feeling into your body, so that it streams down from the head and over the heart.

In the third month a new exercise should become the focus of your practice: developing a certain equilibrium in fluctuations between pleasure and pain, joy and suffering. Swinging between "rejoicing to the skies" and "deep gloom" should be consciously replaced by an even mood, by equanimity. You can take care that no joy carries you away, no pain floors you, no incident drives you to boundless anger or annoyance, no expectation fills you with fear or anxiety, and no situation leaves you stunned or bewildered, and so forth. You should not fear that this exercise will render you neutral or poor in response to life. Instead, you will soon notice that what occurred in you before this exercise is replaced by purified qualities of soul. Above all, by attending carefully you will eventually come to sense an inner tranquility in your body. As in the two other instances described above, you should pour this feeling into your body by letting it radiate from the heart to the hands, to the feet, and finally the head. In this case, this cannot be done after each individual exercise, since really this is not a single exercise but an ongoing attentiveness to your inner life of soul. At least once a day you should invoke this sense of inner peace, and then practice allowing its current to emanate from the heart. Manage the exercises of months one and two in the same way that you handled the first exercise during the second month.

During the fourth month you should take up what is called positivity, as a new exercise. This involves seeking always what is good, excellent, beautiful, and so forth, in all experiences, beings, and things. This quality of soul is best characterized in a Persian legend about Christ Jesus. When he was walking along one day with his disciples they saw a dead dog by the wayside that was already half-decomposed. All the disciples turned away from this ugly sight; but Christ Jesus stopped, reflectively observed the animal and said, "But what beautiful teeth the animal has!" Where the others saw only something ugly and repugnant, he sought the beautiful. Similarly, the esoteric pupil must try to find the positive aspect in everything that happens, and in every creature or person. You will soon notice, if you do, that an ugly exterior conceals something beautiful; that a hidden beauty can be found even in a criminal; and that the divine soul is present somewhere under the surface of a madman. This exercise is somewhat related to what we can call the withholding of criticism. It does not mean calling black white, or white black. But there is a difference between judging things in a way that issues merely from one's own personality, reacting accordingly in sympathy and antipathy, and the stance that enters lovingly into the other being or phenomenon and continually asks, "Why is the other like this, or why does that person act in such a way?" Such a stance inevitably leads to greater efforts to aid what is imperfect, rather than to simply criticize and find fault with it.

The objection that many people's circumstances require them to find fault and judge is misplaced here, for such circumstances mean that they will be unable to undergo a proper esoteric schooling. Many circumstances do indeed prevail that prevent people from undergoing proper and full esoteric training. We should not impatiently demand our own progress despite this, for we can advance only under certain specific conditions. If you take a month to focus consciously on all that is positive in what you experience, you will gradually notice that a feeling slips into you as though your skin has become permeable on all sides, and your soul is opened wide to all hidden and subtle processes in your surroundings, which you previously entirely failed to notice. This is the real point: to combat the lack of attention to such subtle things, which all of us have. Once we notice that this feeling has entered the soul like a kind of happiness or blessedness, we should try to direct this feeling toward our heart, and from there let it stream into our eyes; and from there out into space and around us. If you do this you will notice it gives you an intimate relationship with this surrounding space. It is as if you grow beyond yourself, learning to regard a part of your environment as belonging to yourself. A great deal of focused concentration is needed for this exercise, and above all acknowledgment of the fact that all stormy passions and raging emotions utterly destroy such a mood. The exercises from the first months continue in the way already suggested.

In the fifth month you should then try to develop in yourself the sense of encountering every new experience with a completely open mind. Saying such things as "I've never seen or heard that before; I don't believe it; it's an illusion" embodies an attitude that the esoteric pupil should entirely dispense with. You must be willing to encounter a completely new experience at any moment. All you have previously perceived as natural law; everything that has appeared possible to you, must not act as fetters that prevent you from absorbing a new truth. It is radical to say so, but right nevertheless, that if someone were to come to an esoteric pupil and tell him that the spire of the local church has bent right over in the night, he should not close his mind completely to the possibility that this might be true; that his previous understanding of natural laws might have to be amended to encompass such an apparently unheard-of thing. If, in the fifth month, you pay attention to developing this attitude, you will notice a feeling slipping into you as though something comes alive, something stirs, in the space we spoke of in relation to the exercise of month four. This feeling is extraordinarily subtle and delicate. You must try to attentively grasp this subtle resonance in your surroundings, and let it stream through all five senses; especially through eyes, ears, and skin, inasmuch as the latter contains the sense of warmth. At this stage of esoteric development one should pay less attention to impressions stirring in the lower senses of taste, smell, and touch. At this stage it is not yet really possible to distinguish the numerous bad influences mixed up with the good ones in this domain, and therefore the pupil should leave this for a later stage.

During the sixth month you should try to practice all five exercises systematically in regular and repeated alternation. Gradually this will develop a fine harmony in your soul. In particular you will notice that any dissatisfaction with the world will fade. A mood grows in which the soul is reconciled with all experiences. This cannot be mistaken for indifference; but, on the contrary, the capacity to work in the world in a way that really brings about improvement or progress is dependent on it. Calm insight into things the soul previously had no access to now opens up. A person's gait and gestures will even change as the result of such exercises; and one day you may even notice that your handwriting has acquired a different character. You can then say that you have your foot on the first step of the ladder that leads you upward. Once again, two things must be emphasized.

First, that the six exercises counteract the harmful effect that other esoteric exercises can have, retaining only what is beneficial. [*See note on following page,] And second, that only these exercises really safeguard the positive results of meditation and concentration work. Even ordinary conscientious fulfillment of mundane moral standards is not sufficient for the esoteric pupil, for such morality can be very egotistic. For example, if someone thinks he will be good in order to be regarded as good. Esotericists do not do what is good in order to be seen as such; but because they gradually recognize that goodness alone advances evolution; whereas evil, imprudence, and unpleasantness throw a wrench in the works of this evolution.

———

[*] The "harmful effect" is cited as follows in audience notes for the lecture in Leipzig on July 9, 1906 (in CW 94, *Cosmogony*):

Sleep is the starting point for development of the spiritual senses. When we sleep, our physical and etheric bodies lie in the bed while the astral body and "I" are outside them. If a person starts to perceive spiritually in sleep, then forces that previously took care of regenerating the physical and etheric bodies are withdrawn from the body. These forces have to be replaced by other means to avoid great danger for the physical and etheric bodies. If this does not happen, these bodies and their forces are greatly depleted so that amoral beings can take possession of them. It can therefore happen that although people develop astral clairvoyance, they nevertheless become immoral....

The following principle is important: one can leave a being or a matter to itself the more one has introduced rhythm into it. Thus esoteric pupils have to inform their thought world, too, with a certain regularity. The following is necessary for this:

[an account of the six balancing exercises]

If we develop all these qualities in ourselves, then our inner life is informed by rhythm in such a way that the astral body no longer needs to take care of regeneration during sleep. These exercises establish a state of equilibrium enabling the etheric body to protect and regenerate itself. Anyone who embarks on esoteric development without developing these six qualities will be at risk, and is exposed to the worst entities during the night. Once we have practiced the six qualities for a certain period, we can start to develop our astral senses, and will then begin sleeping consciously. Our dreams will then no longer be arbitrary, but will acquire regularity. The astral world dawns before us.

ADDITIONAL RULES FOLLOWING FROM THE "GENERAL CONDITIONS"

THE FOLLOWING RULES aim to encourage every esoteric pupil to arrange life in a such a way that you can continually observe and govern yourself to see if you are living in inner accord with each requirement. All esoteric schooling, especially when it rises into higher regions, can cause harm and confusion for the pupil when such rules are not observed. Yet you do not need to shy away in alarm from such schooling, if you endeavor to live in accordance with these rules. Nor do you need to be despondent if you find that you are, as yet, fulfilling the requirements very poorly. Inner honesty in your efforts not to lose sight of these rules in every situation in life will be sufficient. But such honesty must, above all, be honesty toward ourselves. There are many who deceive themselves in this respect, believing their strivings are pure; whereas if they reflected more closely on themselves they would find a great deal of concealed and underlying egotism, refined self-aggrandizement. Such feelings often adopt a mask of selfless striving and lead the pupil astray. Serious inner contemplation of ourselves is indispensable. It is something we cannot do too often, to check whether, after all, such feelings lurk in the depths of our psyche. Energetically following the rules discussed below here will increasingly release us from such feelings. The rules are as follows:

First:

No idea should be allowed in my consciousness unless I have carefully examined it.

Just take a moment to observe the many ideas, feelings, and will impulses living in a person's soul. We absorb these through our life and family circumstances, profession, race and culture, the era in which we live, and so on. Such content of the psyche should not be seen as something all people are morally obliged to eradicate. After all, we gain our roots and certainty in life from our culture, era, family, and education; and these sustain us. If we were to reject such things unthinkingly, we would deprive ourselves of this support. For people weaker in their nature, in particular, it would be undesirable to go too far in this direction. Observation of this first rule by every esoteric pupil should be associated, in particular, with developing understanding for all the actions, thoughts, and feelings of others. Following this rule should never lead to lack of restraint or to breaking with everything we acquire at birth and during the course of life. On the contrary, the more we examine our circumstances, the more we will come to see the justification of what lives in our surroundings. It is not a matter of combating and repudiating such things, but of becoming inwardly free through careful examination of all that stands in relationship with our own souls. The strength of our soul will then cast a light over all our thinking and conduct; our awareness will broaden accordingly; and we will acquire the general habit of increasingly allowing the spiritual rules revealed in the soul to speak, rather than blindly obeying the dictates of the world around us. In relation to this rule, one soon sees that if we are to examine everything, this will in particular include occult and esoteric teachings given by an esoteric teacher. We have to understand the nature of such examination. We cannot always examine something directly, but may often have to examine it indirectly. For instance, no one today can check directly whether Frederick the Great actually lived or not. We can only try to discover whether the route by which we have heard about Frederick the Great is reliable or not. We have to start our enquiry at the right place. It is the same with all faith in authority. If someone reports something to us that we ourselves cannot directly ascertain, we will need to check by the means and material available to us, whether this person is a credible authority; and therefore, whether he is telling us things that invoke a sense and intimation of truth. From this example we can see it is important to initiate our inquiries from the right starting point.

A second rule is:

I should nurture in my soul a vivid obligation to continually increase the totality of my ideas.

Nothing is worse for the esoteric pupil than to be happy to make do with a certain number of already existing concepts, and to use these to understand everything. It is infinitely important to keep acquiring ever new ideas. If this doesn't happen, pupils arriving at suprasensory insights would not meet them with well-prepared concepts, and would be overwhelmed; either to their disadvantage, or at least their dissatisfaction. This latter is because, under such circumstances, they might experience higher realities without even noticing it. There are a good number of pupils who could already be immersed in higher experiences, but are unaware of this because they have so few ideas, which means that they entertain quite different expectations of such experiences from the actual reality. While many people might not seek ease and comfort in outer things, they are unwilling to enrich their ideas by forming new concepts.

A third rule is:

I will gain insight into things only when I have neither sympathy nor antipathy toward any truth they may reveal.

An old initiate regularly told his pupils that they could grasp the soul's immortality only if they were equally willing to accept that the soul ceases to exist after death as that it lives eternally. "As long as you wish to live forever," he said, "you can gain no idea of the state you enter after death." This important example applies to all other truths as well. As long as we nurture the least desire in ourselves that things should be a particular way, the pure bright light of truth cannot illumine us. When we practice self-reflection, for example, yet maintain a secret wish that our good qualities will outweigh the bad, then this very wish will produce a pantomime that deceives us and prevents us from reaching real self-knowledge.

A fourth rule is:

I must overcome my wariness of what seems abstract.

As long as esoteric pupils cling to concepts that relate to and draw on the material world, they will be unable to reach any truth about higher worlds. They must endeavor to acquire sense-free ideas. This is the hardest of all four rules, especially because of the conditions that prevail in our time. Materialistic thinking has largely deprived people of the capacity to think in sense-free concepts. We can try to regularly think concepts that never occur as such in the external sensory world, but exist only in approximate form—such as the concept of a circle. A perfect circle cannot be found in the world; it can be conceived only in thought. However, all spherical forms relate to this conceptual circle as their underlying law. The other way forward here is to conceive of a high moral ideal, which no one can entirely realize, but which nevertheless underlies many human deeds as their governing law. No one progresses in esoteric development without recognizing the great significance in life of so-called abstract ideals, and enriching the soul with the ideas that arise from these.

For the Days of the Week

We must attend carefully to certain soul processes that we usually carry out without care or attention. There are eight such processes.

At first, it is naturally best to undertake only one exercise at a time, for instance, over an eight-day period or a fortnight, and then proceed to the second, and so forth, before starting again at the beginning. However, exercise eight is best done every day. Thereby we gradually attain self-knowledge and can also see what progress we have made. Later on perhaps, starting with Saturday, the daily exercise, which requires about five minutes, can be undertaken alongside the eighth. Thus each day is assigned to a particular exercise: thinking on Saturday, resolve on Sunday, speech on Monday, action on Tuesday, actions on Wednesday,[108] and so forth.

---

108. Translator's note: In what follows, Wednesday is assigned to "right standpoint" or "right perspective" rather than to "right actions," which belongs to Tuesday.

Saturday

Attending to one's *ideas* (thoughts). Thinking only significant thoughts. Gradually learning to distinguish the essential from the inessential in one's thoughts; the eternal from the transient; and the truth from mere opinion.

When listening to what others say, trying to become completely still within, dispensing with all agreement/assent, and in particular, all derogatory judgments (criticism, repudiation) even in thoughts and feelings.

This is known as

Right opinion

Sunday

Deciding even the most insignificant things only out of full and considered reflection. All thoughtless deeds and meaningless actions should be kept far from our souls. We should always have well-pondered reasons for everything. And we should certainly relinquish anything that we are not impelled to by some meaningful cause.

Once we are convinced that a decision we make is correct, we should adhere to it in inner steadfastness.

This is known as

Right judgment

Monday

Speech. Only what has purpose and meaning should fall from the lips of someone who strives for higher development. All talking for the sake of it, to pass the time for instance, is harmful in this regard.

Ordinary conversation in which people chat away aimlessly should be avoided, but neither should we distance ourselves from engaging with others. Precisely in daily exchanges, speech should gradually become more meaningful. We can engage in conversation with everyone, but do so thoughtfully, with careful reflection. Never speak without cause! Gladly fall silent. We should try to speak neither too much nor too little. First listen calmly, then engage with what you hear.

This exercise is also called:

Right speech

Tuesday

Outward actions. These should not disturb people around us. When moved to act by our inner life (conscience), carefully weigh up how we can best accord with the good of the whole, the enduring happiness of our fellow human beings, and eternal things.

When we act out of ourselves, from our own initiative, weigh thoroughly in advance how our actions will affect others.

This is also known as

Right action

Wednesday

Mode of living. Living in accord with nature and the spirit, not getting caught up in the externalities of life. Avoiding everything that makes life restless or rushed.

Never being hasty or sluggish. Seeing life as a means to work and develop, and acting accordingly.

This is also called

Right perspective

Thursday

Human striving. Taking care to do nothing that exceeds our powers, but not to omit anything that lies within our powers.

Looking beyond mundane things and each moment, and setting oneself ideals connected with a human being's highest obligations. For instance, trying to develop in accordance with these exercises to be able to better help and advise our fellows, even if not immediately.

This can also be summarized as:

Making all preceding exercises into habitual modes of conduct

Friday

The endeavor to *learn from life* as much as possible.

Nothing occurs without becoming useful experience for life. If we do something wrong or imperfectly, this motivates us to correct or perfect it in future.

We can likewise observe others' actions for a similar purpose of learning (but not unlovingly). And we do nothing without looking back at experiences that can help us in our decisions and actions.

We can learn a great deal from every person, and also from children, if we attend carefully.

This exercise is also known as

Right memory

or in other words, remembering what we have learned and experienced.

Summary

Looking inward from time to time, even if only for five minutes a day, at the same time each day. Here we should reflect upon ourselves, carefully communing with ourselves, and test and shape the principles governing our life. We should ponder our knowledge and capacities (and also lack of them); weigh up our duties; reflect on the content and true aim of life. We should find serious displeasure in our own errors and imperfections, and in a word, seek to discover what is enduring and essential; at the same time undertaking to pursue appropriate goals such as acquiring certain virtues. (We ought not fall into the error of thinking we have done something well, but instead keep striving to emulate the highest ideals.).

This exercise is also known as

Right contemplation

The Twelve Virtues as a Subject of Meditation and for Practice in Daily Life
(Virtues for Each Month)

Assigning of the virtues to the zodiac originated with H.P. Blavatsky, as did the original English terms for the virtues given here. They were translated into German by Rudolf Steiner, who also gave the additional phrase starting with "becomes..." Words in parentheses after the virtue indicate slight differences of interpretation derived from Steiner's German translation.

Aries	April	Devotion	becomes the power of sacrifice
Taurus	May	Equilibrium	becomes progress / advancement
Gemini	June	Perseverance (endurance, steadfastness)	becomes faithfulness
Cancer	July	Unselfishness (selflessness)	becomes catharsis
Leo	August	Compassion	becomes freedom
Virgo	September	Courtesy	becomes tactfulness of heart /sensibility
Libra	October	Contentment	becomes composure
Scorpio	November	Patience	becomes insight
Sagittarius	December	Control of speech control of thoughts, "guard your tongue"	becomes the sense of truth

Capricorn	January	Courage	becomes redemptive power
Aquarius	February	Discretion	becomes meditative power
Pisces	March	Magnanimity	becomes love

Always start practicing each virtue around the twenty-first of the previous month and continue until the first of the following month; that is, "Devotion" from March 21 to May 1, and so forth.[109]

---

109. See note on p. 456.

PART TWO

MAIN EXERCISES
FOR MORNING AND EVENING[110]

The first stage involves developing as many metaphoric ideas and images as possible. One should find satisfaction in the subtle engagement of such activity. This path will only come to rewarding fruition at a relatively late stage. It is, however, a safe path, one that protects the seeker from every phantasm and illusion. The metaphors do not have to be merely pictorial images, but can also be words in which profound and universal truths are compressed and condensed.

(Vienna, March 28, 1910, GA 119)

---

110. See note on page 458 in relation to print reproduction of the exercises. Every exercise bears the date of its transcription (if known) in the top left corner of the page. See the editor's appendix in relation to suggestions for regulating the breath in some of these exercises.

The Essential Nature of Meditative Practice

Transcribed for Professor Hans Wohlbold, Munich, May 1917

THE ESSENTIAL NATURE of meditative practice lies in acquiring the kind of thinking and picturing[111] activity that can raise spiritual reality to our awareness and understanding. The important thing is that we experience activation of the thinking and picturing faculty independently of our physical organization. Experience shows it to be possible for us to think and imagine, etc., without involvement of the normal conditions of thinking bound to corporeality. This moment will arise as we pursue our meditative practice. In particular I advise:

1) A reverse review of the day's events in the evening. This accomplishes a first step in picturing and thinking that is not bound to normal thinking and picturing sequences. Our capacity to think and visualize becomes freer.

2) Concentrating in utter tranquility on a brief thought content. This should be one that can be *surveyed in its entirety*. Rather than mingling it with unconscious or subconscious memory pictures, and so forth, we must really remain in absolutely conscious spiritual activity. Then we allow the thought content to lapse from our awareness, but at the same time try to retain the energy: to remain conscious without thought content for a short period. By doing this we imbue our capacity for insight

---

111. Translator's note: The word Steiner used here repeatedly is *vorstellen*; although it is often used to denote "thinking," it has a stronger sense of imaginative picturing than the word *denken*.

with the tranquil energy it needs to grasp the spiritual, which otherwise seeps away through the mesh, as it were, of our ordinary thinking and does not come to our awareness. I suggest that these two exercises are more suitable for the evening.

In the morning it is good to undertake one of two similar thought concentration exercises. Here pictorial thinking can play the role I described in principle in the second part of *Esoteric Science* (Chapter 5) in relation to the Rose Cross exercise.

To acquire the necessary tranquility of concentrated thinking, it is a good idea to do the six exercises (as supporting or balancing exercises) cited in the second part of *Esoteric Science* (Chapter 5).

Part of the purpose of practice lies in developing greater activity of soul in ourselves than usual. Just as quantitative aspects transform into qualitative ones at critical points of a physical phenomenon, so enhancement of our normal cognitive powers develops a faculty capable of perceiving the world of spirit.

A

Nine groups of exercises

1904 to about 1914

(each group using one meditative verse)

A–1

Exercises with the meditative verse
"More radiant than the sun..."
and meditations
taken from *Light on the Path*

In accordance with the law of continuity in esoteric endeavor, in 1904 Rudolf Steiner drew on the Esoteric School of Theosophy in London, initially giving the verse used by this school: "More radiant than the sun / Purer than the snow / Subtler than the ether / Is the Self / The Spirit of my heart / I am this Self / This Self am I..." along with certain phrases taken from *Light on the Path* by Mabel Collins: "Before the eyes can see..." and "Seek the way...."[112]

In relation to these early beginnings, see *From the History and Contents of the First Section of the Esoteric School 1904–1914*, CW 264.

---

112. Translator's note: In both cases the original English words are given here.

October/November 1904   Archive no. 7074

Meditations.

Morning:
   1.) *Aum*
   2.) Elevation to the higher self through the verse:
       More radiant than the sun
       purer than snow
       finer than the ether
       is the self
       the spirit in my heart
       this self am I. I am this self.[113]

   3.) Contemplative meditation in *Light on the Path*
       a.) 14 days: Before the eye...
       b.)   ”   Before the ear...
       c.)   ”   Before [the voice can speak] in the presence of
                         the masters...
       d.)   ”   Before [the soul can stand] in their presence...

   4.) Devotional dedication to an ideal that is utterly worthy of
       veneration.

Evening:
   Review of the day. Start with most recent experiences and actions in
   the evening and ascend to the morning.

Start of meditation: Tuesday [Thursday], December 8.[114] Until then,
   try the preparatory exercise.

———————————

113. Translator's note: The words of this verse deviate from the English original to reflect the
subtle change to them in Steiner's translation into German.
114. See the editorial notes at the end of this volume for more on this kind of date indication.

Facsimile Archive no. 7074

Meditation.

Morgens:

1.) Aum.

2.) Erhebung zum höheren Selbst durch die Formel:

„Strahlender als die Sonne

Reiner als der Schnee

Feiner als der Aether

Ist das Selbst

Der Geist in meinem Herzen

Dies Selbst bin Ich. Ich bin dies Selbst".

3.) Contemplative Meditation in „Licht a. d. W."

a.) 14 Tage: „Bevor die Auge ...."

b.) "   "   „Je den ..."

c.) "   "   „Je vor den Meistern..."

d.) "   "   „Je vor ihnen stehen...-

4.) Devotionelle Hingabe an das absolut verehrungswürdige Ideal.

Abends:) Tagesrückschau. Anfang mit den letzten Erlebnissen und Handlungen am Abend und aufsteigend bis zum Morgen.

Anfang der Meditation: Dienstag. 8. December. bis dahin vorbereitete Vorübung.

End of 1904   Archive no. 6912/13

Please observe the following in the first few weeks:

I. A morning meditation consisting of the following.

1. Elevating our feelings to the higher self. Here it is *less* a matter of
   learning something theoretical about the higher self than of a vivid
   feeling of a higher nature living within us. We picture the ordinary
   self as a vessel surrounding this higher nature; in other words, seeing
   the latter existing within the lower self as its *kernel*. Having engendered this feeling in ourselves, we speak the following words (not
   aloud but in thoughts) in a prayerful way to the higher self:

> More radiant than the sun
> purer than snow
> finer than the ether
> is the self
> the spirit in my heart
> this self am I; I am this self.

In picturing this very precisely, we should take care that no other
idea or image gets mixed up with it. We should feel the eye of the
soul to be directed only toward the higher self. Gradually we will feel
how a wonderful strengthening issues from the words of the above
lines. We will feel as though lifted out of ourselves and slowly begin
to feel as if the soul grew wings. This is the beginning, on which we
can then build further. This exercise should take between two and
three minutes.

2. We immerse ourselves in the first sentence of *Light on the Path:*

> Before the eye can see
> it must lose the habit of tears[115]

---

115. Translator's note: These quotations from *Light on the Path* are translations from Steiner
rather than the original words by Mabel Collins.

No other thoughts must be allowed entry to the soul. We imbue ourselves entirely with this thought. The meaning of it must then suddenly strike each self like lightning. This will happen quite certainly on a day when we are patient. Utter stillness must reign in the soul for several minutes. The soul must be blind and deaf to all external sense impressions and memory pictures. Again for two-to-three minutes.

3. Then devotion to what we revere as the highest divine nature. Here the *mood* is the important thing. Ardent elevation of the inner gaze and longing for union with this divine nature.

II. In the *evening* before falling asleep, we should undertake a brief review of what we have experienced during the day. It is not a matter of including everything, but of facing and judging ourselves as if we were someone else. We should learn from ourselves. Life should become, increasingly, a lesson we learn from. We begin with the evening and work forward to the morning.

———

Gradually we will notice that our dream life assumes a more regular and ordered character. A *first glimpse* of the spiritual world flows within it. Meditation is the esoteric key to it. It is good to purchase a little notebook and in the morning very briefly write down any characteristic dreams in just a few words. Thereby we gain practice in retaining what streams toward us from higher worlds. This is the first, elementary method which will later enable us to allow spiritual experiences to break through into bright, waking consciousness. Dreams that are *only* reminiscences of daily life, or that arise from bodily states (headaches, heart palpitations, and so forth), have value *only* when they are clothed in *symbolic* form; for instance, if a palpitating heart appears as a hot stove, or an aching brain as a vault in which animals crawl about. Here it is not the content of the dream that has value but *only* the symbolism. The spiritual world first uses the form of symbolism to guide us toward the powers of higher worlds, and we must therefore attend to the subtleties of this symbolism. Depending on your disposition, to the extent you are able to do so, it will also be good if you compare the dreams you become aware of with your experiences the next day. It is very probable that before long your dreams will start to assume a prefiguring character. When this starts to happen, we will speak further of how this can bear fruit for your spiritual life.

Please see how you get on with these suggestions, and in eight days' time let me know how things have gone.

———

Spring 1905   Archive no. 6915-18

Add the following to the previous exercise, the latter to be *retained*, please, until further notice.[116] It should be added at the place where the *"He wills"* streams over the whole surface of the body:

Streams (rays) are to be formed on the body's surface and drawn toward the heart as center point. The whole thing should be done slowly, with consciousness resting calmly on the process.

During this process, meditate on the following thought (from *Light on the Path*):

> *Seek the way*

Then please rest all feeling in stillness within the heart, and meditate on this:

> *Seek the way in inner contemplation*

Then guide the stream back toward the body's surface, and meditate on these words:

> *Seek the way by boldly striding out of yourself.*

✳

✳ ✳

A time will soon come when you perceive the rays described here as real streams of warmth.

These exercises prepare the union between your own personality (microcosm) and the greater world and its secrets (macrocosm) in the

---

116. This is not extant. However, it must have been an exercise based on the formulation "I am – It thinks – She feels - ..." (see next group, A–2)

same way that the exercises given hitherto have prepared the awakening of your own individuality.

In the future, human beings will live in a much more intimate connection with the laws of the world than they do at present. And an esoteric pupil anticipates this evolving intimacy. The head with the brain is only a transitional organ of cognition and awareness. The organ that will really perceive the world in profound and at the same time powerful ways is *potentially prefigured* in the present *heart*. But please note that this is only an initial development, a *potential*. To become an organ of perception and cognition, the heart will have to undergo transformation in the most diverse ways. Yet this heart is the fount and spring of the future stage of humanity. When the heart becomes its organ, cognition will be warm and inward, as today only feelings of love and compassion are. But these feelings, presently only fumbling in dull obscurity, will work their way through into the brightness and clarity that today only the most refined, logical concepts of the head possess.

The true pupil is preparing for these things. And this preparation will take the right course only if one does this with the *sensibility of soul, the inner outlook*, indicated here. This attitude is the mother of the stance one needs. Please be very clear that we will achieve what we ought through our meditative and concentration exercises only when we accomplish them in a way that is informed by great and lofty aims; in full, illumined clarity.

I would ask you always to regard the exercises in this way and to undertake them in this spirit. By doing so you join with the community of spirits who, from present incarnations, are to become the seers and helpers of the future. We can do nothing more helpful for the world's further evolution than to evolve ourselves. This is something, in fact, that we *must* do. And we will have no doubt whatsoever that we *must*, the moment we perceive the truth about our own nature and its relationship with the wider world. This insight, however, is one that can only gradually be acquired. It is a child

of *the will* and of *patience*.

Please try to connect the various discussions we have had this winter with the first four sentences in *Light on the Path*, and freely write down your thoughts in this respect.

You will find that these four sentences

1. Before the eye...
2. Before the ear...
3. Before the voice can speak in the presence of the masters...
4. And before the soul can stand in their presence...

contain an infinite amount; and that the most important theosophical teachings about the world and the self will gradually arise intuitively before your soul, if you live entirely in these sentences. They are in fact not merely phrases but powers that awaken truth, strength, and life, if you give yourself up to them.

*

* *

Write to me regularly every four weeks or so; and as often as you like if something special occurs in your spiritual life: about progress, ideas you have gained, any further elaborations. In each instance my answers will then guide you further. *Peace.*

September 24   Archive no. 5326

I. *Morning meditation.*

   a.) Elevation to the higher self:

       More radiant than the sun
       purer than snow
       finer than the ether
       is the self
       the spirit in my heart
       this self am I
       I am this self.

   b.) Meditation.

     1. Fourteen days: Before the eye can see it must lose the habit
                         of tears

     2.   ”   : Before the ear can hear it must lose its
                         sensitiveness

     3.   ”   : Before the voice can speak in the presence of
                         the masters it must have relinquished the
                         power to wound.

     4.   ”   : Before the soul can stand in their presence, the
                         feet must be washed in its heart's blood.

   c.) Devotion. Dedication to one's highest ideal.

in full wakefulness

II. *Morning meditation.*

> Review.
It is fine to fall asleep! Have I learned enough from
the experience?
Have I acted in such a way that I cannot
conceive of acting better?

> The stance is what counts (not completeness)
> *from the evening back to the morning.*

> Without regret.

As far as possible keep to a fixed time.
No alcohol at all.
Vegetarian diet is not absolutely essential
but is recommended where possible.

———

Spring 1906   Archive no. 3105/06

1.)   More radiant than the sun
       purer than snow
       finer than the ether
       is the self   } *5 minutes*
       the spirit in my heart
       this self am *I*
       I *am* this self.

2.)   On the inbreath: *Seek the way* 1 unit of time
       (deep, tranquil)

On held breath: *Seek the way in*
                 inner contemplation 3 units of time } 3 times

On the   *Seek the way*
outbreath   *by boldly*   2 units of time   5 *min*
(not jerkily)   *striding out of*
                 yourself

14 days: Before the eye can see …
14 days: Before the ear …
14 days: Before the voice …
14 days: Before the soul …

3.) Devotional dedication to one's own divine ideal.   5 min.

Drawing to a close: Month 1: Self-confidence
                        Month 2: Self-mastery
                        Month 3: Presence of mind
                        Month 4: Energy

Evening:

Review of the day:

> In relation to an experience: Did I learn enough from it?
> In relation to an action: Could I have done it better?

Without regret. Merely with the intention of learning from life.
Backward to the beginning. From evening toward morning.

No alcohol.

———————

Archive no. 5349

Decide on the time yourself,
then keep to it

Morning meditation.

    1.) Elevation to the higher self
          with the verse:

          More radiant than the sun
          purer than snow
5 mins.   finer than the ether
          is the self
          the spirit in my heart
          this self am I
          I am this self.

                                  fully wakeful

    2.) Concentration:
          1. 14 days: Before the eye…
5 mins.   2. 14 days: Before the ear…
          3. 14 days: Before [the voice can speak]
             in the presence of the masters…
          4. 14 days: Before [the soul can stand]
             in their presence

5 mins.   3.) Devotional dedication to one's
              divine ideal

Evening:
    Review of the day:
    In relation to all I experienced: Did I learn sufficiently from it?
    In relation do all I did: Would I behave in the same way again
        in the same situation?
    Without regret. In reverse from the evening toward the
        morning

———

Archive no. 3107

Morning

I.)   More radiant than the sun
purer than snow
finer than the ether   *with full*
is the self   *wakefulness*
the spirit in my heart
this self am I
I am this self.

II.)   Thought of left hand and heart, and at the same time picture:
Seek the way

Now stay in the heart and think:
Seek the way of inner contemplation

Now think of the right hand and fold it over the left, at the
same time picturing:
Seek the way by boldly striding out of yourself.

III.)   Dedicating yourself with devotion to what you regard as your
divine ideal.

Evening

Review of the day.
Without regret.
From evening to morning. Backward.
You can fall asleep!!!

———

[Morning]

More radiant than the sun
purer than snow
finer than the ether
is the self
the spirit in my heart
this self am I
I am this self.

*
* *

[Evening]

I am the self
the self am I
the spirit in my heart
is the self
it is finer than the ether
purer than snow
more radiant than the sun.

[drawing]

———

Facsimile of archive no. 3103

Strahlendes als die Sonne
Reiner als der Schnee
Feiner als der Aether
Ist das Selbst
Der Geist in meinem Herzen
Dies Selbst bin ich,
  Ich bin dies Selbst

Ich bin das Selbst
Das Selbst bin ich
Der Geist in meinem Herzen
Ist das Selbst
Es ist feiner als der Aether

Reiner als der Schnee
Strahlender als die Sonne

A–2

Exercises with the meditation
"I am – It thinks – She feels – He wills"

a) Exercises transcribed by hand
b) Cyclostyled exercises (multiple copies)
c) Additional notes/drawings

This formula appears early among the exercises. Initially, it appeared in addition to the meditation usual in the English Esoteric School ("More radiant than the sun..."); and then it accompanied the meditative verse "In the pure rays of the light...," as well as being given on its own.

Probably spring 1905   Archive no. 4401/02

After waking up in the morning, before any other impressions have passed through the soul, guide attention away from all sensory impressions and memories of daily life. One seeks to free oneself entirely from all cares, anxieties, and so forth.

First create this lull and tranquility in the soul, then:

1.) Allow only the following seven lines to live in the soul for five
    minutes:
                More radiant than the sun
                purer than snow
                finer than the ether
                is the self
                the spirit in my heart
                this self am I
                I am this self.

2.) In the second five minutes comes the following:

    1.) Concentrate on the point between and a little behind the
    eyebrows, at the same time meditating:

                        I am

    2.) Concentrate on the interior of the larynx, at the same time
    meditating:

                        It thinks

    3.) Concentrate on the two arms and hands, at the same time
    meditating:

                        She feels

    The hands may be folded during this, or the right hand can
    be placed over the left. After a while one feels how the hands

seek to separate by their own volition. But one must on no account bring this about by self-deception.

4.) Concentrate on the whole surface of the body, at the same time meditating:

He wills

Then concentrate on the pit of the stomach, at the same time meditating:

Divine life.

3.) After all this, five minutes of reverent contemplation of one's own divine ideal.

———

Evening review as previously.

———

January 1906   Archive no. 5328

Morning meditation

I.) More radiant than the sun

     ...

     ...

II.)

   a.) Concentrate on a point between and behind the
       eyes with the meditation: *I am*

   b.) Concentrate on a point in the larynx exactly
       behind its ridge, with the meditation: *It thinks*

   c.) Concentrate on the arms and hands while placing
       right hand over left, with the meditation: *She feels*

   d.) Concentrate on the whole surface of the body,
       with the meditation: *He wills.*

5 Mins.

III.) Devotional dedication to your divine ideal.

Evening: review as previously.

———

[This exercise replaces archive no. 5326, p. 34.]

Archive no. 6857

Meditation should now be allied with concentration, and consists of the same elements as previously.[117] Now, however, the meditation in *Light on the Path* is replaced by the following:

I.)   Concentrate on a point in the head lying behind the middle of the eyes, and meditate:

> *I am.*

II.)   Concentrate on the larynx, and meditate:

> *It thinks.*

III.)   Concentrate on arms and hands (the latter folded or placed over each other) and meditate:

> *She feels.*

IV.)   Concentrate on the whole surface of the body (picturing it objectively to yourself as pliable form), and meditate:

> *He wills.*

———

———

117. The "previous" exercise is not extant.

Archive no. 4415-18

Morning meditation

Part one: More radiant ...

    ...

    ...

Part two:

1.) Slow, calm inbreath with concentration on the phrase: *Seek the way*	This part is of shortest duration
2.) Hold breath and at the same time concentrate on a point between and somewhat behind the eyebrows. Initially immerse yourself fully (contemplation) in the thought *I am*. After a while pass on to concentrating on the phrase: *Seek the way of inner contemplation*. Then once again contemplate the thought *I am*.	This part is of longest duration
3.) Slow, calm outbreath, at the same time concentrating on the phrase: *Seek the way by boldly striding out of yourself*	This part lasts roughly twice as long as the first

Throughout this process of breathing, awareness focuses on a sense of addressing the *breath* itself as "you."

During the *first* inbreath, holding of breath and outbreath, accompany the breathing process with the specified meditations.

During the *second* sequence, accomplish only the breathing process, without thought or feeling.

During the *third*, as for the first

During the *fourth*, as for the second,
And so forth.

After practicing this for a few weeks, during the last sequence (of inbreath, holding breath, and outbreath, this sequence now *not* accompanied by meditation, and so forth), attend in profound stillness and with fine subtlety to the process; observe it spiritually. If you have grown ripe for this, it will now itself tell, reveal something. One has to be patient here; impatience drives away all spiritual revelations.

Part three:

1.) Concentrate on the point between and behind the eyebrows; and meditate

I am

2.) Concentrate on the point inside the larynx (where you feel the voice vibrates from), and meditate

It thinks

3.) Concentrate on both arms and hands (hands folded, or the right placed over the left), and meditate

She feels

Attend here to a warm stream passing through the arms and pouring into the fingertips, where it drives the hands apart like a repelling force.

4.) Concentrate on the whole surface of the body, and meditate

He wills

It is as if you pour out your whole body with this *He wills*.
Attend here to the living warmth that permeates the whole body; give yourself in stillness and tranquility to this sensation for a while.

Part four:

Tranquil contemplation (devotion) of one's divine ideal.

———

Archive no. NB 152

Morning:

1.) Radiant …
     …
     …   … I.

2.) i-b. o-b. h-b. [inbreath; outbreath; hold breath][118]
              Concentrate on forehead point

                    I AM

     i-b. o-b. h-b. Concentrate on larynx

                    It thinks

     i-b. o-b. h-b. Concentrate on arms, hands

                    She feels

     i-b. o-b. h-b. Concentrate on whole body

                    He wills

Inbreath while thinking of
Hold breath and spread in oneself   *I*[119]
Outbreath   } three times
                                         ICH
                                         CH.
3.) Devotion. –
4.) Image of a growing and fading plant

     5 minutes
     _____

[Evening]
8–10 lines of *Theosophy* and one's own thoughts about it.
Review.

_____

118. Inbreath, outbreath, hold breath
119. Translator's note: As becomes clear later, this exercise contains: 1. The "I" (or "J") of Jesus;
2. The word "I" in German (*ich*); and 3. The first two letters of the name Christ. Given here in
German since only the German word for "I" also contains the first two letters of Christ's name.

March 1906   Archive no. 5327

1.) More radiant than ...

    ...   .

2.) *Inbreath:*   Long, deep (lower abdomen
                    draws in, upper body comes out) ⎫
                                                    ⎬ 1 unit of time
    Meditation: *Seek the way*   ⎪
                    (as if spoken to the breath)   ⎭

    Hold breath:
    Meditation: *Seek the way in inner*   ⎫
                    contemplation   ⎬ 3 units of time
                                                    ⎭

    Outbreath: Long (not jerkily)   ⎫
    Meditation: *Seek the way by boldly*   ⎬ 2 units of time
                    striding out of yourself   ⎭

In the first week: do this once
  "   "   2. "   : second week: twice
  "   "   3. "   : third week: three times, after which no increase

                    _____

        I am
        It thinks
        She feels
        He wills

3.) Devotional dedication to your divine ideal

                    _____

Review each evening as always

                    _____

[This exercise replaces archive no. 5328, p. 46]

Evening:

1.) The human being as "I" is Earth existence.
2.) The human being as astral body is Moon thinking.
3.) The human being as ether body is Sun feeling.
4.) The human being as physical body is Saturn will.

Review of daily life

———

Morning:

Concentrate on forehead	:	I am
Concentrate on larynx	:	It thinks
Concentrate on heart	:	She feels
Concentrate on body	:	He wills

———

The exercise listed under archive no. 3164 contains the following as additional explanation:

I am:	I
It thinks:	spirit self
She feels	life spirit
He wills:	spirit human

———

Archive no. 3234

Evening: (12 midday to 12 midnight)

1.) True echo you   10 min.   [drawing, see facsimile]

        |
   I am within you   10 min. (pineal gland)
                   5 min. (larynx)
                   5 min. (heart)

> Tranquil expectancy without thinking or sensing;
> yet with awareness.

Morning: (12 midnight to 12 midday)

Between eyebrows: I am   (12 mins.)

	Hold breath	Outbreath	
Inbreath: It	(larynx)	thinks	5 min.
Inbreath: She	(heart)	feels	5 min.
Inbreath: He	(navel)	wills	5 min.

Likewise here.

[= tranquil expectancy ... as above]

———

Abends. (12 Mittags ∿ 12 Mitternacht)

1.) Wahres Echo Du̎   10 Min.

Ich bin in Dir drin   10 Min. (2. D.)

                5 Min   (K. K)

                5 Min   (H z)

Ruhiger, erwartungsvoller Zustand ohne
Denken ohne Empfinden; doch mit Bewußtsein

Morgens (12 Mitternacht bis 12 Mittag)

A. B. :   Ich bin   (12 Min)

Einatmung : Es [Kehlkopf] denkt   5 Min.

Einatmung : Sie [Herz] fühlt   5 Min.

Einatmung : Er [Nabel] will   5. Min.

                Ebenso hier.

1910 or later   Archive no. 3187/88

Evening

First undertake a review of daily life; picture single episodes of your life in images. Work back from the evening to the morning. It need last only five to seven minutes.

Then, with the sense that *My self flows to me from the world of spirit,* concentrate on the place between the eyebrows, at the same time guiding these words there:

I am

Then, with the sense that *The world of spirit lives as soul in the unspoken word,* concentrate on the larynx, at the same time guiding these words there:

It thinks

Then, with the sense that *The world of spirit engenders its knowledge,* concentrate on heart, arms, and hands, and guide these words there:

She feels

Then, with the sense that *The world of spirit creates its self-awareness within me,* concentrate on the aura that is conceived as enclosing the body in an egg-shape, at the same time guiding these words there:

He wills

The meditation should last between ten and fifteen minutes.

Morning

Meditating on ⊕ as described in *Esoteric Science.*

In addition, the six balancing exercises.

A–2b

The five cyclostyled* exercises given to members of the Esoteric School

originating around 1905/1906

For each individual pupil Rudolf Steiner wrote in his own hand on the cyclostyled* pages both a meditative verse (either "More radiant than the sun..." or "In the pure rays of the light...") and an individual meditative phrase. These latter are compiled on pp. 72–73.

---

* A cyclostyle is a stencil duplicator; also referred to as hectographed.

First thing in the morning, after waking, and before any other impressions of the day have passed through the soul, begin to meditate. Try to develop complete inner stillness and seclusion; in other words guide attention away from all outer perceptions and also all recollections of daily life. Suppress any cares and anxieties you may have; and while you are meditating, create inner peace. To achieve this more easily, spend a short while thinking *only* of a mental image; for example *tranquility*. Then let this fade from consciousness so that you are thinking of nothing. Ensure that you remain fully awake throughout the meditation, allowing no dimming of awareness. Then, for *five* minutes, allow the following seven lines, *and nothing but these*, to live in your soul. Give yourself up to them entirely; and if any other image penetrates the soul, try to return immediately to the content of the seven lines. These seven lines are:

[meditative verse in Steiner's hand:]

> More radiant than the sun
> purer than snow
> finer than the ether
> is the self
> the spirit in my heart
> this self am *I*
> I *am* this self.

After five minutes, guide awareness from these ideas into the following thought:

[meditative phrase in Steiner's hand:]

My strength

Now continue to immerse yourself completely in this thought for a further two and a half minutes; then try to suppress it, but without any other idea being mixed in with it; and remain without any mental

picture at all for a further two and a half minutes, in fully alert awareness, given up entirely to the effect of the above words on your soul:

[here the individual phrase was written again:]

My strength

Then immerse yourself in reverent (devotional) contemplation of your
divine ideal, for a further five minutes.

Time all this by feeling, not by the clock. The whole meditation need
not last longer than around fifteen minutes. Body position should be
as comfortable as possible, so that you are not distracted from inner
attentiveness by tiredness, weariness of the limbs, and so forth.

———————

Evening: Review of the day. Without regret. Back in reverse direction.

———————

First thing in the morning, before any other impressions of the day have passed through the soul, give yourself up to your meditation. Try to become completely still inwardly; in other words, withdrawing attention from outward impressions and also all recollections of daily life. Try also to release the soul from all anxieties and worries that may currently be weighing on you. Then the meditation begins. To make it easier to achieve inner stillness, you can first direct awareness to a single idea, such as "tranquility," immersing yourself entirely in this; and then let it fade from your consciousness so that you no longer have any inward picture or idea at all, but instead allow the content of the following seven lines to become vivid in it. These seven lines should live in your consciousness for only *five* minutes. If other pictures or ideas surface, keep returning to these seven lines in which you entirely immerse yourself.

[meditative verse in Steiner's hand:]

> More radiant than the sun
> purer than snow
> finer than the ether
> is the self
> the spirit in my heart
> this self am *I*
> I *am* this self.

After practicing this continually for five minutes, pass on to the following.

Breathe in calmly and strongly, after which you breathe out with equal calm and strength, without any pause between inbreath and outbreath. Then refrain from breathing for a short while, in other words endeavoring to leave the breath outside the body.

The following time periods or durations should be adhered to, roughly. The duration of the inbreath is up to you; shape the breath for a period that corresponds to your capacity. The outbreath should last twice as long as the inbreath, and the holding of breath three times as long as the inbreath. So if you take two seconds, say, for the inbreath, the outbreath will last four, and the holding of breath six seconds. Repeat this inbreath, outbreath and holding breath *four times*.

During the inbreath and outbreath, do not think of anything, but focus attention completely on the breathing; during the *first* holding of breath, by contrast, focus completely on the point between and a little behind the eyebrows, thus the root of the nose (a little way back in the interior of the forebrain) and fill your consciousness with the words:

I am

While holding your breath the second time, focus on a point inside the larynx, filling your consciousness with the thought:

It thinks.

While holding your breath the third time, focus on both arms and hands. Here you should either fold your hands or place the right hand over the left. At the same time fill your consciousness with the thought:

She feels.

While holding your breath the fourth time, focus on the whole surface of the body. In other words, picture your body as clearly as possible, at the same time filling your consciousness with the thought:

He wills.

(If you continue this concentration exercise energetically for a few weeks, you will feel something at the places you focus on; that is, the root of the nose, in the larynx, a stream in hands and arms, and over the whole outer surface of the body, while concentrating on each place.)

(While focusing on the arms and hands you will feel how a power pushes the latter apart; let them separate. In other words, follow the impulse; but do not suggest this to yourself. It must occur entirely by itself.)

(The phrases above mean the following: in "It thinks," the "it" is universal *world thinking*, which should live impersonally in our words. In "She feels," the "she" means *the* world soul; in other words, we should not feel personally but impersonally in harmony with the world soul. In "He wills," the "he" means God in whose will we place our whole being.)

After accomplishing these four breaths, fill your consciousness for a while with the *single* thought in which you immerse yourself utterly, so that for this period nothing else fills the soul. This thought is:

[meditative formula in Steiner's hand:]

I am steadfast

Then pass on to contemplation, lasting five minutes, of your own divine ideal. This must be done with all devotion (reverence).

This whole meditation need not last longer than fifteen minutes. All times given above should be judged by your feeling rather than by the clock.

Take care that you assume a bodily position which will not distract you, because of tiredness, for instance.

Evening: review of the day's experiences. In reverse.

Extract from archive no. 3929

Supplement to the previous main exercise B

Example of an individually handwritten addition by Rudolf Steiner to the cyclostyled template written in a different hand.

[Transcription of the explanation of the drawing in Steiner's hand (far left of facsimile): eye: the godhead / triangle – spirit human – life spirit / rays – I / illumined clouds: astral body / dark clouds: etheric body / unillumined surroundings: phys. body]

Hectographed main exercise C   Archive no. 3936-38

First thing in the morning after you wake up, try to create complete inner tranquility. Suppress all outer sense impressions and all recollections of daily life. Try also to adopt a bodily position that will not cause any *outward* disturbance, for instance because of the pressure of a limb. By failing to observe this latter point carefully at this stage you would confuse various outward disturbances with effects in the body caused in an entirely justified way from within, through meditation. As far as possible try also to be unaffected by outer conditions such as room temperature, so that you are not disturbed by excessive cold or heat. Then try to concentrate your awareness into a single thought; for example "tranquility." Then let this thought fade from your awareness and for five minutes immerse yourself completely in contemplation of the following lines:

[meditative verse in Steiner's hand:]

> More radiant than the sun
> purer than snow
> finer than the ether
> is the self
> the spirit in my heart
> this self am *I*
> I *am* this self.

Having accomplished this, there follows a sort of repetition of part of the second exercise.[120] With only the ordinary process of breathing, contemplate successively the thoughts "I am," focusing on the root of the nose; "It thinks," focusing on the interior of the larynx; "She feels," focusing on arms and hands; "He wills," focusing on the whole surface of the body. If this isn't too much for you, you can connect these thoughts with the breathing, exactly as in the previous exercise.

---

120. See the previous exercise B

However, since a breathing exercise is to follow, this can be left out here if you do not have the strength to undertake it.

After this, vividly picture (imagine) a plant that you know well, as if it were floating in front of your eyes. It must not be a merely shadowy, generalized image of a plant, but should be imagined in form, color, fragrance, and so forth, intensifying into a complete picture. This image should stay floating there before you while you meditate on the following words and accomplish the following breathing processes. First come three breaths as follows: inbreath (calmly and slowly for as long as you can, for three, four, or five seconds); then an equally calm outbreath (taking twice as long as the inbreath); then hold your breath (the lungs are emptied, the breath outside you, for a period three times longer than the inbreath lasted). As you do this, keep focusing your awareness on the floating image of the plant. On the inbreath think the following intensively as if addressing the plant:

Your death – my life.

On the outbreath, think the following, again in relation to the plant:

While holding your breath, refrain from any thoughts and wait to see whether anything is revealed to you.

Inbreath (any duration); then hold the breath within you (for three times as long as the inbreath); then breathe out calmly (taking twice as long as the inbreath).

On the inbreath, again think the following:

Your death – my life.

While holding your breath think of nothing; on the outbreath think:

My death – your life.

Then, after these six breaths, vividly picture stepping out of yourself in your awareness and leaving the body where it is. Place your soul into the plant as though you were spiritually the plant, and therefore have your own body before you. In doing so, accomplish the seventh breath as follows:

Inbreath (any duration); hold the breath within you (three times longer than the inbreath); then breathe out (taking twice as long as the inbreath).

On the inbreath, think the following as if directing the thought to your own body:

> *My death — your life.*

When holding your breath, think nothing.

On the outbreath, imagine again that you are addressing your own body:

> *Your death — my life.*

Then release your awareness entirely; let it be inwardly still, and fill it for a longer period (as long as you can manage) with only the following *single* thought:

[meditative formula in Steiner's hand:]

> *All above as below*
> *All below as above*

Then contemplate for a while what you acknowledge as your divine ideal. Create a very reverent (devotional) mood toward this ideal.

*
*　*

This whole meditative and concentration exercise need not take longer than twenty to twenty-five minutes.

Evening: Review

Extract from archive no. 3938b

Supplement to the previous main exercise C

Example of an individually handwritten addition by Rudolf Steiner to the cyclostyled template written in a different hand.

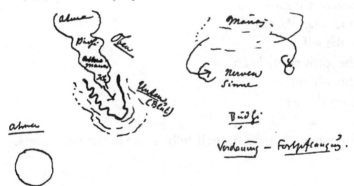

[Atma / budhi / manas / I
Above / below (blood)   Manas / nerves   senses
Atma   Budhi / digestion – reproduction]

Hectographed main exercise D   Archive no. 3939

First thing in the morning, immediately on waking, meditate in the following way:

Establish complete inner tranquility; try to dispel completely all thoughts of your daily affairs. For as long as you meditate, try to completely forget all cares and sorrows. Turn your attention away, also, from all sensory impressions. Become as if blind and deaf to your surroundings, and suppress all memories of ordinary life. Here you need to adopt a body position that will not allow a limb to distract you during meditation, because of tiredness, for instance. Take care also that your surroundings will not distract you by their temperature—heat or cold. Once you are ready, first think only a *single* thought, for example *tranquility*. This focuses your awareness fully, concentrating it in one point. Then let the thought go; that is, let it fade from your awareness so that the latter is entirely free, still in itself and calm. Now, for five minutes, fill the soul entirely with the following verse:

[meditative verse in Steiner's hand:]

> More radiant than the sun
> purer than snow
> finer than the ether
> is the self
> the spirit in my heart
> this self am I
> I am this self.

It is important to immerse yourself fully in the content of these seven lines.

> Then follow seven breaths, thus:
> The first three breaths like this:

Inbreath, then immediately outbreath; then refrain from breathing for a certain time; thus the air is outside you. The inbreath can last as long as you wish (for example two seconds; for as long as your strength allows). The outbreath, though, must then last roughly twice as long as the inbreath, and the holding of breath three times as long. Breathing must be slow and calm. The time it takes is not measured by the clock but by your feeling.

Throughout, picture to yourself very precisely a plant you know well, as if it were floating before you and you were observing it continually. While breathing in think *only* as if you are directing this thought to the plant:

Your death, my life.

While breathing out, similarly, think:

My death, your life.

While holding your breath, refrain from all thoughts and wait to see if anything is revealed to you.

Then follow three further breaths, thus;

Inbreath (any duration); then hold the breath within you (for a duration three times as long as the inbreath); then breathe out calmly (taking twice as long as the inbreath).

On the inbreath, once again think:

Your death, my life.

While holding your breath, think nothing;

On the outbreath, think:

My death, your life.

After completing these six breaths, very vividly picture that you are stepping out of yourself with your awareness and leaving the body where it is. Place your soul into the plant, as if you were the plant spiritually, so that you now have your own body in front of you. Then take the seventh breath as follows:

Inbreath (any duration); hold the breath within you (for three times as long as the inbreath); then breathe out (taking twice as long as the inbreath).

On the inbreath think only as if you were addressing this thought to your own body:

My death, your life.

While holding the breath, think nothing.

On the outbreath again think as if addressing your own body:

Your death, my life,

Then release your awareness entirely again, make it inwardly still, and fill it for a longer period—as long as you can manage—with the following *single* thought:

[meditative formula in Steiner's own hand:]

My strength

Then immerse yourself for a while in what you acknowledge to be your divine ideal. Engender a very reverent (devotional) mood toward this.

*
* *

This whole meditation and concentration exercise need not take longer than fifteen to twenty minutes.

———

Evening: Review of the day. Pictorially, in reverse.

———

Archive no. 3177

A notebook sheet contains the following exercise using a lifeless object:

Picture a colored, lifeless object:

Inbreath:	Your *dark* – my *light*
Outbreath:	My *dark* – your *light*
Hold breath.	
Twice.	

Then place yourself in the object. *Once:*

Inbreath:	My *dark* – your *light*
Outbreath:	Your *dark* – my *light*
Hold breath.	

Supplement to these first four hectographed main exercises A – D:

Below are listed all the phrases which Rudolf Steiner added in his own hand for each pupil (to the cyclostyled texts contained in the archive). Rudolf Steiner noted a number of these phrases in one of his notebooks, under the heading: "Phrases given to each individual." From the extant copies it is clear, nevertheless, that the same phrase was given to several pupils.

> Know yourself
> Stability
> I breathe light in, I breathe light out
> I am steadfast
> I am spirit
> I in me
> I understand the beings
> I will
> Strength in my thoughts
> Strength in me
> All above as below / All below as above
> Light through me
> Light in my thoughts
> Light-filled clarity
> My steadfastness
> My strength
> My vital power
> My soul is
> Tranquility in energy, energy in tranquility[121]
> Tranquility in strength, strength in tranquility
> Calm within me, calm through me
> Soul in the body

---

121. Translator's note: This line and the next are very close in meaning, but employ two subtly different words: *Kraft* (strength, energy, force) and *Stärke* (strength, power). The latter is slightly more static, the former potentially more dynamic.

Soul harmony
Soul power
Soul light illumines me
Soul warmth imbues me
Soul warmth streams through me
Peace of soul
Blessed tranquility
Wisdom's glowing light shines through me
As above so below

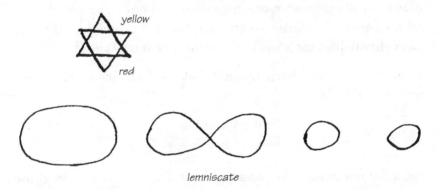

lemniscate

The following commentary in relation to these phrases intended for different individuals is found in notes of the esoteric lessons given in Munich, June 6, 1907, CW 266/I:

After these seven lines [of the meditative verse], we were given a word or a phrase for contemplation. This concentration on a phrase or a word, such as "strength," is very important. It is a kind of watchword, a word of power, carefully adapted to each individual's frame of mind and state of soul. We should let this word or phrase reverberate in the soul in the same way that one strikes a tuning fork. And just as one hearkens to the fading note of the tuning fork, so, after contemplation of the word, we should also let it quietly fade away in the soul and give ourselves up to what this word or phrase has engendered in the soul.

Hectographed main exercise E   Archive no. 7073

Strictly confidential   *Main exercise*
Esoteric exercises

1.) A morning meditation should be undertaken as follows:

First thing in the morning, before doing anything of a mundane nature and before eating, create complete inner tranquility. Direct attention away from all external sensory impressions and ordinary rational ideas. All memories of ordinary events must also fall completely silent. In particular, all life's cares and anxieties must be utterly stilled.

Then, from the completely tranquil soul, the following thought must rise up:

> *Above all as below*
> *Below all as above*

For a full ten minutes (as measured by feeling, not by the clock) live only in thoughts and pictures to be gained by applying this thought to phenomena in the world. It is not initially a matter of forming thoughts and images that are correct, but of activating your thoughts and inner picturing in this direction. But as far as you can, try to form only correct thoughts and images.

After completing this, continue with the following: take seven breaths, the inbreath of each taking only as long as will enable you to accomplish the rest without harmful effect.

Breathe in; and when you have do so, breathe out again immediately; then leave the air outside you, thus suppressing a new inbreath entirely for a while.

Observe the following durations:

> *Inbreath:* as above, optional duration.

Outbreath: twice as long as inbreath.

Holding breath: four times longer than inbreath (to begin with, then gradually intensifying this to ten times longer than the inbreath).

During the first and second period of holding the breath, immerse yourself entirely in the thought:

I am

at the same time focusing on the point at the root of the nose. (You find this point by drawing a horizontal line backward from the point between the eyebrows for about a centimeter.)

When holding the breath for the third and fourth time, contemplate the thought:

It thinks

and focus on the larynx.

During the fifth and sixth holding of breath, contemplate the thought:

She feels

at the same time focusing on the heart.

When holding the breath for the seventh time, contemplate the thought:

He wills

and focus on the navel by picturing rays that penetrate the whole lower abdomen.

While breathing in and out, refrain from any thought.

("It" means: world thinking. "She" means: the world soul. "He" means: the world spirit. But these concepts are only intended as orientation, and should not be present in your awareness during meditation; they would only disturb the mantra-type character of the above phrases.)

Finish this whole exercise by contemplating your own divine ideal with a sense of devotion.

2.) During the day, carry out the balancing exercises described elsewhere.

3.) In the evening, review the day's events, in images,[122] in reverse.

Avoid alcohol altogether. A vegetarian diet is not essential, but is certainly helpful.

———

122. Translator's note: The German word *bildsam* literally means "pliable" or "ductile"; but Steiner seems to use it in alternation with *bildhaft* to indicate a form of thinking that occurs pictorially, in vivid images.

A–2c

Supplementary notes for exercises with the meditation
I am – It thinks – She feels – He wills

Archive no. 346

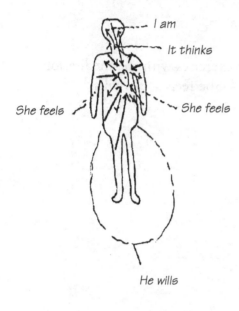

I) I am

II) It thinks

III) She feels

IV) He wills

V   a.) Concentration:
The streams are drawn from the body's
periphery toward the heart:
b.) Meditation: *Seek the way.*

          } Inbreath

VI   a.) Concentration: the soul stays resting
for a while in the heart
b.) Meditation: *Seek the way of inner
contemplation*

          } Breath still

VII   a.) Concentration: The streams pass from
the heart to the body's periphery
b.) Meditation: *Seek the way by...*

          } Outbreath

———

Archive no. 3171

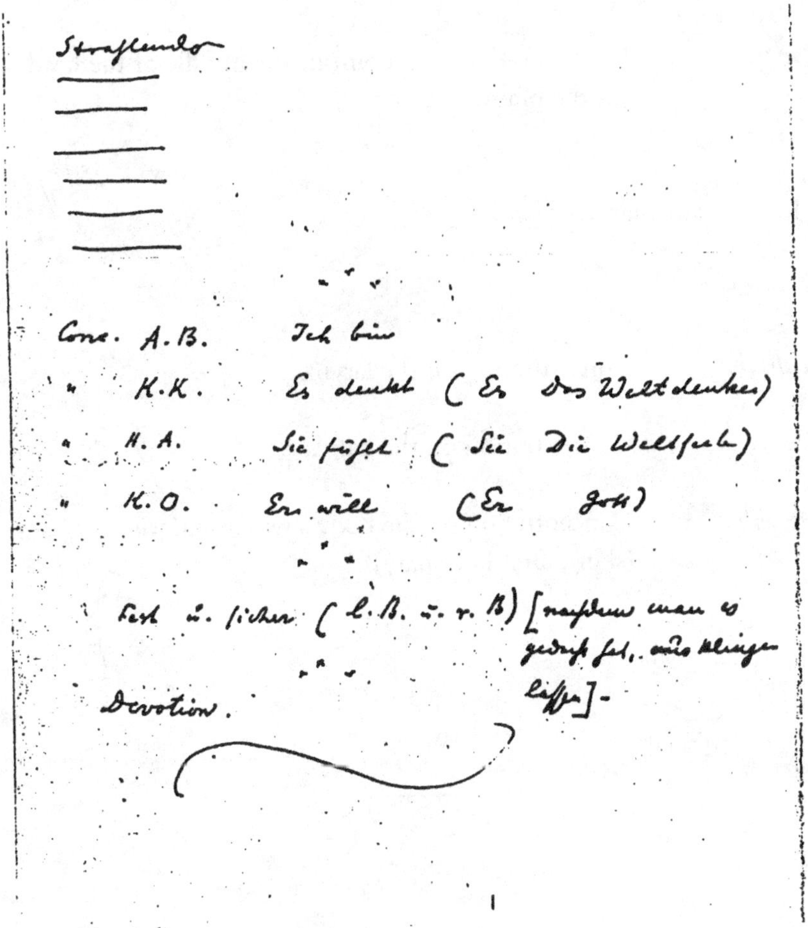
Strahlender

Conc. A.B. Ich bin
" K.K. Es denkt (Es = das Weltdenken)
" H.A. Sie fühlt (Sie = die Weltseele)
" K.O. Er will (Er = Gott)

Fest u. sicher (l.B. = r.B) [nachdem man es gedruckt hat, aus klingen lassen] -

Devotion.

More radiant

Conc. on eyebrows I am
" on larynx — It thinks (It = world thinking)
" hands and arms — She feels (She = the world soul)
" surface of body — He wills (He = God)

Steadfast and sure (left leg = right leg) [after one has [illegible] allow to fade out]

Devotion

Archive no. 357

I am: Concentration on a point in the middle of the head
                   (in the brain).

More radiant than ...

   ...

   ...

It thinks: Concentration on the larynx

She feels: Concentration on the hands[123]

He wills: Concentration on the body's whole surface
                   (skin, outer boundary)[124]

————

————

123. The hands are the organs whereby the feeling human soul elevates itself above the merely feeling animal soul. In the animal the front limbs are not (as they are in us) organs that consciously create karma.

124. This outer boundary is what facilitates our reversal: that is, before we had an external boundary we were outside ourselves; then, with an external boundary we are within ourselves.

Archive no. 356

1.) Organization of the plant – animal organism is brought about
through contemplation of the thought:

I am

_____

2.) More radiant …

...

...   ... I.

_____

3.) Organization of the mental organism is brought about through
contemplation of the thought:

It thinks

[yellow(green)]

gelb(grün)

4.) Organization of the mental-kamic [sic] organism is brought
about through contemplation of the thought:

She feels

[(green)blue]

grünblau

5.) Organization of the astral organism is brought about through
contemplation of the thought:

He wills

[(blue)red
light purple]

_____

Archive no. 4479

More radiant than the sun

...

...   ... self

Surroundings with senses	*Will*
Using hands	*Feeling*
Using larynx	*Thinking*
Using brain	*Am*

light red

I am: with concentration on a point in the
          forehead between and behind eyebrows

It thinks: with concentration on the larynx
               outward-directed

[Southward-directed]
yellow

She feels: with concentration on the arms and
               hands

green

He wills: with concentration on surface of body   blue

He wills   *Concentration on the whole surface of the body*

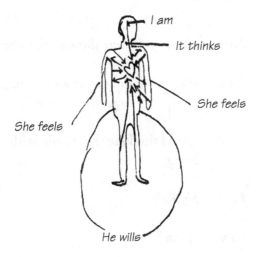

a.) The streams flow from the body's   Concentration
periphery to the heart   Inbreath

    Meditation: Seek the way

b.) Resting of all soul sensibility in   Concentration
the heart   Holding breath

    Meditation: Seek the way of
    inner contemplation.

c.) The streams flow from the heart to   Concentration
the body's periphery   Outbreath

    Meditation: Seek the way by
    stepping boldly out of yourself.

Archive no. 4480

8 days =	*I am:*	feeling your way through the whole organism

8 days =	*I am:*	*It thinks:* feeling your way through the whole organism

World thinking that thinks within the human being

8 days =	*I am:*	*She feels*

8 days =	*I am:*	*He wills*

———

It is *world thinking*
She is the *world soul*
He is the *world will*

The human phys. body
In relation to this, the human being
says *I am*

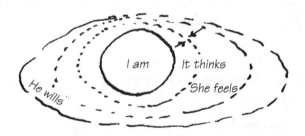

In fact, in the fifth Round, *Jupiter*, the human being
will refer to himself as *It*.
in the sixth Round, Venus, as *She*
in the seventh Round, Vulcan, as *He*

———

Transcriptions

For archive no. 353:

Manas – spirit self / budhi – life spirit / atma – spirit human / 3rd Logos arupa: mental body / he (divine spirit) / atma mental body: she wills / budhi astral body: it feels life spirit (world soul) / manas ether body: I think spirit self / Cogito ergo sum / physical body: am /

I am: mixed / It thinks: gold / She feels: silver / He wills: bronze[125]

> Aum
> I am
>
> More radiant ......

It thinks / She feels / He wills

> devotional

For archive no. 354:

Object – Subject / World-creative thought – thoughts (line, plane, genus, and so
  forth) / Astral light World-creative feeling light of eons of higher kind – Feeling
(joy, suffering. symp. antip.) / World-creative will / light of eons of lower kind –
  sentience (color, light, dark) /
1.) The world-creative thought formed the human organ of thinking
2.) The higher light of eons formed the organ of feeling of the organ of Kama manas
3.) The lower light of eons formed the Indyras or the sensory organs of perception
  (sensation)
It thinks...system of nerves (brain) / She feels...organs of feeling / He wills...organs of perception (senses) / Body with all organs that serve the lower functions. I am

Mental matter / astral matter / etheric matter

For archive no. 355

I am	he	I am
	she wills	More radiant...
	it feels	it thinks
	I think	he wills

The willing spirit of God should will in kama manas, then human beings places their kama manas in the right harmony between themselves and the universe of will (first logos)

The creative world soul should feel in kama (astral) then human beings place their kama in the right harmony with the universal world feeling (second logos)

The universe of thoughts should think in the ether body, then human beings place their ether body in the right harmony with the universal world thought (third logos)

---

125. Translator's note: This would seem to relate to the four kings in Goethe's fairytale *The Green Snake and the Beautiful Lily*.

Cogito, ergo sum

Archive no. 354

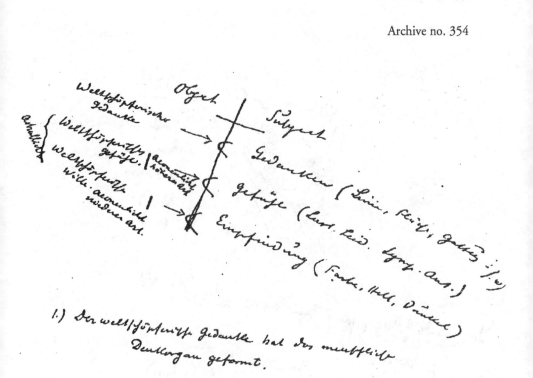

1.) Der weltschöpferische Gedanke hat das menschliche Denkorgan geformt.

2.) Das höhere Aeonenlicht hat das Gefühlsorgan oder die Organe von Kama manas geformt.

3.) Das niedere Aeonenlicht hat die Indryas oder die Wahrnehmungs-Erkenntnisorgane geformt.

Ich bin

Ich bin

er

sie

denkt

fühlt

will

Straße

es denkt.

sie fühlt.

er will

Der wollende Gottesgeist soll in Kama manas wollen, dann setzt

der Mensch hin

Kama manas in die richtige Harmonie

zwischen sich und dem Willens-Universum (1. Logos)

Die ätherische Weltenseele soll in Kama (astral) fühlen, dann

setzt der Mensch hin

Kama in die richtige Harmonie

zum universellen Weltengefühl (2. Logos)

Das Gedanken-Universum soll im Aetherkörper denken,

dann setzt der Mensch seinen Aetherkörper in

die richtige Harmonie

zum universellen Weltengedanken (3. Logos).

A–3

Exercises with the meditative verse
"In the pure rays of the light…"

This verse originated at the beginning of 1906,
and was given in the Esoteric School until around 1914.

End of September 1906   Archive no. 7077-79

First thing in the morning, soon after waking, undertake a meditation exercise before any other impressions pass through the soul. Withdraw all attention from external impressions, becoming very still and inwardly peaceful. During this time all recollections of ordinary daily life must also fall silent, and especially all of life's cares and worries must vanish while you concentrate. To better achieve meditative concentration, first think of a single thought, such as *tranquility*. Once you have succeeded in focusing your whole awareness on this single idea, let it too fade from your consciousness; and for five minutes allow only the following seven lines to live in your soul:

> In the pure rays of the light
> gleams out the godhood of the world
> in pure love for every being
> shines out the godliness of my soul
> I rest in the godhood of the world
> I will find myself
> in the godhood of the world.

After these seven lines have lived in you for five minutes, by strong resolve of will, focus your consciousness on the point between and somewhat behind the eyebrows, as if you were living only in this point, while all else, including your own body, had vanished. In this state of concentration think about something that you wish to accomplish. Then allow this thought to vanish from your mind and think of nothing else except "*I will.*" While doing so, maintain concentration on the same point.

Then do exactly the same again, except that now your concentration is focused on your feet instead of the point previously described. This second part of the meditation should again take five minutes.

Then follow five minutes of reverent devotion to your divine ideal.

*
* *

Evening: Review of the day. In reverse chronological sequence.
            Without regret.

*
* *

Try to practice:
            First month: thought concentration

———————

December 1906   Archive no. 3062/63

First thing in the morning after waking, create complete inner tranquility; turn attention away from all external sensory perceptions; then rid
the soul of all cares and anxieties.

Then (briefly) contemplate the word *tranquility*.

Then let this thought fall away, and for five minutes live in the following seven lines:

> In the pure rays of the light
> gleams out the godhood of the world
> in pure love for every being
> shines out the godliness of my soul
> I rest in the godhood of the world
> I will find myself
> in the godhood of the world.

Then spend five minutes contemplating a single thought:

> During the first month: *self-confidence*
> During the second month: *self-mastery*
> During the third month: *perseverance*

Then five minutes of devotional (reverent) contemplation of your own
divine ideal.

In the evening, before sleep:
Review of the day's events and actions. Without regret; just trying to
learn from life. In reverse.

Read my *Theosophy*.

                              *
                          *   *

In another, identically-worded exercise (archive no. 3059), the following individual formula is given after the verse:

> During the day:
> First week: How do I gain self-confidence?
> Second week: How do I gain self-mastery?
> Third week: How do I gain presence of mind?

———

Archive no. 3056

Main exercise

Morning: *Tranquility*

Then (briefly) contemplate the word *tranquility*.

Then let this thought fall away, and for five minutes live in the following seven lines:

> In the pure rays of the light
> gleams out the godhood of the world
> in pure love for every being
> shines out the godliness of my soul
> I rest in the godhood of the world
> I will find myself
> in the godhood of the world.

*
* *

Tranquility in strength   }   then *fading away* without
Strength in tranquility   }   thinking of anything

*
* *

Devotional contemplation of your own divine ideal

———————
—————
———————

Evening: Review of the day: in reverse.

Hauptübung

Morgens: Ruhe.

In den reinen Strahlen des Lichtes
Erglänzt die Gottheit der Welt
In der reinen Liebe zu allen Wesen
Erstrahlt die Göttlichkeit meiner Seele
Ich ruhe in der Gottheit der Welt
Ich werde mich selbst finden
In der Gottheit der Welt.

✳ ✳ ✳

Ruhe in der Stärke   } dann abklingen, ohne was zu
Stärke in der Ruhe   denken

✳ ✳ ✳

Devotionell sich vertiefen in das eigene göttliche Ideal

Abend: Rückschau auf das Tagesleben: Von rückwärts nach
                                            vorn.

Archive no. 3039

Main exercise

Morning:

Tranquility

then five minutes:

> In the pure rays of the light
> gleams out the godhood of the world
> in pure love for every being
> shines out the godliness of my soul
> I rest in the godhood of the world
> I will find myself
> in the godhood of the world.

then two and a half minutes:

> Light-filled clarity

then for two and a half minutes thinking of nothing, but letting the words "light-filled clarity" fade away.

then: reverent devotion to your own divine ideal.

———

Evening:

> I rest in the godhood of the world
> I will find myself
> in godhood.

Review of the day's events, images, in reverse.

———

Archive no. 6826

Morning:

Five minutes

In the pure rays of the light
gleams out the godhood of the world
in pure love for every being
shines out the godliness of my soul
I rest in the godhood of the world
I will find myself
in the godhood of the world.

*
* *

5 minutes:

I breathe   I   in
I breathe   I   out

*
* *

5 minutes:

Self-reliance	first week
Steadfastness	second week
Assurance	third week

———

Evening: Review of the day. Without regret. In reverse.

———

Archive no. 3070

[Morning:]

Tranquility

In the pure rays of the light
gleams out the godhood of the world
in pure love for every being
shines out the godliness of my soul   5 minutes
I rest in the godhood of the world
I will find myself
in the godhood of the world.

Inbreath	I [126]
Hold breath	ICH
Outbreath	CH

*
* *

Devotional dedication to your own ideal.

———

[Evening:]

Review of the day. In images.
In reverse.

———

———

126. Translator's note: As becomes clear later, this exercise contains: 1. The "I" (or "J") of Jesus; 2. The word "I" in German (*ich*); and 3. The first two letters of the name Christ. I have given it in German since only the German word for "I" also contains the first two letters of Christ's name.

Archive no. 6513

In the *morning* before any other experience of the day, with complete inner tranquility and keeping awareness removed from external impressions, contemplate the following seven lines:

> In the pure rays of the light
> gleams out the godhood of the world
> in pure love for every being
> shines out the godliness of my soul
> I rest in the godhood of the world
> I will find myself
> in the godhood of the world.

This contemplation should last about five minutes, timed by feeling rather than by the clock.

Then picture the image of a growing plant: first the seed which gradually develops a stalk, leaves, flower, and so forth. This image must be such that the plant arises very slowly, taking five minutes (again by feeling, not the clock) to form the complete plant from the original seed.

After this, a further five minutes of devotional dedication; complete reverent immersion in your own divine ideal.

*
* *

Evening: Review of the day. In images. In reverse.

*
* *

Also, during the day the attached balancing exercises [see p.1].

Archive no. 5253

Tranquility

> In the pure rays of the light
> gleams out the godhood of the world
> in pure love for every being
> shines out the godliness of my soul
> I rest in the godhood of the world
> I will find myself
> in the godhood of the world.

10 min.

*
* *

God in me.

———

During the day: Growth and wilting of a plant, concentration unfolding slowly.

———

Evening: First week: Inner nature of the human being[127]
Second week: Life between death and birth.

Review of the day. In images. In reverse.

———

127. The references to "Inner nature of the human being" and "Life between death and birth" relate to chapters in *Theosophy,* CW 9, which bear those headings.

Morning: *Tranquility*

> In the pure rays of the light
> gleams out the godhood of the world
> in pure love for every being
> shines out the godliness of my soul
> I rest in the godhood of the world
> I will find myself
> in the godhood of the world.

*
* *

Vividly picturing   1.) Growing plant
                           2.) Wilting/fading plant

*
* *

Inbreath – I[128]
While holding breath ICH   ⎫
          distributing in body   ⎬   three times
Outbreath CH.   ⎭

Evening:

1.) Read a little of *Theosophy* and spend around a quarter of an hour forming your own personal ideas relating to it.

————

2.) Devotional dedication to your own divine ideal.

————

3.) Review. In images, in reverse.

————

128. Translator's note: As becomes clear later, this exercise contains: 1. The "I" (or "J") of Jesus; 2. The word "I" in German (ich); and 3. The first two letters of the name Christ. I have given it in German since only the German word for "I" also contains the first two letters of Christ's name.

Archive no. 3075

Morning:

Pour out tranquility within you.

Then contemplate the following seven lines:

> In the pure rays of the light
> gleams out the godhood of the world
> in pure love for every being
> shines out the godliness of my soul
> I rest in the godhood of the world
> I will find myself
> in the godhood of the world.

15 to 20 mins.
by feeling, not
by the clock

*
* *

Then   Inbreath I(esus)   consciously
        Outbreath CH(rist)   seven times

Then meditation on the Gospel of St. John
(ongoing). Retain the first 14 verses *every* day.

———

During the day, five minutes of thought concentration. Focus thoughts
on an unimportant object and keep them there for five minutes. (The
same object for a longer period.)

———

Evening:

Review of the day's events. In images. In reverse; from the evening back
to the morning.

Archive no. 4465

Morning: *Main exercise*

     Tranquility

     In the pure rays of the light
     gleams out the godhood of the world
     in pure love for every being
     shines out the godliness of my soul
     I rest in the godhood of the world
     I will find myself
     in the godhood of the world.

*
* *

          Find myself in the universe
          Will myself in the universe
          Form myself in the universe
          Create myself in the universe

Deep inbreath	1	⎫
Deep outbreath	2	⎬ time units
Hold breath	3	⎭

_____

During the first breath, think:
    I know, focusing on the feet
During the second breath, think:
    I am, focusing on the front of the head
During the third breath, think:
    It thinks, focusing on the region of the larynx
During the fourth breath, think:
    She feels, focusing on arms and hands
During the fifth breath, think:
    He wills, focusing on the whole body.

*
*   *

Reverent contemplation of your own divine ideal.

———

Evening: Slow, calm review of the day's events. In reverse.

———

1910 or later   Archive no. 3081

Evening: Review.

          live in after-effect.

                              *
                          *   *

live in a

          In the pure rays of the light   (light – wisdom)
          gleams out the godhood of the world
          in pure warmth for every being   (warmth – love)
          shines out the godliness of my soul
          I rest in the godhood of the world
          I will find myself
          in the godhood of the world.

live in after-effect.

                              *
                          *   *

p. 306 six qualities[129]   *study*

                        ———

---

129. This refers to the balancing exercises in the book *Esoteric Science*, p. 306 in the first edition of 1910. See note on p. 455.

1910   Archive no. 5625

Morning:

For five minutes, to establish equilibrium of soul forces, concentrate on the words:

I am.

Introduce into the soul forces thus brought into equilibrium the image/idea of

with all the feelings and sentiments cited in relation to this in ES [*Esoteric Science*]; then, as if radiating from the Rose Cross, receive the following soul contents:

> In the pure rays of the light
> gleams out the godhood of the world
> in pure activity of wisdom
> divine being experiences itself
> I am resting one with the world's godhood
> I am living in will activity
> I am.

Allow this content to flow back, as it were, into the ☧ ; and for a period, which will necessarily be short initially, growing ever longer, rest in inner tranquility that allows no external impressions and memories to surface.

*
* *

Evening: Picturing of some of the day's events, precisely and pictorially, but in reverse.

Transition to the ☿

Receiving as if from this the same impressions (seven lines above) as in the morning.

Once more tranquil resting in them, if possible until you fall asleep.

————

As balancing exercise, cultivation of the six qualities as described in ES.

————

1910 or later   Archive no. 7115

Evening:

1.) Review. Pictorially. In reverse, five to six min.

2.) An event of the day, such that it becomes self-judgment.

3.)   In the light's pure shining
           May world's godhood gleam toward my spirit

           In pure warmth of heart
           let human godhood shine out toward my soul   } 10 min.
           I rest in the godhood of the world
           let my self apprehend its being
           sustaining itself in the godhood of the world.

                                        (Inner tranquility)

Morning:

                I rest in the godhood of the world
15 mins.   let my self apprehend its being
                sustaining itself in the godhood of the world.

                                        (Inner tranquility)

6 exercises: *Esoteric Science*, p. 306 [130]

————

————

130. Translator's note: Again, this refers to the original German edition and the six balancing exercises.

Abend: 1.) Rückschau. Bildhaft. Rückläufig 5-6 min.

2.) Ein Tageserlebnis so, dass es Selbstbeurteilung wird.

3.) In des Lichtes reinen Strahlen
Erglänze meinem Geist die Ganzheit der Welt.

⊕

In des Herzens reiner Wärme
Erstrahle meine Seele die Ganzheit des Menschen
Ich ruhe in der Ganzheit der Welt
Mein Selbst ergreife sich
Sich haltend in der Ganzheit der Welt

(Seelenruhe)

10 Min

Morgens:

⊕

15 Min:
Ich ruhe in der Ganzheit der Welt
Mein Selbst ergreife sich
Sich haltend in der Ganzheit der Welt

(Seelenruhe)

6 Übungen = Geheime. S. 306.

[Two additional versions of the verse]

1908   Archive no. 3432

> In the pure rays of the light
> gleams out the godhood of the world
> in pure fire of the ether
> shines out I-hood's lofty power
> I rest in the spirit of the world
> I will always find myself
> in the eternal spirit of the world.

1908   Archive no. NB 337

> In the pure rays of the light
> gleams out the spirit of the world
> in pure warmth for every being
> shines out the soul of a life
> I rest in the soul of the world
> I will find my self
> in the spirit of the world.

A–4

Exercises with the meditative verse
"In the pure rays of the light..."

and its reversal as
"In the godhood of the world..."

Archive no. 3061

Morning: Recollecting lines you have read (theos. book)

> In the pure rays of the light
> gleams out the godhood of the world
> in pure love for every being
> shines out the godliness of my soul   } 8 mins.
> I rest in the godhood of the world
> I will find myself
> in the godhood of the world.

———

5 mins.   CHR.

*
* *

Evening: A few lines in a theos. book.

CHR

> In the godhood of the world
> I will find myself
> I rest therein[131]
> the godliness of my soul shines out   } 8 mins.
> in pure love for every being
> the godhood of the world gleams out
> in the pure rays of the light.

———

Review of the day.

---

131. Translator's note: Wherever the word "therein" appears in these verses, this is given in capitals in German as 'in *IHR*' (that is "in IT," in the godhood). This may be because the handwritten IHR resembles or is reminiscent of the CHR with which Steiner often indicates the name of Christ. It would seem wrong in English to capitalize the word "it," which bears no such resemblance.

Morgens: <u>Wiedererinnern der gelesenen Teile.</u> [Hes. ung]

In den reinen Strahlen des Lichtes
Erglänzt die Gottheit der Welt
In der reinen Liebe zu allen Wesen
Erwachet die Göttlichkeit meiner Seele
Ich ruhe in der Gottheit der Welt
Ich werde mich selber finden
In der Gottheit der Welt.

—

8 Min

5 Min: CHR.

Abends: Einige Zeilen in einem Theos. Buch.
CHR

In der Gottheit der Welt
Werde ich mich selber finden
In IHR ruhe ich
Es erstrahlt die Göttlichkeit meiner Seele
In der reinen Liebe zu allen Wesen
Es erglänzt die Gottheit der Welt
In den reinen Strahlen des Lichtes.

8 Min.

—

Rückschau auf das Tagesleben.

May 1909   Archive no. 3053

Morning:

Tranquility

In the pure rays of the light
gleams out the godhood of the world
in pure love for every being
shines out the godliness of my soul   } 10 mins.
I rest in the godhood of the world
I will find myself
in the godhood of the world.

*
* *

Inbreath   I[132] }
Holding breath   ICH   } 3 times
Outbreath   CH   }

During the day: balancing exercises.

———

Evening:

In the godhood of the world
I will find myself
I rest in the godhood of the world
the godliness of my soul shines out   } 10 mins.
in pure love for every being
the godhood of the world gleams out
in the pure rays of the light.

Then review of the day in reverse, in images } 7 to 8 mins.

———

132. Translator's note: As we have seen, this exercise contains: 1. The "I" (or "J") of Jesus; 2. The word "I" in German (*ich*); and 3. The first two letters of the name Christ. I have given it in German since only the German word for "I" also contains the first two letters of Christ's name.

May 1909

Morning:

Tranquility

10 mins.
{
In the pure rays of the light
gleams out the godhood of the world
in pure love for every being
shines out the godliness of my soul
I rest in the godhood of the world
I will find myself
in the godhood of the world.

5 mins.   Illustrious sun spirit enter me

———

During the day: balancing exercises.

———

Evening:

{
In the godhood of the world
I will find myself
I rest in the godhood of the world
the godliness of my soul shines out
in pure love for every being
the godhood of the world gleams out
in the pure rays of the light.

Review of the day

———

Archive no. 3148-51

Evening:

1.) Read a short passage from *Christianity as Mystical Fact*, impressing it on yourself sufficiently to be able to reconstruct it again from memory in the morning.

2.) Vivid reverse picturing of some of the events of the day.

3.) Picturing the setting sun in white light, as though the power of the CHR rays out of this light, accompanied by these words:

> *In the pure rays of the light*
> *gleams out the godhood of the world*

Then let the image of the sun grow yellow-red, as if the love of the CHR were gleaming out in the redness, with the words:

> *in pure love for every being*
> *shines out the godliness of the soul*

Then transform the image of the sun into green, allowing four red roses to appear upon its face below

with the words:

> *I rest in the godhood of the world*

then three red roses above

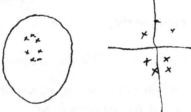

with the words:

I will find myself

then a black cross on the green background with the words:

in the godhood of the world.

Then fall asleep in the mood engendered by these phrases.

Morning:

1.) Recall what you read in the evening from *Christianity as Mystical Fact*

2.) Picture a white cross:

with the words:

In the godhood of the world

Add to this, over the crossbeam, three red roses with the words:

I will find myself

then add four red roses under the crossbeam with the words:

> *I rest therein*

then add a green background with the words:

> *the godliness of the soul shines out*
> *in pure love for every being*

then add a green background with the words:

> *the godliness of the soul shines out*
> *in pure love for every being*

Then add a purple framing, its outer edge fading into indistinctness, with the words:

> *the godhood of the world gleams out*
> *in the pure rays of the light.*

(With the words "godhood" and "godliness" we picture the inner and outer CHR power.[133])

Then, maintaining inner tranquility, remain in expectancy without external impressions and memories. The revelations which the soul is to receive will arise when the time is ripe.

*

*   *

Develop the six qualities

---

133. Translator's note: It is given in this order in the German text, but presumably "godhood" relates to outer and "godliness" to inner power.

Archive no. 3200/01

Every *Evening:*

1.) Read a short passage from *Christianity as Mystical Fact.* Impress it upon yourself sufficiently to be able to reawaken it from memory in detail in the morning.

2.) Reverse picturing of some events of the day.

3.) Vivid picturing of the ⊕
Black cross with seven red roses
accompanied by the feeling:

> "In true endeavor what prevents our ascent to the spirit dies away as the light is extinguished in the black cross; the spirit blossoms in the soul as the seven red roses flower out of the black cross."

Then feel the power of the CHR in the radiance of the roses, and fill the soul entirely with these words (for up to ten minutes):

> *In the pure rays of the light*
> *in the pure warmth of the rays*
> *gleams, shines out the godhood of the world.*

(Fall asleep in inner tranquility, in the mood arising from this exercise.)

Every *Evening:*

1.) Clear recall of what you read the previous evening in *Christianity as Mystical Fact.*

2.) Invoke the ⊕ clearly again within you, with the same feelings as in the evening (the cross white now instead of black, the roses red).

Then (for up to ten minutes) allow these words to live in your soul:

> *The godhood of the world gleams, shines out*
> *in the pure warmth of the rays*
> *in the pure rays of the light*

Then again (for up to ten minutes) develop this feeling:

> *I unite myself with the rays, with the light.*

(Continue to remain for some time in a tranquil state. What is to be revealed to the soul will be revealed when the time is ripe.)

*
* *

Developing the six qualities.

———

New Year 1912/1913   Archive no. 5267

Evening:

1.)   Review of the day as suggested in *How to Know Higher Worlds*.
      About five minutes.

2.)   Rose Cross meditation, lasting about five minutes, followed for a
      further five minutes by:

> In the light's pure rays
> I can gaze upon
> the pure power of all wisdom
> in the wavebeat of the heart
> I can feel
> the strong image of all existence -
> both will I feel.
>
> (Then inner tranquility)

Morning:

> First the Rose Cross meditation.
> Then contemplate the following thoughts:

> Wisdom in the spirit
> love in the soul
> strength in the will
> they guide me
> and uphold me
> I trust in them
> I surrender to them.
>
> (Then inner tranquility)

The balancing exercises as described in *Esoteric Science*

———

Probably February 23 1912   Archive no. 5315

Evening:

> Light's pure rays
> the universal spirit reveals to me
> love's pure warmth
> may universal soul reveal to me
> God deep within me
> in my heart
> in my spirit.

    (Inner tranquility)

Morning:

> In my spirit
> in my heart
> God deep within me
> may universal spirit reveal to me
> love's pure warmth
> the universal spirit reveals to me
> light's pure rays.

    (Inner tranquility)

> Peace
> Truth
> Love

———

A–5

Exercises with the meditative verse
"In the godhood of the world…"
as reversal of "In the pure rays of the light…"

Archive no. 4462-64

In the evening tell yourself: I will submerge myself in an invisible world during the night and will rest within it. This invisible world also contains the source of the highest virtues, especially the highest virtue of all: love for all beings. I must always draw afresh from this source; for increasing perfection is possible only if the invisible is repeatedly led over into the visible. For this reason the source and origin of the visible world can be found only in the invisible realm. All this must now be pictured in images. I picture space illumined by a light; the suprasensory light of the divine spiritual realm. I picture love as a warmth that streams through this suprasensory world. I think of myself as *resting* in this suprasensory world during the night.

All this is now presented to the soul in images in the following seven lines:

> In the godhood of the world
> I will find myself
> therein I rest
> the godliness of my soul shines out
> in pure love for every being
> the godhood of the world gleams out
> in the pure rays of the light.

For five minutes (by feeling, not by the clock) allow nothing but these seven lines and the images of them to live as content of the soul. Then, for a further five minutes, exclude all thoughts whatsoever, and give yourself up entirely to the effect of these seven lines, maintaining complete inner tranquility.

After this, undertake your review of the day.

*
* *

In the morning, after waking and before any other impressions have passed through your soul, revive the seven lines and the images in your awareness, and do so as follows:

> In the pure rays of the light
> gleams out the godhood of the world
> in pure love for every being
> shines out the godliness of my soul
> I rest in the godhood of the world
> I will find myself
> in the godhood of the world.

Again, let these seven lines entirely fill your awareness for five minutes, and then, for a further five minutes, give your awareness up completely to their effect without retaining any thought in your mind.

Then picture a growing plant, allowing this to grow very slowly in front of you leaf by leaf, through to flower and fruit. Picture the force that brings about this growth. Then think this force into your own heart and concentrate upon it for two to three minutes.

*
* *

During the day undertake the balancing exercises as described.

Archive no. 3040

Evening: Review

8 to 10 mins.
{
In the godhood of the world
I will find myself
therein I rest
the godliness of my soul shines out
in pure love for every being
the godhood of the world gleams out
in the pure rays of the light.

*
* *

2 mins.   Peace

*
* *

———————

[Morning:]   Tranquility

2 mins.
{
In the pure rays of the light
gleams out the godhood of the world
in pure love for every being
shines out the godliness of my soul
I rest in the godhood of the world
I will find myself
in the godhood of the world.

*
* *

During the day: thought concentration

Facsimile of archive no. 3040

Abend   Rückblick.

8-10 Min

In der Gottheit der Welt
Werde ich mich selber finden
In IHR ruhe ich
Es erfasset die Göttlichkeit meiner Seele
In der reinen Liebe zu allen Wesen
Es erglänzt die Gottheit der Welt
In den reinen Strahlen des Lichtes

2 Mai.   Friede.

2 Mai.   Ruhe

In den reinen Strahlen des Lichtes
Erglänzt die Gottheit der Welt
In der reinen Liebe zu allen Wesen
Erfasset die Göttlichkeit meiner Seele
Ich ruhe in der Gottheit der Welt
Ich werde mich selber finden
In der Gottheit der Welt.

Im Laufe des Tages: Gedankenconcentration.

Archive no. A 0217

Evening:

Experience the content of light and warmth in symbols; then:

> In the godhood of the world
> I will find myself
> therein I rest
> the godliness of my soul shines out
> in pure love for every being
> the godhood of the world gleams out
> in the pure rays of the light.

(Give yourself up to the effect [of the verse] for five minutes; then review the events of the day for seven to eight minutes)

> Picture the Rose Cross

> May light of worlds live within my heart.

Morning:

> Reawakening of pictures.

> In the pure rays of the light
> gleams the godhood of the world
> in pure love for every being
> shines out the godliness of my soul.
> I rest in the godhood of the world
> I will find myself
> in the godhood of the world.

(Give yourself up to the effect for five minutes. Then: inner tranquility.)

Picture a growing plant, allowing this to grow in thoughts very slowly before you, leaf by leaf through to flower and fruit. Picture the force: how this brings about the growth. Then think this force into your own heart.

(Concentrate on this for two to three minutes.)

Let word of worlds live within my heart.

During the day: balancing exercises

———

12 June 1909   Archive no. 5843/44

In the evening:

I bring to mind the fact that I have received external impressions throughout the day. In the night I will receive no such impressions, but will be in the suprasensory world. Now I will picture the suprasensory world to myself through symbols, so that these symbols awaken my awareness for this world. I will picture the space around me and in me as being filled with suprasensory light, like an ocean of light shimmering in many colors. I will picture warmth, the symbol of divine love, streaming in all directions in this ocean of light. I will think of my "I" in this world, picturing the warmth streaming into my heart. All this I accompany with the following seven lines:

5 mins.

In the godhood of the world
I will find myself
therein I rest
the godliness of my soul shines out
in pure love for every being
the godhood of the world gleams out
in the pure rays of the light.

Then give yourself up very calmly for five minutes to the effect of the exercise.

Then a review of the day as described elsewhere (seven to eight mins.)

*
* *

In the morning:

I inwardly awaken the images of the previous evening and accompany them again with the seven lines, but now in the following sequence:

5 mins.
{
In the pure rays of the light
gleams out the godhood of the world
in pure love for every being
shines out the godliness of my soul
I rest in the godhood of the world
I will find myself
in the godhood of the world.
}

Then give yourself up to the effect for five minutes.

After this, four breaths:

> Inbreath: deep and slow
> Hold breath: so that I have the sense that the breath is
> spreading throughout my body.
> Outbreath: slow, not jerky.

> On the inbreath: Light enter me
> When holding breath: Light in me
> Outbreath: I sacrifice

Give yourself up to the effect of this for a while.

*
* *

During the day: balancing exercises

———

Archive no. 5271

Evening: Summarizing of a short account of theos.
             Wisdom in one phrase or sentence.

5 to 8
mins.

> In the godhood of the world
> I will find myself
> therein I rest
> the godliness of the soul shines out
> in pure love for every being
> the godhood of the world gleams out
> in the pure rays of the light.

⊕

Morning: ⊕

Recall the phrase/sentence of the previous day and live within it for five minutes.

5 to 8
mins.

> In the pure rays of the light
> gleams out the godhood of the world
> in pure love for every being
> shines out the godliness of my soul
> I rest in the godhood of the world
> I will find myself
> in the godhood of the world.

Rest for a while in the echo of these lines, with full inner equilibrium.

_____

During the day balancing exercises.

_____

1910 or later   Archive no. 3179/80

Evening:

> In the godhood of the world
> I will find myself
> therein I rest
> the godliness of my soul shines out
> in pure love for every being
> the godhood of the world gleams out
> in the pure rays of the light.

*

*   *

> Read five or six lines of *Theosophy*
> Review of the day.

*

*   *

Morning:

> Recall five or six lines

> In the pure rays of the light
> gleams out the godhood of the world
> in pure love for every being
> shines out the godliness of my soul
> I rest in the godhood of the world
> I will find myself
> in the godhood of the world.

Let the effect fade away in stillness and inner tranquility.

Six qualities, *Esoteric Science*

———

1910 or 1911   Archive no. 7083

Evening:

    1.) Picturing of some of the events of the day in reverse

    2.)   I rest in the godhood of the world
              I will find myself
              in the godhood of the world
              in the pure rays of the light   5 mins.
              in pure love for every being
              the godhood of the world gleams out
              the godliness of the soul shines out.

    3.)   ⊕

Morning: 1.)   ⊕

    2.)   The godliness of the soul shines out
              the godhood of the world gleams out
               in pure love for every being
              in the pure rays of the light   5 mins.
              in the godhood of the world
              I will find myself
              therein I rest.

    3.)   I am   2 to 3 mins.

*
* *

Balancing exercises as in *Esoteric Science*

———

Facsimile of archive no. 7083

<u>Abends:</u> 1.) Bildhaftes Vorstellen einiger Tageserlebnisse
Rückläufig.

2.) Ich ruhe in der Ganzheit der Welt
Ich werde mich selber finden
In der Ganzheit der Welt
In den reinen Strahlen des Lichtes } 5 Min.
In der reinen Liebe zu allen Wesen
Erglänzt die Ganzheit der Welt
Erstrahlt die Göttlichkeit der Seele

3.) ⊕

<u>Morgens:</u> 1.) ⊕

2.) Es erstrahlt die Göttlichkeit der Seele
Es erglänzt die Ganzheit der Welt
In der reinen Liebe zu allen Wesen
In den reinen Strahlen des Lichts } 5 Min.
In der Ganzheit der Welt
Werde ich mich selber finden
In IHR ruhe ich

3.) Ich bin { 2-3 Min.

× ×

Nebenübungen S. 306 Gheim W///

Before 1913   Archive no. 3127-29

In the evening, first:

One quarter of an hour: read any theosophical material. Read only a little but reflect a lot. Then inwardly summon the following thoughts very vividly:

During the day I received impressions of the external world, and formed ideas and pictures of them. During sleep I will now enter the invisible world. I picture this suprasensory world symbolically as a surging ocean of light, shimmering with colors, in which I immerse myself, and in which I will rest. I picture how all higher virtues come from this suprasensory realm, especially the chief virtue of all: love for all beings. I picture this love symbolically as *warmth* within suprasensory divine spirituality. Warmth—as I picture it—streams through the spirit's ocean of light, which fills the space around me.

All this is now embodied in the pictures described and in the following seven lines:

> In the godhood of the world
> I will find myself
> therein I rest
> the godliness of my soul shines out
> in pure love for every being
> the godhood of the world gleams out
> in the pure rays of the light.

The soul must contemplate these seven lines for five minutes (not by the clock but by feeling). Then, for a further five minutes, exclude all thoughts whatsoever, and try to think *nothing at all*. Instead, give yourself up with inner tranquility to the effect of these seven lines. Give yourself to what then arises by itself in your awareness.

Then do the review of the day.

*
* *

In the *morning*, immediately on waking, before any other impressions have passed through your soul, again take five minutes to bring alive in your awareness all the images and the seven lines, but now in the following sequence:

> In the pure rays of the light
> gleams out the godhood of the world
> in pure love for every being
> shines out the godliness of my soul
> I rest in the godhood of the world
> I will find myself
> in the godhood of the world.

(Again, five minutes' contemplation, then give yourself up to the effect for five minutes)

After this, focus on both your eyes for around two or three minutes, as if you wished to think this thought into them:

Light enter me

Then focus on your heart for two or three minutes, as if you wished to think into it:

Warmth enter me

Conclude this morning exercise by breathing in strongly four times,[134] holding your breath and then breathing out calmly. Picture the following as you do so:

> On the inbreath: Spirit light enter me
> While holding the breath: Spirit light within me
> On the outbreath: I surrender to the world what is in me

---

134. Translator's note: Presumably this means four repetitions of the sequence: breathing in, holding the breath, then breathing out.

Then remain absolutely calm for three to four minutes, without external thoughts, entirely given up to whatever appears in your awareness as the effect of the exercise.

*

* *

During the day do the balancing exercises as described.

———

A–6

Exercises with variations of
"I rest in the godhood of the world…"

Archive no. 3067

Morning:

Five mins.:

> I rest in the godhood of the world
> I will find myself
> in the godhood of the world

> In the pure rays of the light
> gleams out the godhood of the world
> in pure warmth for every being
> shines out the godliness of the soul.

5 to 10
mins.

(*Light* the symbol for wisdom; *warmth* the symbol for love)

*
* *

Evening: 5 to 10 mins.

> In the godhood of the world
> I will find myself
> therein I rest.

———

Archive no. 4424

(Wärme in mich.)

Morgens:
10 Min :   Licht   Wärme
              ◯   ◯

CHRISTUS

Ich ruhe in der gonsheit der Welt
Ich werde mich selber finden
In der gonsheit der Welt

abends :   Licht   Wärme
              ◯   ◯
           Weisheit   Liebe

CHRISTUS

In der gonsheit der Welt   } 10 Min.
Werde ich mich selber finden
In IHR ruhe ich .

──────────

Transcription:

Warmth enter me

Morning: Light   Warmth
10 mins.
              CHRIST
          I rest in the godhood of the world
          I will find myself
          in the godhood of the world.

Evening: Light   Warmth

             Wisdom   Love
             CHRI   ST   10 mins.

          In the godhood of the world
          I will find myself
          therein I rest.

Archive no. A 0051

Evening: Truths contained in *Theosophy*

Morning: After the ⊕ and recollection of truths contained in
            Theosophy:

> I rest in the godhood of the world
> I will live in the soul of the world
> I will think in the spirit of the world

———

Archive no. 7081

Morning:

In the godhood of the world
in the spirit of the world
in the soul of the world
I will seek myself
I will find myself
I assuredly.

Evening:

Assuredly
I will find myself
for I will seek myself
in the soul of the world
in the spirit of the world
in the godhood of the world.

———

Archive no. 6254

Every morning:

> May my soul blossom
> in love for all existence
> may my spirit live
> in the soul of beings
> may my self rest
> in the godhood of the world
> thus will I be.

Every evening:

> I will strive
> to be in the godhood of the world
> may my self rest therein
> may my spirit live
> in the soul of beings
> may my soul blossom
> in love for all existence.

———

Facsimile of archive no. 6254

Jeden Morgen:

> Es möge blühen meine Seele
> In der Liebe zu allem Dasein
> Es möge leben mein Geist
> In der Seele der Wesen
> Es möge ruhen mein Selbst
> In der Gottheit der Welt
> So will ich sein.

⊕

Jeden abend: ⊕

> Ich will mich bestreben
> Zu sein in der Gottheit der Welt
> Ruhen möge mein Selbst in *JHR*
> Leben möge mein Geist
> In der Seele der Wesen
> Blühe möge meine Seele
> In der Liebe zu allem Dasein.

Archive no. 3139

Evening: Look back on day's events.

> In the godhood of the world
> in the spirit of the world
> in the soul of the world
> I will find myself
> rest therein
> live therein
> be therein.

*
* *

[Morning:]

> I will be
> I will live
> I will rest
> I will find myself
> in the soul of the world
> in the spirit of the world
> in the godhood of the world.

———

December 14, 1908   Archive no. 7111

Morning: First week: Nature of the human being
                Second week: Life between death and birth[135]

                I rest in the godhood of the world
                I will find myself   } In images
                in the godhood of the world.

                              *
                           * *

During the day: thought concentration

                           *
                        * *

Evening: Review of the day. In images.

                        ——————

---

135. These two phrases relate to chapter titles in *Theosophy*, CW 9.

1909   Archive no. 3206

In the evening the soul should give itself up entirely for five minutes (by feeling, not by the clock) to the following seven lines:

> I rest in the godhood of the world
> I will find myself
> in the godhood of the world
> love imbuing a soul with warmth
> lets world godhood live therein
> light streaming through space
> is luminous with the godhood of the world.

After these seven lines, remain in a mood of inward devotion for a while.

*
* *

In the morning, spend five to eight minutes contemplating the following lines with your whole soul:

> Luminous the godhood of the world
> when light streams through space
> world godhood lives in the soul
> that love imbues with warmth
> in the godhood of the world
> I will find myself
> I rest therein.

Then spend a few minutes resting in great inner calm and expectancy.

During the day, cultivate the six qualities.

———

1910 or later   Archive no. 3145

[Evening:]

Devotion to a phrase that has been prepared during the day. = A

> In the godhood of the world
> I will find myself
> therein I rest
> may warmth of godhood penetrate
> my being of soul
> may light of godhood penetrate
> my being of spirit.

———

[Morning:]

Repetition of A.

> My being of spirit
> may light of godhood penetrate
> my being of soul
> may warmth of godhood penetrate
> I rest in the godhood of the world
> I will find myself
> in the godhood of the world.

Esoteric Sc.: six qualities

———

1910 or later   Archive no. 5250/51

Evening:

Try to inwardly and pictorially conjure a few of the day's events pictorially, but in reverse sequence; and then invoke the

as described in *Esoteric Science*, allowing the following words to pass through your tranquil soul for around five minutes (possibly growing longer over several months), as if radiating outward:

> In the godhood of the world
> I will find myself
> therein I rest.

(You may wish to organize the exercise so that sleep follows immediately after you have filled your soul with this content.)

In the *morning*

    Start with the

And imagine the following words streaming out from this into the soul (to the location of the heart):

> In the pure rays of the light
> in pure activity of wisdom
> gleams out the godhood of the world
> in pure warmth for every being
> in pure love for every being
> shines out the godliness of souls
> I am within light within love.

(Rest in these pictures for only a brief time to begin with, then longer, for up to ten minutes.)

———

As balancing exercise, cultivating of the six qualities, as described in *E.S.*

———

September 1911   Archive no. 6909/10

Every evening: Pictorial, reverse recall of an event during the day

---

⊕   black   red

In the godhood of the world
rests my soul
rests my spirit
the godhood of the world gleams out
in pure warmth for every being   (warmth, symbol
the godhood of the world shines out   for love)
in the pure rays of the light.   (light, symbol
                                                        for wisdom)

(Allow to resonate in the soul)

During the day:

Saturday: Good and bad strokes of fortune rest in the lap of the
                future.

Sunday: I will note well the good that happens to me each day:
                this shows me what gods have made of me.

Monday: The bad things that sometimes happen to me I will
                endure: they show me what I can still make of myself.

Tuesday: For the way I now live I thank my good destiny.

Wednesday: At moments of misfortune I thank my strength for the
                power which can lead me upward in life.

Thursday: Whoever believes that good fortune alone sustains and advances us, that misfortune alone bows us down, is looking at the day only, and not the year.

Friday: ⊕   black   red

———————

Every morning:

> In the pure rays of the light
> shines out the godhood of the world
> in pure warmth for every being
> gleams out the godhood of the world
> my spirit rests
> my soul rests
> in the godhood of the world.

⊕   white   green[136]

(Then await what occurs in your awareness.)

———

———————————

136. white = cross; green = roses

1910 or later   Archive no. 5252

Evening: Review of the day

              In the godhood of the world   ⎞
              I will find myself   ⎟
              therein I rest   ⎟
              my soul rests   ⎟   10 mins.
              in the spirit of the world   ⎟
              my spirit rests   ⎟
              in the soul of the world.   ⎠

                         ☥

                    ────────

Morning: ☥   white cross
                                        green roses
              In the soul of the world
              rests my spirit
              in the spirit of the world
              rests my soul
              I rest in the godhood of the world
              I will find myself
              in the godhood of the world.

                    ────────

Allow to resonate and fade.

Balancing exercises: *Esoteric Science*

                    ────────

1912   Archive no. A 0070

Evening:

> In the spirit of the world
> may my soul rest
> in the soul of the world
> may my spirit find itself   10 mins.
> in the godhood of the world
> may my self find itself
> therein I rest.

⊕   5 minutes

Morning: ⊕   5 minutes

> I rest in the godhood of the world
> may my self find itself
> in godhood's core of being
> may my spirit find itself   10 mins.
> in the soul of the world
> may my soul rest
> in the spirit of the world.

Contemplation in inner tranquility.

———

A–7

Exercises with the verse
"Steadfast I place myself into existence…"

This verse originated in 1907

December 1907   Archive no. 3038

Morning: Withdraw attention from all sensory [perception] and all
             memories of daily life.

       Tranquility

In the pure rays of the light
gleams out the godhood of the world
in pure love for every being
shines out the godliness of my soul
I rest in the godhood of the world
I will find myself
in the godhood of the world.

*

* *

Conc.   l.l, l.f:[137]   *Steadfast* I place myself into *existence*
      r.l, r.f: *certain* I walk the course of my life
      l.a, l.h: *love* I nurture in the core of my being
      r.a, r.h: *hope* I place in every deed
      Head: *trust* I impress in all my thinking
            these *five* lead me to my goal
            these *five* gave me my *existence*

*

* *

Devotional contemplation of your own divine ideal

———

Evening: Review of the day's events. In images.
           Backward to the beginning of the day.

———

---

137. left leg, left foot ... right arm, right hand

May 1909   Archive no. 3111

Morning:

Tranquility

Left foot	:	Steadfast I place myself into existence
Right foot	:	certain I walk the course of my life
Left hand	:	love I nurture in the core of my being
Right hand	:	hope I place in every deed
Heart		quiet leads me to the goal
		quiet led me into my existence
Head	:	wisdom I seek in all my thinking.

During the day: balancing exercises

Evening:

Head	:	Wisdom I seek in all my thinking
Heart		quiet led me into my existence
		quiet leads me to the goal
Right hand	:	hope I place in every deed
Left hand	:	love I nurture in the core of my being
Right foot	:	certain I walk the course of my life
Left foot	:	steadfast I place myself into existence.

Review of the day.

Morning:

Devotional contemplation of one's divine ideal.

In your light wisdom
in your warmth endeavor
in your strength beauty

*

* *

l.l, l.f:	*Steadfast* I place myself into *existence*
r.l, r.f:	*certain* I walk the course of my life
l.a, l.h:	*love* I nurture in the core of my being
r.a, r.h:	*hope* I place in every deed
Head:	*trust* I impress in all my thinking
	these five lead me to my goal
	these five gave me my existence.

Evening: Devotional contemplation of your own divine ideal
             Review of the day. In images
             From evening back to morning.

Archive no. 3074

First thing in the morning: Start: anytime

    Tranquility

5 mins.:   In the pure rays of the light
               gleams out the godhood of the world
               in pure love for every being
               shines out the godliness of my soul   } in vivid images
               I rest in the godhood of the world
               I will find myself
               in the godhood of the world.

                     *
                 * *

Concentr.   l.l, l.f: *Steadfast* I place myself into *existence*
          r.l, r.f: *certain* I walk the course of my life
          l.a, l.h: *love* I nurture in the core of my being
          Heart region: *fortitude* I plant in my I
          r.a, r.h: *hope* I place in every deed
          Head: *trust* I impress in all my thinking
                  these *six* lead me through existence

Evening: Review of the day. Backward from the evening. Vividly
              pictorial.

Archive no. 3046

Start: waxing moon[138]

Morning:

>*Tranquility*
>
>>In the pure rays of the light
>>gleams out the godhood of the world
>>in pure love for every being
>>shines out the godliness of my soul
>>I rest in the godhood of the world
>>I will find myself
>>in the godhood of the world.

Conc. l.l, l.f: *Steadfast* I place myself into *existence*
   r.l, r.f: *certain* I walk the course of my life
   l.a, l.h: *love* I nurture in the core of my being
   r.a, r.h: *hope* I place in every deed
   Head: *trust* I impress in all my thinking
      these *five* lead me to my goal
      these *five* gave me my *existence*.

*
* *

Devotional surrender to your divine ideal.

Evening: Review of experiences during the day. In images.
     Backward from the evening.

---

138. See note on p. 460.

Facsimile of archive no. 3046

Anfang: Mondzunehmen

Morgens:

Ruhe

In den reinen Straßen des Lichts
Erglänzt die Gottheit der Welt
In der reinen Liebe zu allen Wesen
Erstrahlt die Göttlichkeit meiner Seele
Ich ruhe in der Gottheit der Welt
Ich werde mich selbst finden
In der Gottheit der Welt.

———

Conc. l.B.·l.F.: Standhaft stell ich mich ins Dasein
  „   r.B.·r.F.: Sicher schreit ich die Lebensbahn
  „   l.A.·l.H: Liebe leg ich in Wesenskern
  „   r.A.·r.H: Hoffnung leg ich in jeglich Thun
  „   Kopf : Vertrauen präg ich in alles Denken
             Dies Fünf führen mich aus Ziel
             Dies Fünf gaben mir das Dasein

Devotionelle Hingabe an das göttliche Ideal.

Abends: Rückschau auf die Tageserlebnisse. Bildsam.
           Von rückwärts nach vorn.

Archive no. 3072

Morning:

Tranquility

In the pure rays of the light
gleams out the godhood of the world
in pure love for every being
shines out the godliness of my soul
I rest in the godhood of the world
I will find myself
in the godhood of the world

*
* *

Concentr.   l.l, l.f: *Steadfast* I place myself into existence
              r.l, r.f: *certain* I walk the course of my life

———

During the day: Thought concentration

*
* *

Evening: Review of the day's experiences. In images.
               From evening back to morning.

*
* *

Spend one quarter of an hour on theos. reading

———

Morning:

    "In the beginning..."[139]

    Then:

Conc.	l.l, l.f:	*Steadfast* I place myself into *existence*
	r.l, r.f:	*certain* I walk the course of my life
	l.a, l.h:	*love* I nurture in the core of my being
	r.a, r.h:	*hope* I impress in every deed
	Head:	*trust* I place in all my thinking

           these *five* lead me to my goal
           these *five* gave me my *existence*.

Evening: Review of the experiences of the day. In images.
              From evening to morning.

In a free way: read the Gospel of St. John and reflect on it.

---

139. Translator's note: This refers to the beginning of the Gospel of St. John.

Archive no. 4459

Morning:

Steadfastness:	left leg
Certainty:	right leg
Love:	left arm
Hope:	right arm
Trust:	head

———————

Steadfast I place myself into existence: conc. left leg
certain I walk the course of my life: conc. right leg
love I place in the core of my being: conc. left arm
hope I impress in every deed: conc. right arm
trust I nurture in all my thinking: conc. head
these *five* gave me my existence
these *five* show me the goal.

*
* *

creation
and
revelation

———————

Evening: Review of the day. In images.
    Backward from the evening.

———————

Archive no. 3116

Morning:

Steadfastness:	left leg
Certainty:	right leg
Love:	left arm
Hope:	right arm
Trust:	head

Steadfast I place myself into existence:	conc. on left leg
certain I walk the course of my life:	conc. on right leg
strength flows into my heart:	conc. on heart
love I nurture in the core of my being:	conc. on left arm
hope I impress in every deed:	conc. on right arm
trust I place in all my thinking:	conc. on head
these *six* guide me through *existence*.	

*
* *

Evening: Review of the day's experiences. In images.
              Backward toward morning.

Archive no. 3123

Morning:

Tranquility (2–2 ½ minutes)

Concentrating on left leg, left foot	*Steadfast* I place myself into *existence*
Concentration on right leg, right foot	*certain* I walk the course of my life
Concentration on left arm, left hand	*love* I nurture in the core of my being
Concentration on heart	*strength* I feel in the center of my body
Concentration on right arm, right hand	*hope* I place in every deed
Concentration on forehead and head	*trust* I impress in all my thinking

7-8 mins. {

these *six* always govern my *existence*.

Evening:

Review of the day's experiences. Backward toward morning. In images.

————

A–8

Exercises with the meditative verse
"Light-streaming forms…"
and its reversal as "Consciously steps my I…"

Probably originated 1907

Archive no. 3098, 3100/01

Main exercises for morning and evening.

In the morning, as soon as possible after waking: withdraw attention from all external sense impressions and also all memories of daily life. In this emptied soul first fill yourself with the idea of *tranquility*. It should feel as if you are pouring this sense of tranquility through your whole body. However, this can be very brief (two to five seconds). Then, for about five minutes, fill yourself inwardly with the following seven lines:

> Light-streaming forms
> shimmering ocean waves of spirit
> the soul departed from you
> she dwelt in the divine
> in which her being rested –
> into the realm of life's enclosing mantles
> consciously steps my I.

Try to picture these lines as vividly as possible. In the first two lines, therefore, think of a sea of light in which forms take shape; in the third, fourth, and fifth, picture how the soul emerges from this ocean of light on awakening. In the sixth and seventh lines, think of how we enter our bodily sheaths when we wake up. The *spiritual* content of the seven lines should be felt, and at the same time also, *images* of the whole should be pictured in as vivid a way as possible.

Then follows a breathing process involving *four* breaths: breathe in, hold the breath within you, and breathe out in a time ratio of 1 : 3 : 2 for inbreath, holding breath and outbreath (timed by feeling rather than by the clock). In other words, if you need 3 seconds for the inbreath, hold the breath for 9 seconds and breathe out through 6 seconds. (Or 2 : 6 : 4 or 4 : 12 : 8 and so forth)

Think nothing while breathing in and out, but give yourself up entirely to observation of the breathing process. By contrast, concentrate as follows during each held breath:

First held breath: on point between the eyebrows   with: I am
Second held breath: on larynx   with: It thinks
Third held breath: on heart, arms, hands   with: She feels
Fourth held breath: on surface of the body   with: He wills

Following this, concentrate for two to three minutes on the picture of a
"growing and wilting plant."

To conclude the morning meditation:
            dedicate yourself to a divine ideal

———————

During the day, the "balancing exercises" should be done. Here it is less
important to keep to a particular time of day.

Evening: Meditation on the following seven lines. These should be
handled in the same way as the 7 lines in the morning, but pictured in
the reverse sequence:

> Consciously steps my *I*
> out of the realm of life's enclosing mantles
> to rest in universal beings
> into the divine it seeks its way
> my soul attain this realm —
> the spirit's shimmering ocean waves
> light's streaming forms.

Then review of the day. In images, in reverse.

———————

Archive no. A 4483-86

Evening:

At a point in the day not long before going to sleep, give yourself up
first to the following train of thoughts: Throughout the day I have
received impressions of the physical world and have formed thoughts
about these impressions. In the night I will have no such impressions.
I will be in a world of spirit. I will now paint inner pictures which,
given persistence, are suitable for opening my sensibility to the world of
spirit. I will picture myself surrounded and permeated by a sea of light
of all possible fluctuating shades of color, within which stream diverse
currents of warmth. One of these currents of warmth enters my heart

> (Light – symbol for wisdom
> Warmth – symbol for love)

As I live in these pictures, I contemplate the following seven lines as if
I were actually hearing them spiritually:

> Out of the realm of life's enclosing mantles
> consciously steps my I
> to enter into universal beings
> to dwell in the divine
> my soul attain this realm –
> the spirit's shimmering ocean waves
> light's streaming forms.

For roughly eight to ten minutes (by feeling, not the clock) give yourself
up to these thoughts and to inward hearing. Then, for a further five
minutes, with complete inner tranquility, as if seeing and hearing nothing, allow the after-effect of the meditation to fade away in you. Now
vividly call up a particular event of the evening and picture it in reverse
sequence, as if standing outside yourself. Then take another such event
from an earlier point in the day, a third from still earlier, back to the
morning. These events will join with each other by themselves to create

a tableau of the day within a relatively short time. Exclude all thought of regret, but always picture how you might conduct yourself better in a similar situation in future. Immediately before falling asleep, try to imbue yourself with the thought: The spirit gives me what I most need.

Morning:

In the morning, before any other thought or impression has passed through your soul, try to call up the images of light and warmth from the preceding evening, now with the following seven lines:

> Light-streaming forms
> shimmering ocean waves of spirit
> the soul departed from you
> she dwelt in the divine
> in which her being rested –
> into the realm of life's enclosing mantles
> consciously steps my I.

After meditating on this for eight to ten minutes, again give yourself calmly to the fading after-effect for about five minutes.

Then try to preview roughly how your day might unfold. During the day, take a short time, as your personal need dictates, to undertake one of the exercises described in "Initiation,"[140] especially as this chapter relates to the "six exercises":

> Thought concentration
> Initiative in action
> Equanimity in joy and suffering
> Positivity
> Open-mindedness
> Harmonizing of these five qualities

---

140. This refers to the chapter "Initiation" in *Esoteric Science*, CW 13.

(Don't try to do too much on one day.) Reading matter is left to your own discretion. Reading a certain amount of theosophical content is indispensable for the meditant.

———

Archive no. 3090, 3165

Morning:

> Light-streaming forms
> shimmering ocean waves of spirit
> the soul departed from you
> she dwelt in the divine –
> into the realm of life's enclosing mantles
> consciously steps my I.
>
> > *I am.*

CHR J ST U S [141]

During the day: balancing exercises

Evening:

> Review of the day

CHR J ST U S

> > *I am.*

> Consciously steps my I
> out of the realm of life's enclosing mantles
> to dwell in the divine
> my soul attain this realm –
> the spirit's shimmering ocean waves
> light's streaming forms.

———

141. See following facsimile, archive no. 5310, in relation to these signs and letters.

Archive no. 5310

Translation of facsimile text:

Image of the luminous sun: U [oo]
Image of the warming sun: I [ee]

Light symbol of wisdom
Warmth symbol of love

```
        I      U
CHR     ST      S
```

Archive no. 3091

Morning: *Tranquility*   2–3 seconds

10 mins. {
Light-streaming forms
shimmering ocean waves of spirit
the soul departed from you
she dwelt in the divine
in which her being rested –
into the realm of life's enclosing mantles
consciously steps my *I*.
} in images

*
* *

During the day: balancing exercises

Evening:

10 mins. {
Consciously steps my I
out of the realm of life's enclosing mantles
to rest in universal beings
into the divine it seeks its way
my soul attain this realm –
the spirit's shimmering ocean waves
light's streaming forms.
} in images

Review of the day's experiences. In reverse. Eight to ten mins. In images.

———

Archive no. 5316

Morning: *Tranquility*   2–3 seconds

> Light-streaming forms
> shimmering ocean waves of spirit
> the soul departed from you
> she dwelt in the divine   5 mins.
> in which her being rested –
> into the realm of life's enclosing mantles
> consciously steps my *I*.

*

*   *

Picturing a growing plant
Picturing a dying plant   5 mins.

———

During the day: Thought concentration   5 mins.

———

Evening: Consciously steps my I
out of the realm of life's enclosing mantles
to rest in universal beings
into the divine it seeks its way
my soul attain this realm –
the spirit's shimmering ocean waves
light's streaming forms.

Review of the day. In images. In reverse.

———

Archive no. 3095

Morning: *10 minutes:*

> Consciously steps my I
> out of the realm of life's enclosing mantles
> to rest in universal beings
> into the divine it seeks its way
> my soul attain this realm –
> the spirit's shimmering ocean waves
> light's streaming forms

Review of the day. In reverse.

[Morning:]   *10 minutes:*

> Light-streaming forms
> shimmering ocean waves of spirit
> the soul departed from you
> she dwelt in the divine
> in which her being rested –
> into the realm of life's enclosing mantles
> consciously steps my *I.*

During the day: Strength in me
                       love I nurture in the core of my being   } 5–10
                       trust I place in all my deeds.   mins.

———

Archive no. 3165a, 3093

Main exercise

[*in the evening:*]

Throughout the day I have received impressions of the external physical world of the senses, and formed ideas about these. In the night I will have no such impressions. I will be in the world of spirit. I will now picture the suprasensory world to myself through symbols, so that these gradually lead me into the suprasensory world. I will picture that the space around me and in me is filled with suprasensory light, as if an ocean of light shimmers in diverse colors, and currents of warmth stream through this ocean of light. Let one of the currents of warmth enter my heart. (Light = symbol of divine wisdom; warmth = symbol of divine love). This picture should be sustained meditatively for five minutes, accompanied by the following seven lines:

> Consciously steps my I
> out of the realm of life's enclosing mantles
> to rest in universal beings
> into the divine it seeks its way
> my soul attain this realm –
> the spirit's shimmering ocean waves
> light's streaming forms.

Preserve the impression for three to four minutes in complete inner tranquility.)

After this, review.

In the morning: I re-awaken the pictures of the previous evening. I accompany them again with the seven lines, for five minutes, but now in the following sequence:

> Light-streaming forms
> shimmering ocean waves of spirit
> the soul departed from you
> she dwelt in the divine
> in which her being rested –
> into the realm of life's enclosing mantles
> consciously steps my I.

Give yourself up again for three to four minutes to the impression, retaining inner tranquility.

Then:

Conc.	Between eyebrows	:	I am (2–5 mins)
	Larynx	:	It thinks
	Arms, hands	:	She feels
	Body surface / skin	:	He wills.

After this, devotional dedication to one's own divine ideal (5 minutes).

✳

✳ ✳

During the day: balancing exercises.

———

Archive no. 5322/23

Evening: Review

10 mins.:

[142]Friday: Will-endowing forms
powerful ocean waves of spirit   ♄

Saturday: Light-streaming forms
shimmering ocean waves of spirit   ☉

Sunday: Soul-bestowing forms
warming ocean waves of spirit   ☽

Monday: Soul-surrendering forms
powerful ocean waves of spirit   ♂

Tuesday: Light far-streaming forms
illumining ocean waves of spirit   ☿

Wednesday: Will-living forms
life-surrendering ocean waves of spirit   ♃

Thursday: God-blessed forms
peaceful ocean waves of spirit   ♀

[and each time:]   The soul seeks you
it aspires into the divine
unites her being with it
out of the realm of life's enclosing mantles
step consciously my I.

---

142. Regarding the order of planetary symbols, in an esoteric sense a day begins around six in the evening. That is, Saturday starts at 6 p.m. on Friday evening, which is why the symbol for Satuday (Saturn) adjoins the Friday meditation.

Morning: 1   Consciously steps my I
          2   into the realm of life's enclosing mantles
          3   it comes from the divine
          4   it takes its way into the earthly realm   ⎫
          5   from you the soul departs   ⎬   10 mins.
          6 [143]   ⎭
          7   taken from what preceded

*

* *

5 mins.   ⎰ I am [between eyebrows]
          ⎱ staying in calm inner contemplation for a short while

———

---

143. At lines 6 and 7 of the morning meditation, reversal of the lines for the days of the week may likewise be intended; that is, for Saturday morning: 6. Powerful ocean waves of the spirit; 7. Will-endowing forms.

Archive no. 3099

Evening: *Review*

          Light symbol of wisdom
          Warmth symbol of love

———————

1. Will-endowing
   strength

     2.   Light-streaming forms
         shimmering ocean waves of spirit
         my soul seeks you
         aspires into the divine
         unites her being with it –
         out of the realm of life's enclosing mantles
         consciously steps my I.

3. Soul-bestowing
   warmth
4. Self-enacting
   strength
5. Soul-surrendering
   radiance of strength
6. Light far-streaming
   illumining
7. Will-living
   life-surrender –

} 10 mins.

*
* *

Morning:

     Consciously steps my I
     into the realm of life's enclosing mantles
     the soul united with the divine
     she dwelt in it
     therein her being rested
     in the shimmering ocean waves of spirit
     in light-streaming forms.[144]

} 10 mins.

*
* *

Conc. Middle of eyebrows   I am   4–5 mins.

———————   ———————

144. Translator's note: In the last four lines, Steiner has underlined a single vowel in each line, which cannot be reproduced in the translation. The sequence of vowel sounds in the original is: ei, oo, o and ah.

Facsimile of archive no. 3099

Apd:

Rückblick.

Licht Sinnbild von Weisheit
Wärme , , Liebe
Wille kraftvolles

3 { Seele / Herbende , Erwärmendes

2) Licht ersprossende Gebilde
Erglänzendes Wogenmeer des Geistes
Euch sucht die (meine) Seele
In das Göttliche strebet sie
Mit ihm vereint sie ihr Wesen
Aus dem Reif der Daseinshüllen
Tritt bewusst mein Ich.

10 Min.

4. Selbst einwirkende Kraftvolles
5. Seele opfernde Kraft, schaffendes
6. Licht Sinnbild Erleuchtendes
7. Wille lebende – leben fortsetzendes

ᴧˣᴧ

Magd:

Es tritt bewusst mein Ich
In das Reif der Daseinshüllen
Mit dem Göttlichen einte die Seele sich
In ES weilte sie
In IHM ruhte ihr Wesen
In dem glänzenden Wogenmeer des Geistes
In Licht- ersprossenden Gebilden.

10 Min

ᴧˣᴧ

Conc. A.B.M. Ich bin. 4–5 Min.

Editor's explanations relating to exercise in archive no. 3099:

As the previous exercise (Archive no. 5322/23) shows, the verse "Light-streaming forms…" was also given with variations for the different days of the week, here designated by the numbering 1 to 7. If we apply the suggestions given there, we get the following verses:

Friday evening

Will-endowing forms
powerful ocean waves of spirit
my soul seeks you
aspires into the divine
unites her being with it –
out of the realm of life's enclosing
mantles
consciously steps my I.

Saturday morning   Saturn

Consciously steps my I
into the realm of life's enclosing
mantles
the soul united with the divine
she dwelt in it
therein her being rested –
in the powerful ocean waves of spirit
in will-endowing forms.

Saturday evening

Light-streaming forms
shimmering ocean waves of spirit
my soul seeks you
aspires into the divine
unites her being with it –
out of the realm of life's enclosing
mantles
consciously steps my I.

Sunday morning   Sun

Consciously steps my I
into the realm of life's enclosing
mantles
the soul united with the divine
she dwelt in it
therein her being rested –
in the shimmering ocean waves of spirit
in light-streaming forms.

Sunday evening

Soul-bestowing forms
warming ocean waves of spirit
my soul seeks you
aspires into the divine
unites her being with it –
out of the realm of life's enclosing
mantles
consciously steps my I.

Monday morning   Moon

Consciously steps my I
into the realm of life's enclosing
mantles
the soul united with the divine
she dwelt in it
therein her being rested
in the warming ocean waves of spirit
in soul-bestowing forms.

Monday evening

Self-enacting forms
powerful ocean waves of spirit
my soul seeks you
aspires into the divine
unites her being with it –
out of the realms of life's enclosing mantles
consciously steps my I.

Tuesday evening

Soul-surrendering forms
strength-radiant ocean waves of spirit
my soul seeks you
aspires into the divine
unites her being with it –
out of the realms of life's enclosing
mantles
consciously steps my I.

Wednesday evening

Light far-streaming forms
illumining ocean waves of spirit
my soul seeks you
aspires into the divine
unites her being with it –
out of the realm of life's enclosing
mantles
consciously steps my I.

Thursday evening

Will-living forms
life-surrendering ocean waves of spirit
my soul seeks you
aspires into the divine
unites her being with it –
out of the realm of life's enclosing
mantles
consciously steps my I.

Tuesday morning   *Mars*

Consciously steps my I
into the realms of life's enclosing mantles
the soul united with the divine
she dwelt in it
therein her being rested –
in the powerful ocean waves of spirit
in self-enacting forms.

Wednesday morning   *Mercury*

Consciously steps my I
into the realm of life's enclosing
mantles
the soul united with the divine
she dwelt in it
therein her being rested –
in strength-radiant ocean waves of spirit
in soul-surrendering forms.

Thursday morning   *Jupiter*

Consciously steps my I
into the realm of life's enclosing
mantles
the soul united with the divine
she dwelt in it
therein her being rested –
in the illumining ocean waves of spirit
in light far-streaming forms.

Friday morning   *Venus*

Consciously steps my I
into the realm of life's enclosing
mantles
the soul united with the divine
she dwelt in it
therein her being rested –
in life-surrendering ocean waves of spirit
in will-living forms.

A–9

Exercises with meditations on
the Gospel of St. John

Between around 1906 and 1923

Appendix: Two exercises for
the Christian-Gnostic path of schooling

Archive no. 3157

Evening: 1.) Review of the day

2.) Transform the Gospel of St. John into images

3.) Meditation:

> In the beginning was the Word
> and the Word was with God
> and one[145] God was the Word.

Morning: 1.) Repeat the evening image

2.) Meditation:

> And may the Word be in me
> and in my soul be the Word
> and my will arise from the Word.

———

145. Translator's note: Steiner's formulation of *"ein Gott war das Wort"* is not commonly found in any German translations of the Bible. Readers may prefer to stay with the King James translation, "And the Word was God." I have used "one" here, rather than "a," because in one of these versions (Archive no. 7089/90) the word *Ein* is emphasized with a capital.

Archive no. 6827

Morning: 7 first lines of the Gospel of St. John

[In the beginning was the Word
and the Word was with God
and one God was the Word.
The same was in the beginning with God.
There where all arose, it was;
and nothing arose
except through the Word.]

In the pure rays of the light
seek my waiting soul
communion with God.

Evening: Review of the day

Communion with God
seek my waiting soul
in the pure rays of the light.

(Inner tranquility). –

———

Archive no. A 0062

Evening:

> In the beginning was the Word
> and the Word was with God
> and one God was the Word
> and the Word –
> let it live in the heart
> in the heart of your being
> within your I.

Morning:

> Within your I
> in the heart of your being
> let the Word live
> the Word of spirit.
> And the Word was with God
> and one God was the Word.
> In the beginning was the Word.

———

Archive no. 6802

Evening:

> In the beginning was the Word of time
> and the Word of time was with God
> and one God was the Word of time
> and the Word of time –
> let it live in *you.*

———

Morning:

> And the Word of time
> let it live in *me.*
> And one God was the Word of time
> and the Word of time was with God.
> In the beginning was the Word of time.

———

Archive no. A 0066

Evening:

    1.) Review   5–6 minutes

    2.)   In the beginning was the Word
          and the Word be within me
          and the Word work within me
          and the Word bear me
          in worlds of spirit
          in depths of soul.

Morning:

        Be the image
        of my self.
    In my depths of soul
    strong powers of the spirit
    like bright rose-stars
    upon the black wood of the cross.

———

Archive no. 5320

Evening:

Review.

Let my soul rise up
to far breadths of worlds
let my soul descend
into deep heart-ground
let it seek there to experience
breadths of worlds
in depths of heart.

(Inner tranquility)

Morning:

In the beginning was the Word
and the Word was with God
thus be the Word in me
and my soul with the Word.

(Inner tranquility)

———

Archive no. 3228

Evening:

1.) Review

2.) Place yourself into the moon-illumined sphere of night;
     and feel there:

> In the beginning was the Word
> and the Word grows to wisdom
> and dwells within my head
> and the Word is Christ
> and lives within my heart.

Morning:

Place yourself into the sun-resplendent sphere of day;
     and feel there:

> There lives within my soul
> the Word that is the Christ;
> there lives within my spirit
> the Word, that grows to wisdom;
> beginning and ending of all things:
> that is the wise love of the Christ.

In addition: the 6 exercises.

———

Archive no. A 7084R

In the beginning was the Word ...

Morning:

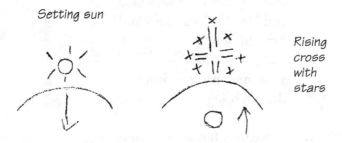

Christ speaks: Let my Word live in your heart

Evening:

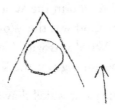

I, speaking to Christ: Let your Word live in my heart.

In the beginning was the Word ...

———

October 1919   Archive no. 7089/90

Evening: Review of the day

> Picturing the rising sun; feeling as if Chr. Spoke from it:
>
> | In the beginning was the Word | 1 |
> | and the Word was with God | 2 |
> | and One God was the Word | 3 |
> | hear the Word | 4 |
> | and you will hear | 5 |
> | your inner nature's own | 6 |
> | deepest being | 7 |

After this: wait with empty but wakeful awareness.

Morning:

> Picturing the setting sun. It leaves behind the Rose Cross.
>   The 7 roses resound:
>
> | Your deepest being | 7 |
> | within your inner nature | 6 |
> | you hear it | 5 |
> | resound to you in the Word | 4 |
> | and One God was the Word | 3 |
> | and the Word was with God | 2 |
> | in the beginning was the Word | 1 |

After this: wait with empty but wakeful awareness

Balancing exercises: Thought concentration
                          Initiative in action
                          Equilibrium of joy and suffering
                          Positivity
                          Open mindedness
                          Harmonizing of these 5 qualities

———

October 1919   Archive no. 7091/92

Evening: Review of the day. 3–4 minutes

> Standing on a hill. Sun at the zenith. Feeling that the sun resounds. A further feeling that the Chr. speaks from the sun so that it resounds through you:

In the beginning was the Word	1
and the Word was with God	2
and one God was the Word	3
and may the Word be	4
the core of your own being	5
in speaking I	6
within you speaks the Word.	7

After this: waiting with empty but wakeful awareness.

Morning: Standing on a hill. Sun at nadir. You have the feeling that it resounds beneath the earth.

Speaks the Word within you	7
so it is I	6
may core of your own being	5
be the Word	4
and One God was the Word	3
and the Word was with God	2
in the beginning was the Word	1

After this: waiting with empty but wakeful awareness. –

Supporting exercises: 6 exercises
                         Thought concentration
                         Initiative in action
                         Equilibrium of joy and suffering
                         Positivity
                         Open mindedness
                         Harmonizing of these 5 qualities

———

1923   Archive no. 7113

In the morning: Chapter 8 of the Gospel of St. John[146]
                           Verses 12–59

In the evening: Devout and reverent will I be
                           before the spirit beings
                           who within the dark of night
                           harbor my soul.

1st day often   :   Let peace guide me
2nd day often   :   With love I shall do what I should
3rd day often   :   God accompany my life

                           ———

---

146. Another exercise, Archive no. 6804, states: "Every evening: meditate on one sentence from John's Gosp., chapter 8, verses 12–59."

Appendix

Two exercises for the
Christian-Gnostic path of schooling

The only extant exercises for this schooling path are the following two. Whether additional ones were given is not known. It is not very probable, because under modern conditions, this path is almost impossible to pursue, as it requires complete withdrawal from ordinary life. (See also, for instance, CW 95 and 99.).

Archive no. 3192

Christian-Gnostic meditation.

I. Early in the morning after waking, before any other impressions have passed through the soul, try to free your awareness entirely from all memories of daily life and turn attention away from all external impressions. Having achieved this inner stillness, allow only the following to live in the soul:

> The five first verses of the Gospel of St. John. –

II. In the first two weeks, attempt to conjure before you the whole of your past in order to know yourself fully by this means.

After these two weeks, go through the whole of the St. John's Gospel, living entirely in one chapter each day for 7 days.

Thus in the first 7 days:	Chap. 1 from verse 6 to the end
" second 7 days:	Chap. 2
and so forth.	

Once arrived at Chapter 13, try with

The washing of the feet	to immerse yourself in feeling how every higher being owes its existence to lower ones, to which it must bow itself in humility.
The scourging	to feel that you have the capacity to stand upright in relation to the scourges of life; that is, in the face of all sufferings and pain.

The crowning with thorns	to feel that you must stand upright even in the face of all derision and scorn.
The crucifixion	to feel that your own body is something alien that you bear, and to which you are externally attached.
The mystic death	Here you experience the curtain which still conceals the spiritual world, but then also how it tears so that you can see into the world of spirit.
	Here you learn to look upon the depths of evil and wickedness: descent into hell.
The entombment	Feeling of being one with all earthly beings and the earth itself in which you are immersed.
The resurrection	This can only be *experienced* since the words of ordinary language are inadequate to describe it.

IIII. Then conjure the figure of Christ Jesus before the soul and pass on to the following thought as the subject of long contemplation:

I, in your spirit.

*
*   *

Evening: Review of the whole of the day.

I and III are the same every day; only II changes every 7 days as described.

After completing the cycle of II, start again from the beginning, and so on.

After a longer period one can experience the following inner and outer symptoms described on the path of Christian development:

Outer:	Inner:
Feeling as if your feet are surrounded by water.	Experience of the vision that you are yourself accomplishing the washing of the feet.
A feeling of burning, etc. on the whole skin.	You see yourself being scourged.
You feel pain in the head.	You see yourself wearing the crown of thorns.
The stigmata points redden during meditation.	You see yourself being crucified

———

Archive no. 3223-3226

It is necessary to meditate *every* morning, throughout *one* year, in the following way:

1st month: complete immersion for half an hour in the words of the
Gosp. of John,   1:1 and 2
2nd month: likewise   1:3
3rd month: "   1:4
4th month: "   1:5
5th month: "   1:6
6th month: "   1:7 and 8
7th month: "   1:9
8th month: "   1:10
9th month: "   1:11
10th month: "   1:12
11th month: "   1:13
12th month: "   1:14

This to be followed by an additional meditation throughout the weeks of the year:

1st day (Sunday): complete immersion for 15 minutes
in: First book of Moses (Genesis)   1:1-5
2nd day Monday: "   1:6-8
3rd day Tuesday: "   1:9-13
4th day Wednesday: "   1:14-19
5th day Thursday: "   1:20-23
6th day Friday   "   1:24-31
7th day Saturday   "   2:1-3

The designated length of these and all exercises should not be governed by the clock but by the feeling of time we acquire. The content of all biblical texts that belong to the above meditation must as far as possible be transformed into an image and conceived pictorially. For instance, in

1:1-2 of the Gospel of St. John, picture a mighty sphere within which all substance is in motion so that it forms itself in accordance with the wise meaning of the "divine Word" resounding through it. My lectures contain the building blocks of esoteric Christian tradition, which can guide the soul in transforming biblical words into the right, authentic images. As far as possible, adhere to these foundations.

After the above morning meditation, add the following *each* day for *at least* quarter of an hour, in deep meditation:

"I try to understand: that in the first third of cosmic evolution, Christ was the leader of a host of spirits in whose lap I lay unconscious; that to attain consciousness I had to separate myself from this host until, through Yahveh's preparation, my soul reached the point of being able to consciously receive the Christ forces; now I can receive these if I turn my spiritual gaze on the Christ who became flesh, and can take up his being into mine."

At the same time keep in mind that the being of Christ is represented in the Gospel of St. John.

*
*　*

During the day, contemplate the four parts of the Mass:

1. Evangelium: picture that through this, "God's Word" comes to human intellect.
2. Offertorium: picture that you voluntarily offer up to God what you already contain of God's being in yourself.
3. Transubstantiation: picture that what human beings offer up is transformed into something wholly divine.
4. Communion: picture yourself united with God.

When, in real priesthood, we attend Mass with *these* thoughts, what is suggested here is magically accomplished.

*
*　*

In the evening, we should develop the 7 qualities of the Christian mystic:

1. Feeling of true humility: All higher life owes its existence to the lower: plant to the stone, animal to the plant, the higher human being to the lower. Picture: Washing of the feet: Christ bows down to the apostles.

2. Feeling of forbearance: In patience I will bear all pain and suffering in life. Picture: Scourging.

3. Feeling of courage: I will stand upright, even if the things I hold most sacred are reviled. Picture: Crowning with thorns.

4. Feeling of independence from the body. Picture: Bearing the cross: (I will bear my body as something alien, like the wood of the cross.)

5. Feeling of mystical death: (I will learn to live within what of me is not my body, over which death has no power.) Picture: Hanging on the cross.

6. Feeling of burial and resurrection. (I regard the whole earth as my body.)

7. This feeling of the Ascension follows by itself from the previous qualities. There are no human words to express it.

Following this, in the evening: review the day's experiences in reverse sequence; start with the last experience of the evening and conclude with the first of the morning.

*
* *

Outward rules: Practice abstinence in as many ways as possible; abstaining from any desire, so that one no longer desires a previously desired object, leads a step further toward *gnosis*.

*
* *

The exercises are continued until new ones are given; but after some time the student should tell me in what direction he feels moved to aspire.

———————

Study is necessary: everything that can lead to contemplation of cosmic evolution and the nature of the human being.

———

B

Exercises with individually composed meditative verses

B–1

Exercises of unknown date

Archive no. 4487/88[147]

In the evening I seek an answer to the question: In what way is warmth the symbol for love?

Contemplate this question each evening for a week. Then each evening for a week: In what way is light the symbol for wisdom?

In week 3: In what way is air the symbol for intelligence?

She[148] should give the answer to this that she wishes, and always try to see how the answer to the three grows better over the three weeks.

This is followed by recall of one event during the day which she pictures very vividly and in reverse. Thus, if one takes off a [hat], it is pictured as being replaced on the head. Then she should form the idea: When I move my left hand, it is in reality my soul that moves it; when I move my right hand, the same soul moves it. The soul orders and governs the movements of my hands. Now, replacing the picture of my limbs with the great phenomena of nature, I form the thought: the divine spirit [relates to] the phenomena of nature as my soul does to my limbs. Then I try to speak the following words to this divine spirit, slowly and clearly:

> You are world intelligence
> You are world wisdom
> You are world love
> I am in you as one of my limbs in me.

Then she should try to fall asleep.

---

147. Text in Marie Steiner's handwriting; drawing in Rudolf Steiner's handwriting. The text was probably dictated by Rudolf Steiner.

148. Translator's note: it is not clear who is referred to here.

In the morning, waken these ideas once more, and speak the following inwardly:

> I am in you as one of my limbs in me.
> You are world love
> You are world wisdom
> You are world intelligence.

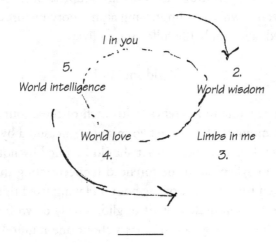

Archive no. 3215/16

Evening, where possible after completing all the day's work, so that
    the soul entertains no other thoughts between undertaking the
    exercise and falling asleep. The thoughts invoked by the exer-
    cise should slowly fade away.

1. Close yourself off from all outward impressions; live only and
entirely in your own soul, suppressing all memory pictures. In the soul
thus emptied, allow only the following to live:

World soul in I.

Become entirely one in awareness with each of these four syllables for
about half a minute. After these two minutes (measured by feeling, not
by the clock), locate thinking (that should be filled by nothing except
the above four syllables) in the forehead (concentrating there entirely,
and abstracted from the rest of the body). Having fixed thinking in the
forehead for two minutes, allow it to glide slowly down from the head
to the right foot (in a stream that lasts about one minute); from there
allow the same thought to pass through the body into the left hand
(again one minute) and from there to the right hand; from there (again
one minute) to the left foot; from there (one minute) back to the head;
from the head let it glide into the heart; and focus there for as long as
you can continue to maintain the thought (not too long, two to three
minutes).

   Then remain calmly self-enclosed, hearkening to your own soul.

   The thought, "World soul in I," is to be felt in such a way that awareness is directed to the effect or action of tangible world forces within
the human soul.

Morning, once again such that between waking up and undertaking the exercise, no other thoughts, daily worries, and so forth, intervene. For about four minutes contemplate the thought

I in world soul

With this reversal of the evening thought, undertake the same exercises as in the evening.

(All these processes must be solely inner ones. No kind of cramped, physical tension, and so forth, should occur. Everything must be undertaken with full self-monitoring by [waking consciousness[149]])

----

149. The end of the text is missing.

Archive no. 3242/43

In the evening, after finishing all work so that no daily concerns, and so forth, intervene between this exercise and falling asleep: fill the whole horizon of your awareness with a serious thought derived from your worldview, summarizing it in just a few syllables.

For instance, think for a few minutes about how the world soul lives in the human soul, so that tangible thoughts about this pass through the soul, and give the whole of this reflection a devotional character. Rather than just thinking these truths, *sense and feel* them. Then summarize them thus:

> World soul in the I

Concentrate the whole of your awareness on such an idea, which is thus the outcome of a sequence of thinking and feeling; fill yourself with it so that you exclude all other thinking, feeling, and sensing.

Then fill your whole bodily form entirely with this thought by allowing it to glide from the head through the body into feet and hands (taking about ten minutes for the whole process—by feeling, not by the clock).

The position of the body, and so forth, is essentially of no importance. All that matters is to be in a position in which nothing can distract your attention. The longer you can allow the exercise to inwardly reverberate without other thoughts intervening, the better (without overdoing it).

In the morning, after waking, repeat the whole sequence of the exercise.

You can undertake the same process for many days; you will make most progress if you have the patience to work with the *same* thoughts for weeks on end. And then vary it.

Archive no. 3214

Morning:

5 mins.:   Everything that happens around me, and
             everything that happens to me is necessary.

             Concentrate on the eyes: I will regard
             everything around me in this way.

5 mins.   Concentrate on heart, arms, hands: I will do in
             this way everything that should be done by me.

5 mins.:

1. forehead

3. right hand   4. left hand

bright yellow color

2. left foot

5. right foot

Strength in me.

*
* *

During the day: thought concentration five minutes.

*
* *

Evening: Read seven or eight lines of *Theosophy*; then make them fully
your own for a quarter of an hour.

Brief review of the day. In images, in reverse.

———

Archive no. A 0069

Evening:
Image of the sun that has just risen, starting to resound. From its tone develop the following meditation processes, which we picture hearing with the heart as though with a soul organ of hearing:

> Within your inner nature
> lives the guiding
> spirit-borne
> soul-filled
> > human being.
> Thinking he grasps light of worlds
> in active will he offers up human love.

(The exercise should be done every two or three days, as desired; but in a regular rhythm.)

Morning:

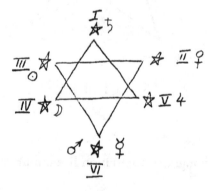

Speak as follows:

For star I: In active will I offer up human love

For star II: Thus I connect with the universe

For star III: Thus in the universe the I sustains itself

For star IV: Thinking I grasp light of worlds

For star V: Thus a universe grounds itself in the I

For star VI: Thus lives in the I a universe

Keep the whole star form in your mind, speaking to it:

I–IV: *I* lives love-offering *thus* in the
light of worlds of love.

———

Archive no. 3236/37

Morning:

Concentrate on a line that passes through the body in this way:

*The line does not pass through the spine but a little **in front** of it, through the body.*

Then meditate on what is contained in the following words:

>Warming light enters me from above
>Heaviness of earth spreads warming light in me and shapes me

Then, for some while, maintain the thought:

I am

Then think of *nothing*, but *wait* with empty awareness for what comes.

Evening: Try to concentrate on your own bodily feeling in the following stages:

> I am my head
> I am my throat
> I am my arms
> I am my ribcage
> I am my heart
> I am the blood that circulates in me
> I am my lungs

Then concentrate on the breath in the following way:

> Concentrate on inbreathing and sense the indrawing breath as

$$I \text{ [ee]}$$

> Concentrate on the inhaled breath filling the body and sense this as

$$A \text{ [ah]}$$

> Concentrate on outbreathing and sense the breath leaving the body as

$$O$$

Do this in *seven* successive breathing cycles; then concentrate on the interior of the head (point a)

and feel there as if the word Iao [ee-ah-o] resounds; sustain this tone for one to two minutes, then think of nothing, but wait for what comes with empty awareness.

———

Archive no. 3238

Stream of light from the middle of
eyebrows to the nape of the neck: I [ee]

Stream of light passes along
spinal column: A [ah]

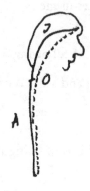

seven times,
each for
2 minutes
(14 mins.)

Light stream within from the spinal
column back to the center of eyebrows: O

I A O   goes into me through me out of me
I A O   creates forces in me through me out of me
I A O   lives weaving in me through me out of me

as often
[as]
possible

Mood: I A O as the name of Christ
         This is connected with the secret of how Christ
         works in the human being.

———

Archive no. 3173

Morning: a number of breaths:

Inbr.:   Attraction pours energy through all things.

Outbr.:   Repulsion inwardly strengthens all things.

Midday: a number of breaths:

Inbr.:   Every thing works upon every thing

Outbr.:   Every being is reflected in every being.

Evening: a number of breaths:

Inbr.:   Every being reveals itself.

Outbr.:   Every being lives in itself.

———

Archive no. 7087

The previous exercises[150] during waxing moon.
These exercises during waning moon.

Morning: Above ....everywhere ....spirit

    Breathe 3 times slowly

           Below .... everywhere .... soul

    Breathe 3 times slowly

           Within ... stronger and stronger .... strength

    Breathe 3 times slowly

           (Inner tranquility)

Evening: Light around me .... Light in me

    Breathe 3 times slowly

           Heart .... Light gives strength

    Breathe 3 times slowly

           Heart .... Into the body

    Breathe 3 times slowly

    (An inner sense as if you felt light streaming out as strength)

---

150. Using the verse "In the godhood of the world...:, see p. 123 ff.)

(Die bisherigen Übungen bei zunehmen Monde)
(Diese Übungen bei abnehm. Monde)

Morgens: Oben .... überall .... Geist

    3mal langsam atmen

      Unten .... überall ..----- Seele

    3mal langsam atmen

       Innen ....·····stärker und stärker .... Kraft

    3mal langsam atmen

      (Seelenruhe)

abends: Licht um mich .... Licht in mir

    3mal langsam atmen

    Herz .... · · - - - - - Licht giebt Kraft

    3mal langsam atmen

    Herz ..· - - - - - -- - --In den Leib

    3mal langsam atmen

    (So in der Seele empfinden, wie wenn man
        fühlen würde das Licht als Kraft hinströmen)

Archive no. 3230

In the morning:

> I discern the thought image
> of my being
> in my head;
> I think the feeling rhythm
> enlivening my being
> in my heart;
> I feel the willpower
> strengthening my limbs
> throughout my body.

At midday:

> Let stream
> the strength of my right eye
> into my left arm
> and the strength of my left arm
> into my right leg –
> let stream
> the strength of my left eye
> into my right arm
> and the strength of my right arm
> into my left leg.

Before sleep:

> I shall
> depart from my body –
> my feeling follows me
> my will enters the spirit realm
> strength permeate my will
> awakening let it take strong hold of all limbs – – –

————

Archive no. 6911

In the morning immediately after waking:

1.) Inner surging soul light –
from the ether's unending periphery
you drew life of spirit –
from harmonies of the stars   } 5 mins.
life powers resounded to you –
you enter into the body's enclosure
to mirror the spirit's reflection.

2.) 5 mins.: Above, light as thought: *I was*
      In the head, light as thought
         (like the aura in the head): *I am*
      From the head, raying light: *I will be.*

} morning

Midday: repeat part 2

Evening:

One week: Nature of the human being[151]
Second week: Between death and a new birth

Inner surging soul light –
you depart from the spirit's reflection
you step out of the body's enclosure –
the powers of life will resound to you   } 5 mins.
in the harmonies of the world of stars –
spirit life you will draw
from the ether's unending periphery.

Review of the day.

---

151. Nature of the human being, in *Theosophy*, CW 9.

Archive no. 3233

Evening: 1st day: Summarize an insight in a
brief sentence
Transform it into a mathematical
or physical symbol.

Breathing;   Inbreath: assimilation of the symbol   10
                      by the head.   mins.
Hold breath: Store away the symbol.
Outbreath: Picture retaining symbol
           within you as you allow air
           to leave you without symbol.

Morning: Repeat the same exercise.
Wait with inner equanimity of soul,   15
without outward impressions or   mins.
memories of life on the physical
plane.

Evening: 2nd day: Summarize an insight in a sentence.
Transform it into a plant symbol.

Breathing: Inbreath: assimilation of the symbol
                     by the heart
Hold breath: Store away the symbol
Outbreath: Picture retaining symbol
           within you as you allow air
           to leave you without symbol.

Morning: Repeat the exercise and wait as on
the first day.

Evening: 3rd day:　Summarize an insight in a brief sentence.
　　　　　　　　Transform it into a symbol in the animal
　　　　　　　　kingdom.

　　Breathing;　Breathe in the symbol through the larynx.
　　　　　　　　Hold breath: Retain the symbol
　　　　　　　　Outbreath: Picture that symbol
　　　　　　　　　　　　remains within
　　　　　　　　　　　　you and empty air leaves you.

　　Morning:　Repeat as on the other days.

　　　　　　　　———

No alcohol. No lentils, beans, or peas.

———

Archive no. 4440

Evening:

> The power of my heart
> I receive into my soul
> then Christ is with me
> I give him dwelling in me –
> I think through him
> I feel with him
> I will with him.

———

Morning:

> The power of my head
> I receive into my spirit
> then godliness is in me
> I bear it in me
> I bear it as thought
> I bear it as feeling
> I bear it is as will.

———

Archive no. A 0213

Morning:

    I see the sun
    the luminous radiant one
    shining into my soul
    beaming into my heart
    I feel sun everywhere
    warming me
    M – e[152]

Evening:

    My heart shines
    over my head shines a star.
    Heart and star shine to each other
    I feel soul warmth
    in shining stars
    in warmth of heart.

———

152. Translator's note: This is untranslatable, and must be used as each person sees fit. In German the last line is: *"M – ich"* which echoes the word *"mich"* (me) on the previous line, but is subtly altered to contain *"ich"* ("I"). In English, one could either say "M – e" [ee], which would echo the German sound of *"i"* in *"ich"*; or "M – I" with an emphasis on the English first person singular.

Archive no. 3178

Morning:

When my eye opens
to receive the light of day
after night's quiet has strengthened me
let my heart with strength of will
feel strongly how life and courage
from God's wide world stream
their gift into my limbs.
And let me know each moment
that lofty powers divine
bless and bear through life
everything in me I can feel
and everything I do with all my will.

Evening:

When my eyes close
and leave the light of day
after the work of daily life's been done
let me strongly feel
how God's wide world
blesses and receives me
how lofty powers divine
enduringly preserve my life and courage.

———

Archive no. A 4006

Morning:

the ♀ for about five minutes,

then live in the following thoughts:

Light flooding around me
image of spirit's creative power
gentle warmth within me
image of soul's apprehending power –
thus I connect
with world depths
with spirit heights.

(Then inner tranquility)

Evening: Usual review

then five to ten minutes

Also the six exercises [the balancing exercises]

———

Archive no. 6654

Evening: 5 mins.

> Feeling round me strengthening light
> strengthening light that courage lends
> lends also strength
> strength that imbues me
> so that with it I
> can find my own
> self-experiencing within.

———————

Morning:

> So that I within my own
>   self-experience
>   truly find myself
> penetrate me
>   power of spirit
>   light divine
>   warmth of soul.

———————

Archive no. A 0111

Courage exercise

Morning:

> Hidden courage of my heart
> stream brightly
> into my head!
> I *am*, I
> *think, feel, will.*

Evening:

> *Thinking, feeling, will*
> is my *being.*
> In my head
> work brightly
> the hidden courage of my heart!

———

Archive no. 3993/94

[Evening:]

Great all-encompassing spirit
who penetrates worlds
who infuses human beings –
penetrate what I may see
feel what I can know
let my I raise itself to you
work its way up from below
to see your creating
work its way down from above
to live your seeing
let it feel its way within existence
into loving world being
uphold itself in feeling
In YOU great all-encompassing spirit.

[Morning:]

In YOU great all-encompassing spirit
let my I
uphold itself in feeling
feel its way within existence
to loving world being –
to live your seeing
let it work its way down from above
to see your creating
work its way up from below
so that it comes to feel what it perceives
so that it penetrates what it knows
through YOU
who infuse human beings
who penetrate worlds
great all-encompassing spirit.

———

Archive no. 7085/86

First the usual evening review   *Evening*

> Spirit of worlds
> bearer of sublime goodness
> bearer of all-embracing world laws
> bring light
> and the word of spirit
> into my soul
> so that she reveal
> my spirit
> who I am myself
> through timeless duration
> through all breadths of space.

———————

Morning

> Through all breadths of space
> through timeless duration
> I am as self
> in the spirit
> therefore be revealed
> my spirit
> to me as soul
> as spirit word
> as spirit light
> that comes
> from the bearer of all-embracing world laws
> from the bearer of sublime goodness
> from
> the spirit of worlds.

————

Archive no. A 0103

Morning:

> Spirit of worlds
> guide me:
> shining in thinking
> warming in feeling
> strengthening in will
> I live in him
> rest in him.

Evening:

> Immanent I
> finds in me
> thinking I.
> Thinking I
> draws living strength
> from power of worlds
> within me.

———

Evening:

1.) Review

2.) Picture yourself placed into moon-illumined night; there experience the following in *feeling*:

> In the beginning was Yahveh
> and Yahveh was with the Elohim
> and Yahveh was one of the Elohim
> and Yahveh lives in me.

Then picture the moon-illumined night transforming into sun-radiant day; and there experience in *feeling*:

> And Christ in me
> and Christ is one of the Elohim
> and Christ is with the Elohim
> Christ will be at the end.

———

Morning:

First, sun-radiant daylight – feeling experience in evening twilight mood:

> Christ will be at the end

Then picture sun over your head:

> and Christ is in me

Then picture daylight – feeling experience in morning mood:

> and I am in a world permeated by Christ.

Six balancing exercises alongside this

———

Archive no. 3135/36

Morning.

In the beginning was Y ...
and Y ... was with the El ...
and one of the El... was J...
and may Y... live in my soul

> Wait with attentiveness   with empty
> Attend in waiting   awareness

Evening, after
the review

Y...is my breath
and with the breath J... enters
the house prepared for him
and his house is my body
my body is the house of the El...
and Y... hallows himself in warmth
and Y...is hallowed in warmth
Chr.

———

Facsimile of archive no. 3135/36

Morgens.

Im Urbeginn war J...
Und J... war bei den El....
Und der El.... Einer war J...
Und J... wohne in meiner Seele

       Wachend wachen ⎫ mit leerem Bewußtsein
       Wartend wachen ⎭

Abends nach
der Rückkehr

J... ist mein Athem
Und Mit dem Athem zieht J...
   In sein vorbereitet Haus
Und sein Haus ist mein Leib
Mein Leib ist der El... Haus
Und J... heiligt sich in Wärme
Und J... ist geheiligt in Wärme
    Chr.

Archive no. 6640

Evening: 1.)   Review

2.)   My soul in world-breadths sense
divine creative strength
my soul in heart-depths feel
spiritual power of love
be sevenfold emblem for me
of my sign
me in you.

(Tranquility in the soul)

Morning: In love
peace
stillness
let my work
unfold strongly
for me
through the day.

———

Archive no. A 0029

Evening:

> Unending spiritual power works
> through breadths of space
> eternally soul being lives
> through cycles of time
> within the sea of space
> and course of time
> weaves my everlasting self.

Morning:

> Sevenfold
> spirit light
> shines resplendent
> bestowing strength
> entering
> me
> potently.

———

Archive no. 4414

Evening:

Review

In world-breadths willingly
weave the core being of my soul
within the spirit warmth
of world-weaving feel
the inner being of the soul
and guide uphold sustain
M – e[153]

(Inner tranquility)

———————

Morning:

In hands let strengthen
in hearts let work
universal human strength
and soothing me release –
to bear me in myself –
the spirit's germinating strength
I in me.

(Inner tranquility)

———————

———————

153. Translator's note: This is untranslatable, and must be used as each person sees fit. In German the last line is: *"M – Ich"* which contains the word *"mich"* (me), but is subtly altered also to contain *"ich"* ("I"). In English, one could either say "M – e" [ee], which would echo the German sound of *"i"* in *"ich"*; or "M – I" with an emphasis on the English first person singular.

Archive no. 4399

In the evening:

Swimming aloft
from depths of worlds   } meditate in more picturing way
the sun of Christ

its light is spirit   — meditate in picturing-feeling way

it shines in the universe
it acts as spirit in me   } meditate in feeling way
it lives in my I.

———

In the morning:

It lives in my I
it acts as spirit in me   } meditate in more feeling way
it shines in the universe

it is the light of spirit   — meditate in picturing-feeling way

it is light of the sun of Christ
from depths of worlds   } meditate in picturing way
from which it swims aloft.

———

Archive no. 3294

[Evening:]

Beings made manifest
in breadths of space enclose
the life of my soul power V
from clarity of light
springs up through spirit depths
the true worth of the soul
life's strong power.

[Morning:]

Life's strong power
the true worth of the soul
springs up through spirit depths
from clarity of light –
the life of my soul power's
enclosed by breadths of space
and beings made manifest.

———

Archive no. A 0104

Evening: Review. 4–6 minutes

> Seven bright stars of roses
> upon the black cross wood
>   be for me the image
> of spirit strongly shining
>   within the dark of soul
> seek my soul
> in dark the light.
>   (Inner tranquility)

Morning:

> Sunlight flows through space
> spirit light flows through the soul.

6 exercises

———

Archive no. A 0023

Evening:

Picture the Rose Cross

You my soul
look upon this sign
let it signify for you
the universal spirit
filling breadths of worlds
working through time's cycles
working everlastingly in you.

(Inner tranquility)

Morning:

Picture the Rose Cross

In this sign
stand my thinking
stand my will
stand my feeling
let its meaning
live in my heart's depths
live in me as light.

(Inner tranquility)

———

Archive no. 3068

Evening: Review of an event in the day – and self-evaluation –
Theosophy five or six sentences

Entering you
my soul life
entering you
my spirit striving
all my existence
       given up to you

_____

Morning:

Given up to you
all my existence
my spirit striving
entering you
my soul life
       entering you.

Recalling the five or six sentences

Spend a quarter of an hour contemplating them.

_____

Archive no. 6252

Evening: 1.) Review. In images. In reverse

2.)

Up to
15 mins.   {

In this your sign
O Christ Creator of worlds
show your soul's
      light
      life
      strength
      word.

(Inner tranquility)

Morning: First picture light before you
then let this light enter the heart:

Then:

10 – 15
mins.   {

Light of the world
light of the spirit
enter the depths of my soul.

———

Archive no. A 0216

Evening:

In looking up
to this sign
may I feel
strength of the universal spirit
light of the universal spirit
wise Word of the universal spirit –
may all this live in me.

(Inner tranquility)

Morning:

Strength of the universal spirit
light of the universal spirit
wise Word of the universal spirit –
may all this live in me
kindle in me
inner strength of God
that holds and bears me up.

(Inner tranquility)

———

Archive no. 7103

Evening: 1.) Review. In images. In reverse. 5–6 mins.

2.)   Let my thinking sink
into the depths of my soul
let my feeling open
into wide spirit realms   } 10 mins.
and so in me unite
soul depth and spirit expanse
within my feeling thinking.

(Inner tranquility)

Morning:

Sevenfold
glows
rose-stars' light
sevenfold   } 10–15 mins.
will
I
strive

(Inner tranquility)

———

Facsimile of archive no. 7103

Abend: 1.) Rückschau. Bildhaft Rückläufend. 5–6 Min.

2.)
Es senke mein Denken sich
In meine Seelentiefen
Es weite mein Fühlen sich
In weite Geistesräume
So einige sich in mir
Seelentiefe und Geistesweite
Im fühlenden Denken
— (Seelenruhe)

⎫
⎬ 10 Min
⎭

Morgens:

⊕

Siebenfach
leuchtet
Rosensternenlicht
Siebenfach
will
ich
streben.

⎫
⎬ 10–15 Min.
⎭

(Seelenruhe)

Archive no. 5314

Evening: 1.) Review. Backward from evening to morning

2.) Blue of the sky with many stars

> Devout and reverent my soul
> send out into the breadths
> of space a feeling gaze
> and let this looking drink
> light love life
> from spirit worlds
> and send into my depths of heart.
>> (Inner tranquility)

Morning:

> May this symbol's
> speech to me
> of lofty universal spirit
> fill my soul
> at every time
> in every moment of my life
> with light love life.
>> (Inner tranquility)

6 balancing exercises

———

Archive no. 3229

Evening: 1.) Review. In images. In reverse.

       2.) Seek my soul
           to sink into and sense yourself –
           upon your ground your spirit lies
           within your spirit works the spirit of worlds
           within all this I am
           thinking feeling
                living.

                             (Inner tranquility)

Morning:

In you O universal letter
I perceive
the sevenfold workings of the spirit
in seven rose stars
and life's dark paths
in black cross wood
          in all of this I am.

                  (Inner tranquility)

––––––

Archive no. 3232

In the evening: first picture an experience of the day in reverse.
          then imagination of the

          Original powers uphold me
          spirits of fire free me
          spirits of light illumine me
          so that I reach toward spirit existence
          so that I feel soul beings
          so that I overleap uncertainties
          so that I stand above abysses.

Then try to immerse yourself in the following:

          Let Christ live in me
          and transform my breath
          and warm my circling blood
          and shine into my being of soul.

   Calmly rest within yourself:

In the morning:

          Imagination on the mountain. Being received.

          Invoke

          Head of mine harden universal spirit
          free from it for me the living light of thought –
          dry my larynx the soul of breezes
          pour into it the sense of spirit word –
          dwell my spirit guide within my heart
          and there unite with me
          so that I swim live weave in spirit-soul existence.

———

Facsimile of archive no. 3232[154]

Am Abend : Erst ein Tageserlebnis rückwärts vorstellen.
dann Imagination des

☩

Urkräfte ballet mich
Geister des Feuers befreiet mich
Geister des Lichtes erleuchtet mich
~~Dass ich~~ ~~theile lange~~ ~~Ungewissf~~
~~Dass ich~~ ☩

Dass ich greife nach Geistessein
Dass ich fühle die Seelenwesen
Dass ich schreite über Ungewissheiten
Dass ich sehe über Abgründen

dann versuchen ganz sich vertiefen in :

In mir lebe der Christus
Und wandle meinen Atem
Und wärme meines Blutes Lauf
Und leuchte meinem Seelenwesen .

Ruhiges Verharren in sich :

Am Morgen:

Imagination auf Berg. Empfangenwerden.
Vorstellen ♄
Mein Haupt erhärte Weltengeist
Und Befreie mir daraus Gedankenlichtesleben
Meine Kehle verdorre Luftseele
Ergiesse in sie geisteswortessinn
Mein Herz bewohne du mein Geistesführer
Da Eine du mich mit Dir
Dass ich schwebe lebe webe in Geistesseelensein

weisses Gewand. Roter Gürtel und
Gehänge. Rotes Stirnband.

⅛ Ave frater
Gros eae et aureae
⅛ crucis
⅛ Benedictus deus qui dedit
notis signum

---

154. See appendix for a comment on the facsimile addition to the exercise.

Archive no. A 0107[155]

In the evening:

1.) Retrospective glance at the events of the day.
      In pictures. Going backward.
            10 minutes

2.)   Try, thou my soul
         To penetrate into thy depths,
         In thy depths acts creatively
         The world spirit's life-force,
         The world spirit's wisdom-light,
         The world spirit's will-power;
         I belong to this all.
               5 minutes (Quiet of the soul; feeling of expectation.)

In the morning:

         Thou, symbol of the world's activity,
         Thy seven shining rose-stars
         On the black wood of the cross
         Shape seven rays of spiritual activity
         In the dark entity of the world
         In the depths of my soul
         I[n] this quiet feeling.
               (Quiet of the soul. Expectation.)

-----

155. Translator's note: The exercises under this archive number, on this page and the next, are originally in English. It is not clear whether Steiner himself wrote them in English, but I have retained the form of English given in the original, including initial capitals and punctuation, with a few small corrections.

Wednesday evening:

1.)   Retrospective glance on the other days.

2.) a) Concentration on the point between the eyebrows
(half a centimeter in)

I am

b)   Concentration on the throat

It thinks

c)   Concentration on the heart, arms, fingers

She feels

d)   Concentration on the bodily form

He wills

Saturday morning: the same
The 6 qualities

———

Archive no. 4467

Evening: 1.) *Review*

2.) Contemplation of:

> To light-filled spaces
> rise aloft my soul –
> into time's creating
> flow forth my spirit
> within me seek
> self's core of being,
> the you in I.

   with the feeling that the source of the "you" radiates and flourishes from the crossing point (shining out in the 7 roses)

Morning: Imagination:

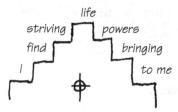

Inbreath: Living I
Holding breath: Weaving the self
Outbreath: Giving oneself to the universe

Guiding thought: What one experiences within oneself in sensing (feeling), is truly concentrated being of the spirit hierarchies within one's own being, just as the eye's activity in the eyeball is the concentrated being of weaving light.

———

Archive no. 4468

Evening: Sunrise:

resounding: 3–4 minutes

Sun:
{
World thoughts
shining
and their shining
feel
in your heart
bright
strong
}

                      grow inwardly very tranquil.

Morning: Sunset

I:
{
strong
bright
in my heart
I feel
your shining
for in you shine
world thoughts
}

                      grow inwardly tranquil.

———

Archive no. A 0007

Evening:

Do the review. Then picture the setting moon,
and within it the cross with roses:

> Christ's light
> from great stars
> streams into my heart.

Morning:

Picture a blue flower that grows ever bigger.
Then stand still *before* this flower:

> May Christ's power of life
> germinate in my soul.

Enter right into the flower…
Allow the image to fade away,
and remain calm and quiet for a few minutes

———

Archive no. 6859

Evening: Above my head stands a star,
from the star resound the words:

Christ who nurtures your heart
is powerful in your soul
he gives you potent life
hear him in the spirit
he comforts human beings
he holds your I in his hand.

Morning: Rising sun:

My heart receive from you (Christ)
the power of the Word
that formed the world.

———

Archive no. A 0212

Evening:

        Picture:

        Bear the spirit of my will
        through your power
        to the spirit of worlds.

Morning:

        Picture (above your head):

        My heart receive from you (Christ)
        the power of the Word
        that formed the world.

———

Archive no. 6446

Evening:

Rising[156]

Light of universal wisdom I send into your heart

Inner tranquility

Morning:

Sinking

Light of universal wisdom I receive into my heart. –

Inner tranquility

_____

_____

156. In the handwritten text there is no indication of what or who rises and sinks, but presumably the sun is meant. See archive no. A 6632, p. 342.

Archive no. A 0005[157]

In the morning:

Picture to yourself that you are in the midst of cosmic space surrounded by Light, and that a voice comes to you from the four points of the compass (a single voice but coming from four different directions) speaking to you:

> Be a strong I.
> Give thy heart to the Spirit of the World.

(Be very quiet in your soul after this meditation.)

In the evening:

Review the day in backward order from morning till evening.[158]

Picture to yourself that you are in the midst of cosmic space, surrounded by Darkness, and that you are speaking to the Full Moon in the East:

> I will be a strong I.
> I will give my heart to the Spirit of the World.

(Be very quiet in your soul after this meditation.)

———

157. Translator's note: This text was originally in English, and no amendment has been made to it.
158. Translator's note: This is presumably an error, and should read "from evening to morning."

[Evening:]

The whole system in calm and quiet; let this tranquility remain a little in your feeling then picture the sun shining without luster on the horizon, and meditate:

>   The red streams will-strengthening through my being

Then picture the sun as blue:

>   The dark blue offers no resistance to my will

The whole exercise need take no longer than 3–4 minutes, but can be repeated again after quarter of an hour.

Morning:

>   The night strengthened my will

to the blue sun; then to the red:

>   The red strengthens me as being of will

Same length of time as in the evening.

———

B–2

Exercises of known date

(around 1910 to 1924)

1910 or later   Archive no. 3167

Evening: 1.) Review. In images. In reverse.   4–5 mins.

2.)   ☦

> Look up my soul
> to the black wood of the cross
> to seven bright rose-stars
> they unite with the image
> of the deep ground of the universe   } 10 mins.
> they unite with the image
> of the high universal spirit.

(Inner tranquility)

Morning: ☦

> Black wood of the cross
> dark depths of soul
> bright rose-stars
> eternal spirit light   } 15 mins.
> I with You
>   O
> universal spirit.

(Inner tranquility)

Balancing exercises: *ES*

———

Facsimile of archive no. 3167

Abends: 1.) Rückschau. Bildhaft. Rücklaufend. 4-5 Min.

2.)   ✠

Meine Seele blicke auf
Zum schwarzen Kreuzesholz
Zu sieben hellen Rosensternen
Sie eine sich mit dem Bilde
Der Welten untergründe
Sie eine sich mit dem Bilde
Des hohen Weltengeistes

                    (Seelenruhe)

} 10 Min.

Morgens,   ✠

Schwarzes Kreuzesholz
Dunkle Seelentiefen
Helle Rosensterne
Ewiges Geisteslicht
Ich mit Dir
· O,
Wellengeist

                    (Seelenruhe)

} 15 Min.

Nebenzb - : ghW. S. 306.

1910 or later   Archive no. 7104

Evening: 1.) Review. In images. In reverse. 5 mins.

        2.)

                My soul have will to see
                in the seven bright rose-stars
                sevenfold-manifest spirit power.

                              ⋮

                My soul have will to see
                in the black wood of the cross
                darkness of worlds as the ground of light

                              ⋮

                    this in me
                                (Inner tranquility)

Morning:

                As upon the black wood of the cross
                seven rose-stars reveal themselves, shine forth
                so let the deepest ground of my soul
                reveal the sevenfold soul starlight:
                wisdom – light – certainty
                composure – inner quiet – fortitude
                    I safely upholding myself in me.
                                (Inner tranquility)

Balancing exercises in *Esoteric Science*

                    ———

Evening:

    1.)   The review of the day as described in Part 2 of
               Esoteric Science. 3–4 minutes.

    2.)   Place yourself into light-filled space, imagining
               yourself pervaded by light. At the same time picture
               the light speaking the following words in your heart:

> One with light I stand
> in you
> as world wisdom
> that gives you
> strength and peace
> for soul for spirit
> and for your I.
>
> > 3–4 minutes, then dwell for
> > a while in inner tranquility

Morning: Place yourself before the image of the setting (not
               rising) sun, and speak the following words out of your
               heart to the being of the sun:

> May my I
> of spirit and soul
> seek strength and peace
> in you
> O world wisdom
> which you
> live one with light.
>
> > 3–4 minutes, then dwell for
> > a while in inner tranquility.

———

1910 or later   Archive no. A 0114[159]

In the evening:

> *I go into the spiritual world* (3 or 4 minutes)

Imagination:

> *Black cross*   (wood changed by fire into coal)
> *7 roses*   (color: pink-violet)

This symbol is to tell you:

> So as out of the black cross
> The red roses,
> So out of the darkness of the world
> The clearness of Christ's life.

> (keep this thought for 10 minutes, seeing the cross)

In the morning:
Retrospective look on the events of the preceding day.
Imagination of a white cross consisting of white
gleaming sunlight – 7 green roses.

---

159. Translator's note: This was in English and the original English words, punctuation, and capitalization have been retained.

So as the green life
In the white sunlight,
So Christ's life
In the course of man's evolution.

(15 minutes)

6 exercises in *Esoteric Science*

———

1912   Archive no. 3231

Evening:

> May warmth enter me   (whole body)
> may light illumine my spirit   (head)
> and pour into my heart   (heart)
> thus will I find myself
> thus through spirit power
> be myself in me
> and rest in God's wide world.

                                        (Inner tranquility)

Morning:

Spirit light refresh the core of my being

                                        (Inner tranquility)

Sunday, 9 a.m.:   In the spirit of humanity I feel
                    united with all esotericists. –

———

Facsimile of archive no. 3231

abend:

☩

Wärme dringe in mich   (ganzer Körper)

Licht erleuchte meinen Geist (Kopf)

Und ergieße sich mir in mein Herz (Herz)

So will ich mich finden

So durch Geistes Kraft

Mich in mir selber sein

Und ruhen in Gottes weiter Welt

                              (Seelenruhe)

☩

Morgens

Geisteslicht erquicke meines Wesens Kern.

                              (Seelenruhe).

Sonntag 9 Uhr: Im Geiste der Menschheit fühle ich mich
                mit allen Esoterikern vereint. —

April 1912   Archive no. 5325

Morning:

   1.) Contemplation of the thought that human beings can
        raise themselves above themselves.

   2.)

            In the sign of Christ
            I see the power
            that should lead me
            out of my own being
            into the light realm of the spirit
            into the love world of the soul –
            there may I find myself.
                        (Inner tranquility)

Evening: Review. In reverse

            May my soul
            take up the world of spirit
            and may Christ's spirit lead her.

6 exercises: *Esoteric Science*

Sunday, 9 a.m.: In the spirit of humanity I feel
                  united with all esotericists

———

13 April 1912   Archive no. A 0049

Evening:

> I in you.[160]
> You fatherly human soul
>   I seek you.
> I turn outward from myself.
> You motherly spirit of worlds
>   take me up.
> My soul seeks you!

Morning:

> Toward far worlds may my soul
>   turn to seek you
>   motherly spirit of worlds.
> Inward into me may my soul
>   turn to seek you
>   fatherly human soul.
> I from you.

———

160. Translator's note: The "You" in the first line of this verse is the plural form. It is likewise plural in the last line of the subsequent morning verse.

13 April 1912   Archive no. 3169

Evening: 1.) Review, in reverse

                        Light in my I

                2.) 3 or 4 or 5 sentences[161]

                            ⊕

Morning: ⊕

                Recalling the sentences
                and meditating on them.

                        (Light in my I)

Sunday 9 a.m.:   In the spirit of humanity I feel
                 united with all esotericists

                        ———

---

161. 3, 4, or 5 sentences from a spiritual-scientific text.

April 1912   Archive no. A 0020

Morning: Star between the eyes turned toward Christ:

                        The power of your Word
                        the love of your Word
                        be in my soul
                        be in me.

Evening: Star in the heart, voice of Christ:

                        The power of my Word
                        the love of my Word
                        live in your soul
                        live in you.

                            _____

April 1912 or May/June 1913   Archive no. A 0033

Evening:

> Meditation on the Rose Cross
>
> This symbol points me to
> life's victory over death.
> I will feel within me
> the meaning of this sign.
> It will raise me up
> and raised up bear me
> through all life's spheres.

Morning:

> In the beginning was the Word
> and may the Word be in me.
> And the Word was godly
> and with godly power
> may the Word imbue me.
> And one God was the Word
> and may the Word endow my will with the
>   power of God.

During the day: the balancing exercises

———

April 1912 or May/June 1913   Archive no. 6906

Evening: Review – in images, in reverse

        Picturing darkening space

           From the senses' realm
           light vanishes –
           let brightly rise
           from my soul depths
           the light of spirit
           so that I find my goals in life
           and walk the paths of love.

Morning: So that I walk the paths of love
           and find my goals in life
           through spirit light that shines
           from my own soul's depths –
           bend down to me
           from the light of worlds
           that shines out in the realms of space.

6 balancing exercises

———

April 1912   Archive no. 5808

Evening: Review

> Thinking of the star-bright night, with the words:

>> In the darkness shines out light.
>> In my heart shines out love.

Morning: Thinking of the rising sun, with the words:

>> In the world works wisdom
>> and yearning for wisdom works
>> in human life of soul.

———

April 1912   Archive no. 3181

Evening: 1. Review. In images, in reverse, 5–6 minutes

2.   Learn to feel my soul
      how the spirit works
      in all beings and all existence
      learn to feel my soul   } 10 mins.
      how from spirit realms
      you came to sense existence
      to manifest the spirit.

                    (Inner tranquility)

Morning: ⊕

                    Sense my soul the meaning
                    of this symbol
                    and draw power
10 mins   {   and draw light
                    from everything
                    that you can feel
                    arising in it.

                    (Inner tranquility)

6 balancing exercises from Esoteric Science

_____

18 April 1912   Archive no. 5812-15

In the evening, not too long before going to bed:

Undertake a brief review of the day, lasting four to five minutes. This should run backward, by first picturing what you experienced in the evening and then working back toward the morning's experiences. Following this, try picturing an event that occurred many years ago, one you remember so well that you can evoke it vividly as reality before you. Having conjured this image very vividly in your mind's eye, try to picture how you would behave now in relation to this experience, and see if you can imagine what these same experiences would give rise to, if you could reawaken them and engage with them as you are today. Try to keep a clear image in mind of what would thus follow from the experience; then contemplate (meditate on) the following thought:

> *One day I will encounter a similar such experience (though probably only in a future incarnation) and will then need to conduct myself in a way I did not know how to before, but now know how to.*

You can use the same experience in this way for many weeks in succession; and then take another and do the same again for many weeks. Through this meditation a time will eventually come when the insight arises in the soul, as though in an image, that karmic residues remain from all experiences, and that these must inevitably realize themselves in future lives. While forming the picture of such an experience, it is important to exclude all other thoughts from your mind; then you will acquire awareness of the spiritual workings of karma.

Having undertaken this meditation, try (right away on the first evening of doing it) to pass on to meditative contemplation of feelings arising from the following words:

> Departing now from sensory perception
> and freed from body's use
> my soul seeks to have knowledge
> to rest in spirit existence

> to live in spirit light
> to work in spirit love
> spirit in me; I in spirit.

Try to focus awareness entirely on what you can feel with these words, excluding all other thoughts. Then try to free awareness entirely from these ideas *also*, and allow admission to nothing else. When you have succeeded in doing this, pictures or thoughts will come to you as gift from the world of spirit, either in imaginative form (in shapes and forms) or inspired (non-figurative).

* * *

In the morning try to meditate for a quarter of an hour (in the same way as described for the evening with the seven lines above) but now with the following thoughts:

> I seek my true I
> and strive into the undefined
> where it (my I)[162] can find itself
> where it finds its self-
> sustaining being:
> no sense appearance nor corporeal power
> but standing within itself alone.

After this meditation, do the same as after the seven lines for the evening, and something similar will occur.

* * *

The exercises described in books (especially the Rose Cross) can be done alongside if time allows. In particular it is important to do the six [balancing] exercises described in *Esoteric Science*.

———

162. Translator's note: It is not clear whether the words in parentheses are meant to be part of the verse. It may only be an explanatory parenthesis and not intrinsic to the meditation.

18 April 1912   Archive no. 5816-19

In the evening, not too long before going to bed:

Undertake a brief review of the day, lasting four to five minutes. This should run backward, by first picturing what you experienced in the evening and then working back toward the morning's experiences. Then take one of the day's events that you have recalled and picture it very vividly, like an object before your eyes. This picturing capacity will gradually improve over time, so that it becomes an imaging, imagining faculty. Then focus awareness entirely on the following words:

> What I experienced in the day
> stands now spiritually before me
> so place yourself now too my I
> spiritually before the image:
> feel as you felt before it
> in the day and be
> with it alone.

Then try to pass on to meditative contemplation of the following words, feeling everything that can be felt in response to them:

> I will learn
> within the I of spirit
> to be as in my body
> to feel as in my body
> to love as in my body
> in light will I live
> in light will I perceive.

Try to focus awareness on what one can feel with these words, and exclude all other thoughts. Then try to free awareness entirely from these ideas *also,* and allow admission to nothing else. When you have succeeded in doing this, pictures or thoughts will come to you as gift from the world of spirit, either in imaginative form (in shapes and forms) or inspired (non-figurative).

✳
✳ ✳

In the morning try to meditate for a a quarter of an hour (in the same way as described for the evening with the seven lines above) but now with the following thoughts:

> I seek my true I
> and strive into the undefined
> where it (my I)[163] can find itself
> where it finds its self-
> sustaining being:
> no sense appearance nor corporeal power
> but standing within itself alone.

After this meditation, do the same as after the seven lines for the evening, and something similar will occur.

✳
✳ ✳

The exercises described in books (especially the Rose Cross) can be done alongside if time allows. In particular it is important to do the 6 [balancing] exercises described in *Esoteric Science*.

———

———

163. Translator's note: It is not clear whether the words in parentheses are meant to be part of the verse. It may only be an explanatory parenthesis and not intrinsic to the meditation.

20 April 1912   Archive no. 5810/11

Morning: Review of the day before.
                  In reverse. In images. 4–5 mins.

                ⊕   (ES)[164] Blue background behind the RC

Seek my soul
devoted reverence for the spirit of worlds
in breadths of space
and seek my soul
love's gifts, the shoots of truth within my heart
at all times
with all my strength.
                  (Inner tranquility)

During the day: the six exercises

Evening: 1. Peace   ⎫   With all my strength at all times
           2. God in me ⎬   seek love's gifts, the shoots of truth
                              within my heart
           3. Truth   ⎭   and seek my soul in breadths of
                              space to feel the godhood of the
                              world.
                                      (Inner tranquility)

––––––

164. ES: *Esoteric Science:* The Rose Cross meditation described there. See p. [475] in this present volume.

May 1912   Archive no. 3141/42

Evening: 1.) Review. Backward from evening to morning.
                 In images (5–6 minutes)

         2.) Image of bright space that grows
              ever darker; white cross with
              7 green roses

                  In this symbol I perceive
                  the all-encompassing spirit revealed
                  a part of whom is my own being –
                  awaken sacred longing   } 15 mins.
                  within my soul's profoundest depths
                  to sense to feel to know
                  self's spirit in the spirit of worlds.

                           (Inner tranquility)

Morning: Image of dark space that grows ever
                brighter; black cross with red roses:

                  I seek to penetrate
                  the depths of my soul
                  so that from shrouds of darkness may arise
                  the spirit's light   } 15 mins.
                  and waken in me
                  the spirit of this symbol
                  to which I give myself.

                           (Inner tranquility)

                  _____

6 balancing exercises

Sunday 9 a.m.: In the spirit of humanity I feel
               united with all esotericists

                  _____

End of 1912 or later   Archive no. 3184

Evening: 1.) Review. In images. In reverse. 5–6 mins

            2.)   ⊕

                    I will gaze aloft
                    to the black wood's cross
                    and give my soul into the power
                    of the spirit of worlds
                    as the black cross gives itself
                    entirely to the light

                    I in me.

                                            (Inner tranquility)

Morning: I give myself up
                    to world breadths

                            ⋮

                    I give myself up
                    to depths of soul

                            ⋮

                    World breadths and depths of soul –
                    may they sustain me
                    in my being.

                                            (Inner tranquility)

ES: 6 exercises

                    ———

Facsimile of archive no. 3184

Abend: 1.) Rückschau. Bildhaft. Rückläufend. 5–6 Mai.

2.) ✠

Aufschauen will ich
Zum schwarzen Holzeskreuze;
Und im Weltengeiste macht
Mit eigner Seele mich ergeben;
Wie das schwarze Kreuz
Dem Lufte ganz sich giebt

Ich in mir

(Seelenruhe)

Morgens:

Ich gebe mich hin
Den Weltenweiten
⋮

Ich gebe mich hin
Den Seelentiefen

⋮

Weltenweiten und Seelentiefen
In meinem Wesen
Sie mögen mich fallen
(Seelenruhe)

Hsw. s. 306

New Year 1912/1913   Archive no. 0068

Evening:

> Feel my soul in the wide universe
> how spirit shines its wisdom-weaving light
> feel my heart as you grow warm the spirit's
> strongly working love
> and resting in the world ocean's pure
> divinity may my being's deepest core
> feel how the I of worlds sustains my I.

Morning:[165]

> How the I of worlds sustains my I
> be felt within my being's deepest core
> resting in world ocean's pure
> divinity
> and feel my heart as you grow warm the spirit's
> strongly working love
> and feel my soul
> how spirit shines its wisdom-weaving light
> in the wide universe.

———

———

165. The text of the first verse is contained in a letter, while the second verse has been reconstructed in line with the indication in this letter to "reverse its sequence." The time suggested for each meditation is a quarter of an hour.

New Year 1912/1913   Archive no. 6803

Evening: 1.) Review of the day. In images and in reverse.
                   Roughly 5 minutes

            2.) Evoke the following images:

                 1. The Rose Cross, roughly 2–3 minutes
                 2. A shining, five-pointed star. While picturing this
                    (for 2–3 minutes) feel the star as an image of the
                    human soul.
                 3. A circle with its centre (2–3 minutes); while
                    picturing this, feel it as the symbol of the world
                    spirit revealing itself within the human soul.

      The rest of the evening meditation should involve using your
      own thinking to increasingly understand the meaning of these
      three images.

Morning: The following meditation, lasting roughly 15 minutes:

                 The soul of worlds reveals itself
                 upon the world body's cross.
                 Its five rays shining live
                 through wisdom love the power of will
                 through sense of universe and I
                 and thus it finds
                 within itself the spirit of the world.

      Afterward, inner tranquility and silent attentiveness.

As accompanying exercise the six exercises in *Esoteric Science.*

———

January 1913   Archive no. 7037

Evening: 1.) Review. In images. In reverse –

        2.) Raise yourself intuiting my soul
             to the workings of the spirit of worlds
             in the spreading realms of space –
             turn my soul intuiting
             to the workings of the spirit of worlds
             in the depths of my own realms of soul:
             I in me and I in all.

                                        (Inner tranquility)

Morning: I in me and I in all:
               in the depths of my own realms of soul
               to the workings of the spirit of worlds
               turn my soul intuiting
               in the spreading realms of space –
               to the workings of the spirit of worlds
               raise yourself intuiting my soul.

                                        (Inner tranquility)

                        ———

Evening: *Review*

My soul O sense how death
creates itself from consuming fire

my soul O sense how life
engenders itself in shining weft

and so you are within
the secret death of fire
the hidden weft of life.

Morning: God creating my spirit
spirit giving birth to my soul
soul warming my breath
breath enlivening my body
body pushing forth my *corpus* from itself:
and so I wrap myself within sense being.

So hülle ich mich ins Sinnensein

Around 1913   Archive no. 7034

Evening: 1.) Review. In images. In reverse   5–6 mins.
         2.) Picture the following:

               Space as sphere spread out on all sides
               Then contracting to become a point
               Then contracting further

         3.) *Meditation:*

               From universal spaces
               reality penetrates
               glowing warming into my heart
               vanishes in the heart
               – from nothing it will
               shine out spiritually anew
               and reveal myself in me.

                                        (Tranquil expectancy)

Morning: 1.) Picture the following.

               Point. Space shines out on all sides
               Into the endless. Lost. Then
               returns again as far as the point.

         2.) *Meditation:*

               I feel myself within my being's core
               my being shines out
               into all breadths
               in the void I feel myself void
               I will perceive myself again
               – into ever firmer form contracts
               new being's power in my being's core.

                                        (Inner tranquility)

6 balancing exercises in ES

                    ———

1913 or later   Archive no. 7033

Evening: Review

                    Picture: bright space that gradually grows dark

> From the light of space
> senses' brightness fades
> into the light of the soul
> may spirit's brightness enter –
> seek it my soul
> find it my soul
> in truth clarity love.

                                        (Inner tranquility)

Morning: Picture dark space that grows brighter

> Turn my soul toward
> the upper realm
> to seek you mothering spirit of worlds
> turn my soul toward
> the lower realm
> to seek you fathering soul of earth:
> I in you, you in me.[166]

                                        (Inner tranquility)

                        ———

---

166. Translator's note: The "you" in this line is plural.

Morning:

> My soul be guided up
> to feel you mothering soul of worlds,
> my soul be guided down
> to think you fathering soul of earth –   } 10 mins.
> I your creature being
> receive from you in me
> light love truth.

(Inner tranquility)
5 mins.

————

Evening:

> Mothering spirit of worlds
> fathering soul of earth   } 10 mins.
> I through you, in you.

(Inner tranquility)

Review of the day – from evening back to the morning – 5 mins.

6 balancing exercises: ES

————

May/June 1913   Archive no. A 0116

Morning: 1. Peace (5–10 mins.)
                2. God in me
                3. Light in me to become *strength*

Evening: My soul turn upward
                to seek you mothering spirit of worlds
                my soul turn downward
                to seek you fathering soul of earth.

Balancing exercises: ES

———

3 June 1913   Archive no. 7102

Evening: 1.)   Review. In images. In reverse. 4–5 mins.

          2.)   As the rays of sun
                brightly enter my eye
                so enter the spirit that in this

                appears to me
                illumining and warming: enter
                my truth-seeking soul.

                                        (Inner tranquility)

Morning: Within my heart
                    warmth of soul
                within my head
                    light of the spirit
                in my whole being
                    the power of God:
                so will I feel.

                                        (Inner tranquility)

6 exercises, ES

                        ———

June 1913   Archive no. A 0094

Morning:

Review of the previous day, in reverse, in images 4–5 minutes

My soul yearn upward
to you O mothering spirit of worlds

✝

my soul yearn inward
to you O fathering soul of worlds   } 15 mins.

⊕

within this symbol
let me draw the strength
of the spirit of the world.

Inner tranquility

Evening: 1) Meditation: peace
                2)   "   God in me   } 15 mins.
                3)   "   Light of truth

6 exercises

————

June 1913   Archive no. 5842

Evening:

> Seven bright rose-stars
> upon the black cross wood
> seven strong powers of soul
> entering life's commotion:
> strength of soul
>   soul stillness
>   quest for wisdom
>   love's power
>   composure
>   attentiveness
>   confidence:
> with this sign I inscribe them in my soul.
>
>   (Inner tranquility)

Morning: Review of the day. In images. In reverse.

   Meditation:

> As child my body raised
> itself up through its power
> and always thus the spirit raises
> itself up through soul power:
> from child simplicity
> to spiritual certainty
> may it always seek its way.
>
>   (Inner tranquility)

6 qualities, ES

———

Facsimile of archive no. 5842

Abend:

☩

Sieben helle Rosensterne
Auf schwarzem Kreuzesholz
Sieben starke Seelenkräfte
In des Lebens Wirrnis
Seelenstärke, Seelenruhe, Weisheitsproben
Liebekraft, Gelassenheit, Aufmerksamkeit,
Mit dem Zeichen schreib ich in die Seele sie.
(Seelenruhe).

Morgens: Rückschau auf das Tagesleben. Bildhaft
Rücklaufend.

Meditieren:

Als Kind richtete mein Leib
Durch seine Kraft sich auf
So stets richtet der Geist
Durch Seelenkraft sich auf
Vom Kindeseinfall
Zur Geistessicherheit
Suche stets er seine Bahn
(Seelenruhe)

6 Eigenschaften Geheimwissenschaft.

June 1913   Archive no. 5247

Evening: 1.)   Review. In images. In reverse.   5–6 mins.

         2.)   Think soul of spreading breadths of space
                   and feel spreading powers of spirit
                   think soul of your own depths
10 mins.   and feel deep grounds of soul
                   thus fathoming yourself
                   within yourself and in
                   the universe.

                                  (Inner tranquility)

Morning:

                   This symbol
                   of the victory of life
                   over the power of death
                   be sign of how in me
                   the power of soul
                   eternally
                   vanquishes all powers of death.

                                  (Inner tranquility)

ES: 6 qualities

---

7 June 1913   Archive no. 5841

Evening: 1.) Review. In images. In reverse.   5 mins.

         2.)   With strength of soul
                  turn my inward life
                  toward this sign.

                  I will inscribe its meaning
                  deep into my heart
                  so it becomes
                  the star over my life.

                                    (Inner tranquility)

Morning:

     Meditate:

  Sunday: Light as symbol of wisdom

  Monday: Warmth as symbol of love

  Tuesday: Breath as symbol of the spirit penetrating me

  Wednesday: My blood moves within me
                 as in the universe the elements

  Thursday: As clouds bless the earth
                 so grace of spirit blesses me

  Friday: As the sun pure in the morning
                 so rises my soul on awakening

  Saturday: ⊕

6 qualities as in ES

———

24 August 1913   Archive no. 5804

Morning:

> Light in the wide worlds around me
> in the light the spirit reveals
> itself to me
> my soul seeks the spirit
> because it is spirit of the spirit itself:
> if I know myself I follow only myself
> when I place thinking, feeling, and will in the service
> of the spirit.

Evening:

> My soul will now step forth
> from the sensory world
> into the world of spirit
> – strengthened by powers
> that flow to it from the world of spirit
> in the morning it will step back
> into the sensory world.

———

9 September 1913   Archive no. 6616

Evening: 1.)   Review. In images. In reverse.   4–6 mins.

                2.)   ⊕

6–10
mins.

Bright rose-stars
on the black cross wood
        be an image for me
of the deep soul powers
that shine for me
in the soul's dark ground
        in me my godly self.

                        (Inner tranquility without images)

Morning:

In breadths of worlds the sunlight shines
in depths of spirit light of soul holds sway.

10 mins.   (Inner tranquility without images)

6 exercises

———

October 1913   Archive no. 5268

Evening: 1.)   Review. In images. In reverse.   5–6 mins.

            2.)   ☦

                     Be for me
                 symbol of the soul
                 the soul bears within it
                 seven powers of the spirit   ⎫
                     as shine   ⎬   10 mins.
                 seven rose stars   ⎭
                 on black wood of the cross.

                                 (Inner tranquility)

Morning: First inwardly revive the evening meditation and then
              focus thoughts for about 10 minutes on the following:

                     Spirit of God
                 in my spirit
                 my spirit
                 in my soul
                 my soul
                 in my body
                     thus I am.

                                 (Inner tranquility)

6 exercises: Thought concentration
               Initiative in action etc.

                        _____

9 November 1913   Archive no. 6630

Evening: 1.)   Review. In images. In reverse.   4–6 mins.

              2.)   ⊕

                        Upon the black cross
                          bright rose-stars
                              image
                        in my depths of soul
                    strong shining powers of spirit
                             reality
                             in me

                                    (Inner tranquility)

Morning:

                    Sunlight pervades universal spaces
                    spirit light pervades worlds of soul.

                                    (Inner tranquility)

6 supplementary exercises

                         ———

November 1913   Archive no. 0024

Evening:

    1.) Review, in images, in reverse 5–6 mins.

    2.)   You my soul
           feel
           in you
           spirit powers divine
           they lead you beyond you
           into your self.

                        (Inner tranquility)

Morning:

        ⊕   as in ES

6 balancing exercises

———

circa 1913   Archive no. 7116

Evening: 1.) Review. In images. In reverse. 4–6 mins.

       2.)   What am I?

> In my body of substance
>   as vessel
> is my etheric body
>   as oil
> from which is nourished, as is the flame
>   my soul body
> and shining like the flame's light lives my I.

                      (Inner tranquility)

Morning:

> Shining light of worlds through space
> radiant light of spirit through the soul.

                      (Inner tranquility)

6 exercises

———

circa 1913   Archive no. A 0100

Evening: Review

                    [Drawing of lamp – see facsimile on next page]

                    Be the symbol
                    of my I that shines
                    within the astral body of flames
                        the flame lives from oil
                    as my astral within my etheric body
                        they rest in the sensory body
                    as the oil does in the lamp.

                                        (Inner tranquility)

Morning: ⊕

                    Bright rose-stars
                    upon the black cross wood
                    be the symbol
                    of my soul's
                    strong powers divine
                    and shine within me in the dark
                    ground of my soul.

                                        (Inner tranquility)

                    ———

Facsimile of archive no. A 0100

Frau Käthe Galsterer

Abends. Rückschau

2 ————————Schale

Sei mir Sinnbild
Meiner Ich, das leuchtet
Im astralischen Flammenleibe
Die Flamme lebet vom Öl
Gleich meinem astralischen im aetherischen Leibe
Sie ruhen im Sinnenleibe
Wie das Öl in der Schale   (Seelenruhe) —

Morgens
⊕
Heilige Rosensterne
auf schwarzem Holzkreuz
Seid mir Sinnbild
Meiner Seele
Starke Gottesgeisteskräfte
Strahlen im dunklen ... rund
In mir.
(Seelenruhe)

17 April 1914   Archive no. 6519

Evening: Review of the day

      Then: In the spirit will I live
               live with my whole being
               will feel
               the spirit
               in the all-sway of the world
               and in the striving
               of the human soul.

Morning: The usual exercise.[167]

———

167. Unknown.

May 1914   Archive no. 4003/04

Evening: 1.) Review. In images. In reverse. 5–6 mins.

2.) Feel the ♁ as though diffused throughout
the world then ever smaller until it stands
before your soul:

10–15
mins.

In breadths of worlds feeling spiritually
I intuit the sign
of the creative spirit of worlds
source of all light
and of all goodness and beauty:
let it pour into me
sustaining me within myself.

(Inner tranquility)

Morning:

As in the light
of the warm sun
work forces of outer worlds
so work within the thinking
that can sustain my soul
the powers of worlds of spirit
and I in them.

10–15
mins.

(Inner tranquility)

ES: 6 qualities

21 June 1914   Archive no. 7095/96

Evening: 1.) Review of the day. In images. In reverse.

2.) Deep contemplation of the feelings that the following
words can invoke in the soul:

> The senses fall silent
> memory is hushed
> stillness descends around me
> calm breathes upon all being
> you my soul
> sense in silent calm
> the sway of weaving spirit.

(Then remain in inner tranquility)

Morning: Contemplation of the feelings which the following
words invoke in the soul:

> The eternal weaves
> stirring in temporal existence:
> my soul feels lifted
> and rises from death's rigidity
> the eternally living
> flowering
> of the divine will to evolve.

(then feel the sense of these words
in the symbol of the

and remain for a while
with entirely empty soul.)

———

1914 Archive no. A 0076

Evening: 1.) Review. In images. In reverse 5–6 mins.

2.) Into my soul
     my I you enter
     feel yourself in her
     seek, yearn for the divine:
     you within her –
     and so I grasp myself
     seeking me in myself.

                    (Inner tranquility)

Morning:

                    In
                    me
                    I
                    find
                    me
                    as
                    self.

                    (Inner tranquility)

6 balancing exercises

———

1913 or later   Archive no. 7035

Evening: 1.)   Review. In images. In reverse

       2.)   Picture of the   ☥

> Seven rose-stars I see shining
> on the black wood of the cross
> may they fill me full of strength
> so at first hand I can feel
> seven universal powers in me
> working there
> within my being human.

(Inner tranquility)

Morning: Picturing the   ☥

> Raise yourself
> my soul
> seek spirit's heights
> feel them — they
> will one day shine
> toward you when
> your soul grows ripe.

(Inner tranquility)

Esoteric Science: six balancing exercises

———

Abends: 1.) Rückschau. In Bildern. Rücklaufend.

2.) Vorstellung des ☩

Sieben Rosensterne sehe ich leuchtend
An dem schwarzen Kreuzesholze
Mögen sie mich kraftvoll machen
Dass ich erlebe und empfinde
Sieben Weltenkräfte in mir
Die da wirken
In meinem Menschenwesen
(Seelenruhe)

Morgens: Vorstellung des ☩

Erhebe dich
Du meine Seele
Suche Geisteshöhen
Fühle sie
Sie werden dir
Leuchten einst
In deiner reifen Seelenzeit
(Seelenruhe)

Geistes-Geheimwissenschaft: Sechs Übungen.

Evening:

Climb a mountain at dawn in spirit.
Witness the sunrise. The sun speaks:

> Hear the words of the universe!
> In words of the universe your I takes root

>> Wait with attentiveness
>> Attend in waiting.

Morning:

With the sun take the path around the earth passing from sunrise to
sunset. These words sound forth:

> Hear the words of the universe!
> within the human being there lives
> living existence
> and living existence
> is borne by universal waves
> in the river of evolving life
> as I into the universal I

>> Wait with attentiveness
>> Attend in waiting.

———

May 1919   Archive no. 6613

Morning: Image of the setting sun:
            as it sinks the sun speaks:

> You see for sensory appearance
> day change to night:
> in spirit think of true existence
> and then you enter spirit day
> and the eclipsing of the senses
> is God's brightness –
> feel it in you!

Evening: Image of the rising sun:
                  I speak:

> Light of my life
> light of my soul
> light of my I
> bear me from the body into spirit!

———

circa 1919/20   Archive no. 5274/75

Evening:

      1.) Review

      2.) Imagine the world of stars in the blue sky

> My I will be
> in spirit-filled space
> it will have departed from
> the body of flesh
> will weave
> in God's spirit
> filled with strength.

Wait calmly.

Think of him with the given meditation.[168]

Morning:

Imagine the sun
– the sun sounds forth into the heart:

> Christ is with you
> he fills your heart
> Christ is in you
> he fills your soul
> Christ in around you
> he fills your spirit
>   feel him.

Wait calmly

---

168. "Him" clearly refers to a person who has passed away, and the meditation in question is the one on the following page.

Picture face

———————

Picture hands, touching

———————

Come soul to me
I wait
come into my thoughts
they wait
come into my feelings
they wait
my I waits.

—————

circa 1920   Archive no. A 0009

Evening

Picture yourself climbing a mountain. Arriving at the summit, you see the sky with the setting sun.

Inwardly speak the words:

> "Christ light remain in my heart"

In the morning, on awaking

Feel yourself standing on a broad plain, with the sun overhead. The sun's rays pervade your whole body.

Speak to yourself:

> "Christ light is in my heart"

Focus on image and words for 4 minutes, and then dwell in the mood for about 3 minutes.

———

25 May 1920   Archive no. 7088

Evening: Review

      Find yourself in me
      from eternity
      you are in me
      but find yourself in me.

                      Wait with attentiveness

Morning:

      In me
      find yourself
      you are in me
      from eternity
      so find yourself in me.

                      Wait with attentiveness

6 exercises

———

12 April 1921   Archive no. 6908

    Evening: Review

              ———

Picture the sun over your head—the sun speaks:

    In you lives light
    grasp hold of the light
    grasp hold of it with love.

    Morning:

Picture 7 stars over your head—the stars speak:

    You live in light
    feel your way into the light
    grasp hold of it in clarity.

              ———

November 1921   Archive no. A 0078

> *Evening:*   Review

> Rose Cross – picturing it

> Meditate:

> In my heart
> may light of worlds live.

> *Morning:*

> Rose Cross – picturing it

> Meditate:

> In my heart
> may Word of worlds live.

6 exercises

———

November 1921   Archive no. A 0021

Evening: *Review*

     ⊕ Rose Cross meditation

> You my I
> approach this image.
> Seek within you strength
> seek within you love
> seek in you yourself.
> Vow to this image before you
> to be strong.

Morning:

     ⊕ Rose Cross meditation

> Vow to this image before you
> To be strong.
> Seek in you yourself
> seek within you love
> seek within you strength.
> approach this image
> you my I.
>   (Inner tranquility)

(The six balancing exercises)

———

1.) *Evening* 4–5 minutes review of the day (in reverse chronological
                sequence)

2.) *Evening:* The following meditation:

4–5 mins.

I feel myself within illumined space
        (picture the light-filled world all around you)
light weaves my ether body
        (picture your own body composed of light)
I feel myself within the world of colors
        (picture a sea of colors in which you yourself
        are immersed)
the spirit's world of colors gives me my soul
        (picture your own soul)
in light and color
thinks, feels and wills
my self.

3.) *Morning:*   Picture a black cross with seven
                 shining stars:

                 Meditate the following with this:

4–5 mins.

My self
thinks, feels and wills
through light and color
I rest quietly
within my higher self
my I
in Christ.

Alongside this, the six exercises: thought concentrations, and so forth,
as in *Esoteric Science*.

———

April 1922   Archive no. 5269

Evening

1.) Review of the day in reverse chronological order.
4–5 minutes.

2.) First concentrate on the idea:

I think things and facts.

Hold fast to this thought for about a minute, excluding all other thoughts.

Then concentrate on the idea:

My thinking flows in time.

Again hold fast to this idea for a minute.

After this preparation, concentrate on the following successive meditations

I follow the flow of thinking
I will perceive my will within my thinking
3–4 mins.   I will find my I in my thinking will
I will live as I in my thinking will
I await release of the I by the I

Then inner tranquility.

Morning:

rot
(bleu)

> Picture a blue disc surrounded by red
>
> Then transform into a red disc with blue surround.
>
> Transform back into the first state.
>
> Do this seven times in succession.
>
> In inner observation discover how this gradually renders thinking mobile and inwardly free, ultimately releasing it into a body-free condition. Having prepared this state of soul, now apply it to concentrating on any simple object, observing how this inner activity becomes something other than it would have been without this preparation

4–5
mins.
for the
whole
exercise

Timed according to feeling of course (not by the clock)

The 6 exercises as in Part II of *Esoteric Science.*

———

Evening: Universal light within you

Morning: My light within you
               O universal spirit.

circa 1922/23   Archive no. 3189, 3191

Evening:

> To you O spirit of worlds
> my soul
> turns reverently

> Path. Hill.   ⊕

> may your shining power
> send into me
> sevenfold
> inward hold

>   *

> I   am
> left   right

Morning: Path. Hill.   ⊕

> May your shining power
> send into me
> sevenfold
> inward hold
> so that I find myself
> within you
> find you within me.

———

circa 1922/23   Archive no. 7041

Evening: Review

                    In the glory of universal wisdom
    ☽   let the strength of my soul unfold. –

Morning:

                    In the glory of universal love
    ☾   let the strength of my spirit unfold. –

                    _____

                              Facsimile of archive no. 7041

circa 1922/23   Archive no. 7114

Evening:

> Stand in a broad plain
> It is twilight
> *Above appears a star: (Chr.)*
>
>> Your strength   your wisdom
>> your light   your Word
>>   enter
>> my human soul
>>   so that
>> strong and full of wisdom   love
>>   it live.
>>
>>> *Inner tranquility*

Morning:

> Stand on a hill.
> It is dawn.
> The sun rises a little.
> *The countenance of Christ:*
>
>> My strength   my wisdom
>> my light   my word
>>   I give
>> to your yearning human soul
>>   so that
>> strong and full of grace and thanks
>>   it can live.
>>
>>> *Inner tranquility*

———

May 1923   Archive no. A 0038

Evening:

Review

Picture: the heart and a small light in the heart

Meditate:

Divine	light illumine	me
Divine	power strengthen	me
Divine	love warm	me

Inner tranquility

Morning:

Picture: the sun outside shines upon me

Meditate:

Divine	love warm	me
Divine	power strengthen	me
Divine	light illumine	me

Inner tranquility

———

Evening: Review

Picture: a sunbeam passes;

then like waves

Meditate:

The light and the warmth of the divine
universal spirit enfold me.

(Inner tranquility)

Morning: Picture: a long path before me; at the end I meet
Christ, who says:

The power of my Word strengthen your soul.

(Inner tranquility)

———

May 1923   Archive no. A 0012

Evening: Review

                    Picture: The sun shines over your head and the light
                    of the sun passes through your whole body.

                    Meditate:

                         The light of the spirit of worlds strengthens me.

                                                     Inner tranquility

Morning: *Picture:* The same as above, but with moon instead
                    of sun.

                    Meditate:

                         I will be strong in every occurrence in life.

                                                     Inner tranquility

                              ———

Evening: Review

    Picture: starry heavens

    Meditate:

        Starlight enter my heart
        heart's power strengthen my eye
        my eye strengthen the inner light of my soul.

                        Inner tranquility

Morning:

    Picture: The sun shines in the East

    Meditate:

        The light of the sun enter my eye
        spirit's light strengthen my soul
        soul strength empower my heart.

                        Inner tranquility

———

26 May 1923   Archive no. 6632

In the evening:

>   Slowly rising sun
>   Christ speaks from it:
>
>>   As bright light shines through
>>   the breadths of space
>>   so let wise will shine through
>>   the powers of your soul
>>   – act with these powers
>>   and you will find the path
>>   that bears you forward rightly in your life.
>
>   Review in inner tranquility

In the morning:

>   Setting sun – Rose Cross
>
>>   As the power of my heart
>>   imbues my limbs
>>   so let my will imbue
>>   all deeds of my soul
>>   I will follow this
>>   guideline of my life
>>   that gives me energy
>>   gives me strength.

———

1923   Archive no. 7157[169]

Morning:

> Thinking on a star, which is over your head:

>> By the shining
>> of the star
>> over my head
>> I will hold
>> the power
>> in my heart
> to help the powers in my soul.

>>> 3 – 4 minutes

Evening:

> Thinking the Christ comes to you from the sun,
> and the Christ speaks to your heart:

>> I give you
>> my graceful word
>> and my loving power
>> and you will
>> make progress
>> in your soul
> and in your I.

>>> 4 – 5 minutes

---

169. Translator's note: These two meditations are in English in the original. I have retained the English wording but made two corrections.

17 October 1923   Archive no. 5270

Morning:

My love and my
strength I give to your
heart.

Evening

Rising sun

Your love and your
strength fill my
heart.

———

Think in the morning of a star in the East,
which speaks to the heart:

> Feel the light of the spirit
> that shines out from the darkness
> into your eye of soul
> – it gives living strength
> it warms soul depths
> it is the being of your being
> you are therein.

Thinking in the evening of the earth as a great, green star shining in
the universe.
   Let the heart say:

> With the light of the earth
> that prays to the Christ sun
> let the prayer
> of my warm heart unite
> so that I find
> spirit in the light of spirit
> soul breath in breath of worlds
> human power in earthly life.

———

1924   Archive no. 3183

Evening: I will see
a little sun
within my heart
the little sun
shines through my body
I feel it warm
within my body.

Morning: My heart
beats well
and what it streams
through my body is good:
morning   evening   always.

———

1924   Archive no. NB 275

I think of my heart
streaming strength
strength that powerfully courses
into hand and foot   Evening
and warming streams
through all my body.
I live in this strength.

———————

I live in the power of the sun
which powerfully streams
through my body
Morning   and warming flows
through foot and hand
– may its power bear my I
through realms divine.

———

Easter 1924   Archive no. 7060

Evening, after the review

        [drawing, see facsimile on next page]

        From grace
        may wisdom flow to me
        may wisdom bring love to birth in me
        and love partake
          of grace
        love create beauty for me
        and beauty bring me grace.

                    (Inner tranquility)

Morning: A star over the head
          Christ speaks from the star:

          ————

        Let your soul
        be carried
        by my strong power
          I am with you
          I am in you
          I am for you
          I am your I.

               Inner tranquility.

          ————

Facsimile of archive no. 7060

Abend nach der Rückkehr

Aus Gnade
Fliesse mir Weisheit
Weisheit gebäre mir Liebe
Liebe nehme Teil
An Gnade
Liebe schaffe mir Schönheit
Schönheit bringe mir Gnade
(Seelenruhe)

Morgens: Ein Stern über dem Haupte
Chr. spricht aus dem Stern

Lasse tragen
Deine Seele
Von meiner starken Kraft
Ich bin bei dir
Ich bin in dir
Ich bin für dich
Ich bin dein Ich.

May 1924   Archive no. 6620

Evening: 1.) Review 4–5 mins

2.) I picture a star that stands in the sky above my head and
shines light through my whole body. I imagine feeling inwardly
illumined by it — and then meditate (4–5 mins.):

> Starlight, helper
> in my stability
> in my strength
> in my certainty
> soul of starlight
> being of Christ
> live within me
> I live through light.

(Grow very inwardly tranquil)

Morning:

existence   (4–5 mins.)
　　✗
✗　　✗
strength   beauty   5 stars shining bright in the dark sky

✗　✗
wisdom   depths of soul
(love)

> Original power of existence
> waken the power of the world
> in rightful beauty
> through light of wisdom
> within my depths of soul
> mercifully
> from its dark ground.

(Inner tranquility)

———

August 1924 Archive no. 6639

Evening: 1.) Review

2.) Picture a single star in the heavens

4–5 mins. {
Light from wide expanses of the cosmos
your beams shine round me
through me
into me
in the light I feel spirit —
may it bear me
as human being through time and eternity.

———————

Morning:

4–5 mins. {
In
my
heart
shines
God's light
brightly upward
to my head.

2-3

———

24 August 1924 Archive no. 7068/69[170]

Morning:

    Picture to yourself:

in thought, shining blue and red in alternating colors.
Then meditate:

> I will
> send my thoughts
> to thee
> messenger of gods
> and be
> in thy being
> for time and eternity.

(Then rest inwardly)

Morning:

    Review of the day.

Keeping in your thoughts the image of the sun,
hear the sun speak:

> In harmonies
> with the planet sphere
> I speak
> as Christ's representative
> to thine heart:
> "The word of God
> streams in my light."

Then 5 minutes quiet meditation.

———

170. Translator's note: The verses on this page were originally in English, and the original
wording has been retained apart from a few corrections.

C

Further meditations
without indication of "morning / evening"

C – 1

Exercises of unknown date

Archive no. 4422

What is soul strength to me?

What is life strength for me?

What is light of spirit for me?

Lead down into the tips of toes

---

warm, red ground   : love
roses: green   : life
cross: white shimmering light : knowledge, insight

Archive no. 3193

As the roses from this   ☦   white/green

       so Christ's light

         from the light of the world

———————

☦

black / red

                 As the roses from this

                        cross, so Christ's light

                 from the darkness of the world.

———

Archive no. 3174

10 cm before me, at forehead height, a point:
My I occupies this point.
I am present there in clear consciousness.
I am not within the boundaries of my body.

Now I look in spirit above my head:
From the top of my head a line passes through the spine.
Around this line another coils or spirals
to the bottom of the spine
then turns around and returns to the top of my head.

The straight line is stability.
The first coiling line is tranquility.
The second coiling line is certainty.

- - -
- - -

To myself and the I in the heart.

———

Thursday

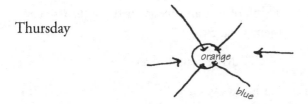

I am I   (the first I everywhere
                the second I within)

The human soul lives enclosed within itself, bearing in itself concentrated light like bright light locked up in a pane of glass. Facing the human soul stands the whole world: dark unknown like the blue of the sky. But what is unknown comes. The human soul must feel this coming like the extinguishing of itself. Sensing this self-extinguishing is followed by the right to recreate oneself anew from the outer world that has been absorbed:

I am I.

———

Archive no. 3217

I: First minute   Think of legs and feet as if trying to stretch them in spirit:

            My strength lives

      Withdraw again

II: Second minute   Think of arms and hands as if trying to stretch them in spirit:

            My will lives

      Withdraw again

III: Third minute   Think of eyes and ears as if a fine air fills them:

            My I lives

      Withdraw again

Once again   II
Once again   I

This grows strong in me
as spirit divine.

———

Archive no. 5254

Form the idea:

I am calm and still

without any tension, and calmly, transpose this into your feet
and for a while think *only* of the feet (forgetting the rest of the
body altogether), pouring into them the above idea, as though
in thoughts.

———

Archive no. 4002

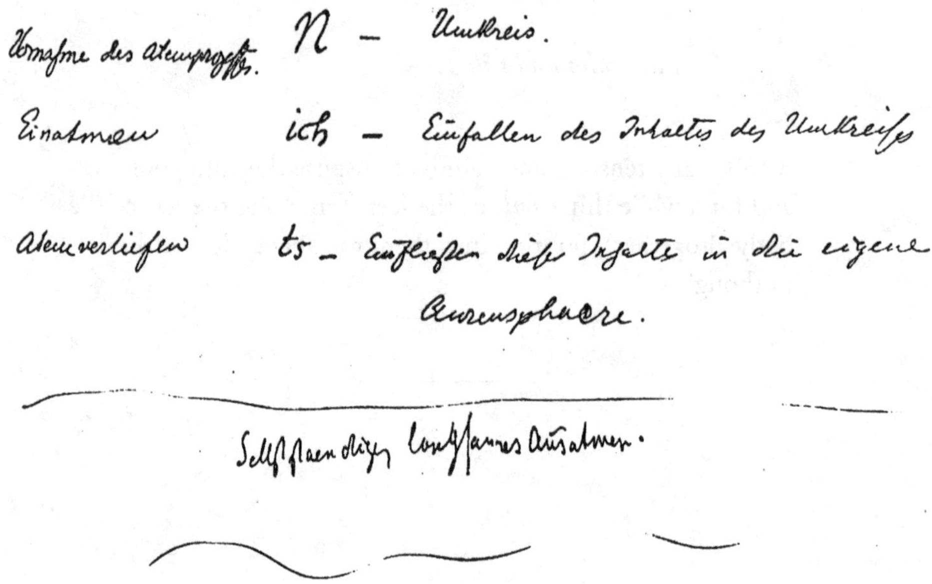

[handwritten facsimile in German]

Transcription:

The breathing process	N	–	periphery
Breathing in	I	–	influx of content of periphery
Deepen breathing	ts	–	influx of this content
			into one's own aura sphere

Self-directed slow outbreath

Archive no. 5282

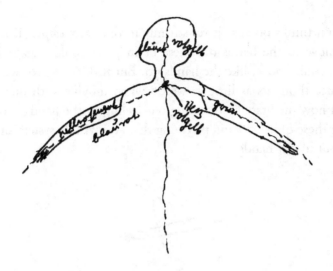

Picture being divided down the middle

　　left side *orange* and arm and hand are *green*

　　through hand and arm pass:

　　1) Living peace weaves into me

　　right side light *purple*, arm and hand are light *pink-red*

　　2) Power of tranquility works into me

　　From nape of the neck to the heart together:

　　3) Light's working warms me

　　and through into the head:

　　4) And illumines me

――――――

Archive no. 5280

The brain thinks because it rests firmly in the bony *corpus*; if its parts could move as the hands do, these brain parts could engage in will activity; could move, like the hands do. But if this were so, we would experience thoughts as little as we do when moving with our hands. We can now meditate by directing our feeling to the hands and arms, holding these quite still and picturing that an invisible system of forces works out of our hands:

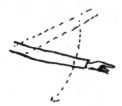

Raising of the ether hand: angeloi comes to me

Lowering of the ether hand: archangeloi leads me

Circulating the ether hand: archai works upon me.

———

20 mins.

Red   green
Black   white

When red is green, then let
the green fade

Hear name

C – 2

Exercises of known date

The first three of these meditation texts date back to the time before the official founding of the Esoteric School in May 1904. For this reason, exercise Archive no. 5299 was included in this section, despite being a morning-evening exercise.

circa 1903/04   Archive no. 364

Extend the index finger and feel therein a cosmic I [ee][171]

Form an angle with the hand and feel therein: A [ah]

Move the hand toward the thumb and touch the thumb with the index finger, and feel therein: O

I A O

With the index finger on the thumb form snake and staff of Mercury

☿ and feel therein ☿ E [eh]

One fist is U [oo]   O with point at centre is Ö [oe] ⊙
Double I [ee] is Ü [ue]   pointed A [ah] is Ä [ae]

☽ with index finger gives the feeling of AU

Saturn: ⁓

Sun: Here in the ether the body is inscribed in accordance with the nature of the letters.

Moon: Here in the astral body the desires are placed into the limbs.

Earth: Here the script is rendered indecipherable through the growing intensity of desires.

———

171. Translator's note: This refers to the sound I (ee) rather than the name for myself.

circa 1903/04

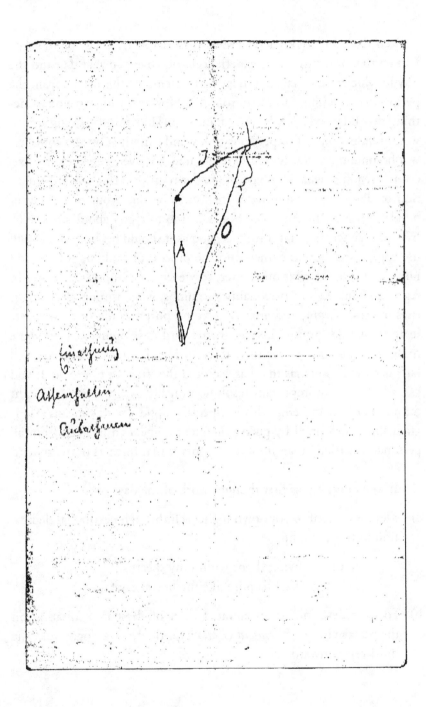

I. Each day, undertake a review of personal experiences of the day. Picture the most important experiences you have had that day and the way in which you behaved in relation to them. All this occurs from the perspective of wishing to *learn* from life. How can I improve on something that I did today? Ask yourself questions like this. By doing so you won't render yourself impervious to joy and suffering; on the contrary, will become more subtly sensitive. Do not, however, get stuck in anxiety and regret at what you have done, but transform this into the intention of doing everything better in future. Become your own "master builder." Just as the latter will not succumb to regret about a house he has built, lamenting that it isn't as good as it should be, but instead will use experiences he has gathered in the process of building a less good house to make the next one better, so we can work upon ourselves. In regret and anxiety our personality succumbs, while through learning it rises upward. Regret and anxiety serve no purpose; the time we waste in them should be used instead for upward development. The whole thing need take no longer than three to four minutes. Then you will fall asleep with a manas that has acquired the strength to evolve. If you can add to this an important resolution for life or also a good thought for another human being, this is especially good. By this means one is gradually transformed by giving the manas, liberated in sleep from all personal constriction, an important content that furthers development.

II. In the morning, as first thought work of the day:

a) Elevate yourself to your own higher self through devotional dedication to this thought:

> I am the living shoot within my sheaths.
> My higher self is pure like the purest crystal.

b) Focused devotion to an elevated thought. Best is meditating on the passage in the *Bhagavad Gita*, chap. III, Karma Yoga, from the third verse onward:

As I have already previously told you...

Always only *one* verse. Stay with a *single* verse for two weeks. After two weeks choose the next one, and so on.

In this meditation, and likewise in the preceding elevation of yourself to your higher self, the field of vision must be entirely pure. Keep yourself *entirely* free of *all* other thoughts. If one such surfaces, it must be dismissed energetically.

c)   Devotional mood toward what is the most sacred thing for you. (The creative universe, God, And so forth, depending on how you personally have learned to esteem and name the highest.)

As part of the morning meditation, 8–10 minutes.

Patience and endurance, and absolute seriousness are needed. It is essential to create a mood in which the spirit feels this meditation to be as much a self-evident need as the body feels its physical needs. And then wait until something is given to you. To all will be given when the time is right.

A start can be made now, on April 16 (no sooner) and then again on May 16.

———

1.)   More radiant ...

       ...

       ...

2.)   Inbreath, outbreath, holding breath

           I am, poured through the body.

       do this *three* times in succession, during which the "am" should
       really accompany the whole process.

       Inbreath, outbreath, holding breath

           It – which in fact really means "I."
           It is

       again, do this *three* times

       Inbreath, outbreath, holding breath

           The inner is

3.)   The streams within the body.

                              *

                          * *

After the meditation, immerse yourself in contemplation and allow the
following forms to work upon you:

Fig. 1:
What does it mean to vanish into
oneself and to arise again from this
vanishing?

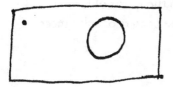

Fig. 2:
How does the point become circle
and the circle become point?

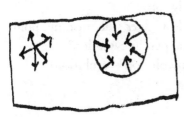

Fig. 3:
What is inner, what is outer?
What is higher, what is lower?
What is matter, what is spirit?
What is physical substance,
what is ether?

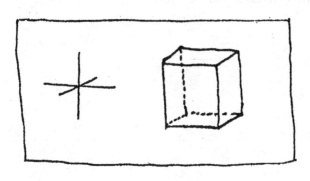

Fig. 4:
What is astral?

Fig. 5:
How do the spirits of feeling work
upon the bearers of substance?

Fig. 6:
How does the turning point
happen in evolution?
(involution – evolution)

Picture this as if the lines were whalebone
strips in the above position whose force/
tension however opposes/resists this position
continually.

———

End of August 1906   Archive no. 6860-62

Immerse yourself fully in the thought:

Impersonal higher self

Here it is not a matter of contemplating some idea predetermined by someone else, but of trying to form the best picture of the "higher self" that is possible at one's current stage of development.

Now place this picture, as it were, in the head's interior, roughly where the pineal gland is located. Transpose your awareness there for awhile, and fill it entirely with the above thought, "impersonal higher self." Thus for awhile imagine that your own being is contracted in the pineal gland, and that you are yourself the above thought. Banish all else from your awareness.

Having done this for awhile, guide this thought slowly in a straight line from the pineal gland to the start of the spinal cord, at roughly the point where the brain passes into the spinal cord. Then lead it from there downward roughly in the region of the spinal cord to the point that is called K (kundalini). Having imagined that one has there thoroughly infused the above thought with kundalini power, lead it slowly upward again, along the spinal cord, to a point in the interior of the head: roughly at the point (B) of the small cerebellum (occiput). Now guide this thought (impersonal higher self) in two lines from this point to both eyes, allowing it to stream out through these into infinite space. Then draw them back in again through the eyes and lead them to point B. Repeat this by leading the thought from B to both ears, allowing it to stream out through them into infinite space and then leading it back through the ears to B again.

Having imagined that the thought "impersonal higher self" has twice been led through universal space and has filled with its content, lead the thought, thus enriched, back from B through the spinal cord to K, imbue it in imagination with spiritual fire and then lead it *very slowly* to the throat (larynx level); so slowly that the time it takes to rise from K to this point will be about 20 minutes. Arriving there, think intensively:

I am not you.

I, the thought of the higher self after all the paths that it has taken in the meditation.

You, the ordinary I, with which one does not identify at this moment.

1907 Archive no. NB 467

Day One: *I am* is the core of my being

> for *four* days

Day Five: *I* will immerse myself in other beings

> for *seven* days

Day Twelve: I will penetrate the other beings

> for *seven* days

Day Nineteen: There is much that *I* cannot overcome

> for eleven days

Day Thirty: *I* will not relinquish hope in the darkness.

———

circa 1907 Archive no. NB 5287

Concentr. on left leg, left foot	=	Steadfast I place myself into existence
Concntr. on right leg, right foot	=	Certain I walk the course of my life
		7 times a day

———

Try to picture a ray of red light entering the brain via the left eye (at a);

This passes through the head to the right side of the spinal column (at b), then descends the spinal column in spirals (c, d, e, f, g, h);

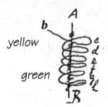

As it spirals allow it to change into *yellow* and then *green;*

Then lead it back again in spirals around the spinal column, allowing it to become first *blue* and then *violet*; as violet ray it arrives at a point c as far to the left of the spinal column as b previously was to the right; then let it pass through the head, emerging via the right eye as violet ray (at d).

This exercise should be done slowly, taking 10–12 minutes.

Before embarking on the exercise, meditate on this thought: The line AB which runs straight down through the spinal column, represents the sub-conscious I; after the exercise, meditate on the thought that the same line represents the super-conscious I.

Do this exercise on Sunday, Monday, Tuesday; then the usual exercises on the other four days of the week: - - -

Commentary

By incorporating these exercises into your meditation, you engage rhythmically with certain powers in the macrocosm. Ancient powers in the cosmos, that have once existed and will exist in future, are always simultaneously present; or in other words, exist only germinally at present. All forces are, at a certain level, ordered so that they flow into the microcosm (the human being) in a spiral form.

In the red parts of the ray one has Saturn forces
In the yellow parts of the ray one has Sun forces
In the green parts of the ray one has Earth forces
In the blue parts of the ray one has Jupiter forces
In the violet parts of the ray one has Vulcan forces

(The Moon forces and the Venus forces are not included since they would cause a retardation of evolution.)

By incorporating these forces into yourself through the described meditation, you will indeed gradually be able to feel the movements of the two-petalled lotus flower, and will find yourself in possession of spirit hands which spiritual beings can touch.

———

circa 1907   Archive no. 3219

1. Look at yourself from without so that you draw a line like a color-
   less ray of light passing from the crown of the head downward in
   the direction of the spinal column;
   > let the following thought run the length of this line:

   From there your being

2. Look at yourself from without so that you draw a line like a blue
   ray of light passing through the center between the eyebrows, and
   winding itself snakelike around the first ray of energy you imagined;
   > let the following thought run the length of this line:

   Thus my seeing

3. Look at yourself from without so that you draw a line passing
   through the larynx as if a dull tone (o or oo) were winding itself
   around the first ray of energy you imagined;
   > let the following thought run the length of this line:

   Thereby my strength

———

circa 1907   Archive no. A 0086

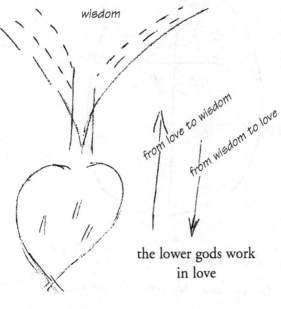

Upper gods
the upper gods work in

wisdom

from love to wisdom

from wisdom to love

the lower gods work
in love

lower gods

Love I bear in the core of my being
hope I nurture in every deed

———

1910   Archive no. NB 198

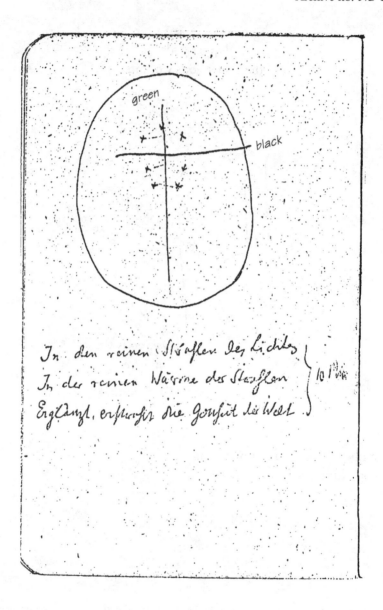

In the pure rays of the light
in the pure warmth of the rays   10 mins.
gleams, shines out the godhood of the world.

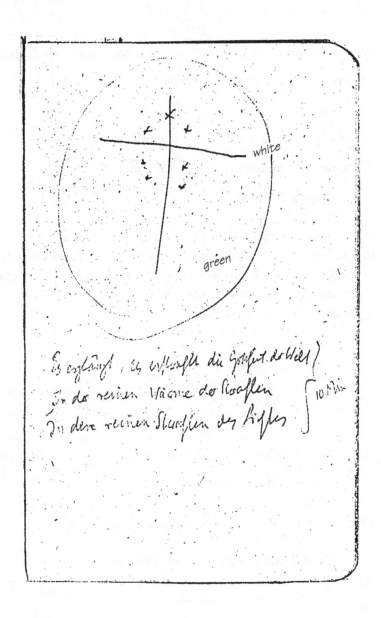

The godhood of the world gleams, shines out
in the pure warmth of the rays
in the pure rays of the light.

10 mins.

September 1912   Archive no. A 7071

I) After the morning meditation and before the evening meditation:

    1) Breathe in deeply and say: *Yahveh*;

    2) Pause

    3) Speak the same word in reverse on the outbreath

    Take around 2 minutes for these 3 moments.

        Repeat 2 to 7 times

II) To the morning and evening meditation add inner contemplation
    of the "Sistine Madonna": picture that she gradually diminishes in
    size and enters your heart, while *strength* streams out from the main
    figure and the small heads in the background.

————

1914   Archive no. 3131

Breathe in Yahveh, filling yourself entirely with

    the power of the name –

Then picture lotus flowers growing in spirals from it

    Thus flower the star form of my body

————

2 September 1922   Archive no. 7106

Look into the sun as imagination and think that
the sun (Christ) is saying:

In the beginning was the Word
may the Word live in *you* (heart).

———

circa 1923   Archive no. A 5351

Seven-week exercise[172]

    1. I understand the world

    2. I know what existed before the world

    3. I enter divine existence – love shines

    4. I grasp divine existence – love comprehends

    5. Divine existence streams into me

    6. Love fills me entirely

Each phrase should be practiced for a week. In week seven do all six together.

————

————————————

172. Given in response to a request for developing the lotus flowers.

circa 1923   Archive no. A 0084

Inner tranquility

Practice these sounds:

R S K G ch h f n l t d P B M

from outside in toward the [ear] so that the first consonants in this sequence are heard more with the outer ear, the last more with the inner

I [ee] U [oo] O E [eh] A [ah]

The vowels in this series must only resonate inwardly so that they acquire ever growing powers and creatively fill the physical ear from within outward

Christ speaks

Rose Cross

———

Night

breathe in silently

I am in breadths of worlds –   breathe out

and my own being is vast –   breathe in

my eye is the space of heaven –   breathe out

and the life threads (nerves) end   hold breath

in the stars –   breathe in slowly

the stars in my universal eye –   breathe out slowly

and my pupil is the moon –   hold breath

I see   breathe in slowly

I see the firmament –

and a point –   breathe out quickly

is the firmament –   breathe in quickly

the firmament is my soul –   hold breath

my I-bearing soul –   breathe out

breathe in silently

breathe out silently

———

September 1924   Archive no. 5272

Alle 3 Tage :

In die Strahlen der Sonne
Tönet mein Herz
m i i n

In den Glanz des Mondes
Spricht meine Seele
O s a l e m ,

I O (tönt in Ihrem
Rückgrat)

<u>Every three days:</u>

Into the rays of the sun
  my heart resounds
    m i i n[173]

Into the radiance of the moon
  my soul speaks
    O s a l e m
      I O (resonates in your spinal column)

---

173. Translator's note: Presumably these letters should each be sounded separately, as together they have no meaning.

C – 3

A few pages with notes on
"lotus flowers – chakras" / "kundalini"

See the editor's commentary on starting on page 451 in relation to these notes.

The effect of all earthly activity on the astral body:

This earthly activity signifies the development of the lotus flowers by the human being *himself.*

Four-petalled lot.	: external sciences	: Raven
Six-petalled lot.	: psychology: sensory-moral	
	: action of color	: Occultist
Eight-petalled lot.	: history	: Warrior
Twelve-petalled lot.	: study of religion	: with the name of the race[174]
		: Sun hero
Two-petalled lot.	: theurgy	: Father

The pupil is the embryo of the astral body, and *mother earth* discharges him.

The pupil retrospectively perceives what humanity has so far worked through.

Learning has the effect of making each lotus flower – previously merely sensitive – *will-endowed.*

For instance concentration on the will:
    Deflection of the idea so that,
    while retaining full awareness,   samadhi
    the spirit sinks down into the will *without* idea

———

---

174. Name of the people or nation, as in "Persian."

When the lotus flowers are developed
without the influx of wisdom: ahrimanic

When mobility is developed
without influx of morality: luciferic

———————

Luciferic: the lotus flowers function
      but they turn only toward everything
      that accords with the personality; they turn
      toward the latter's own ahrimanic element.

———————

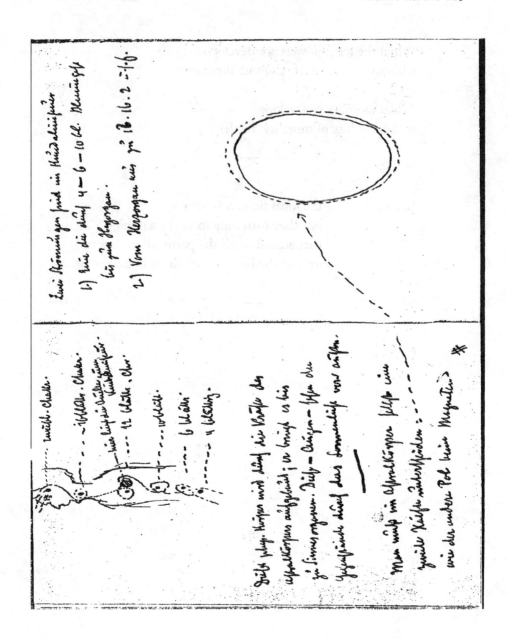

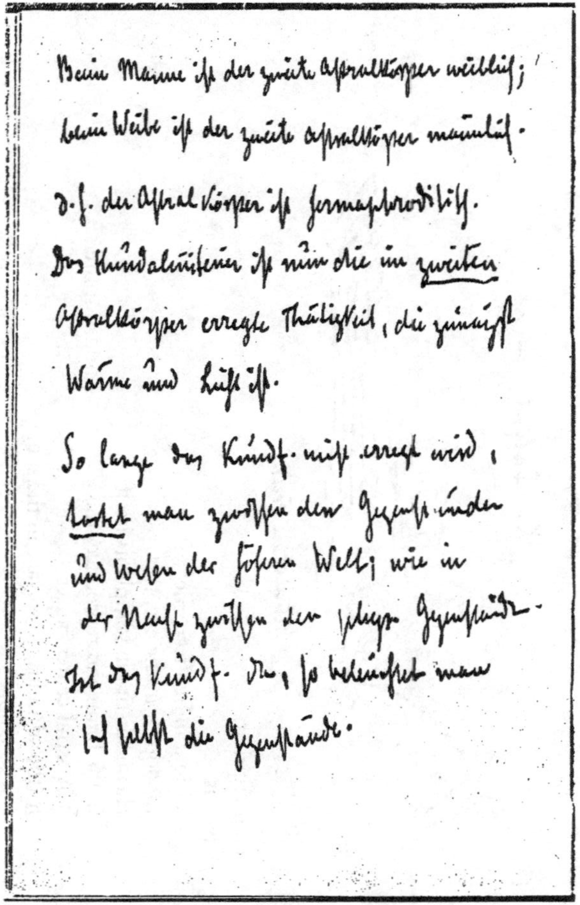
Beim Manne ist der zweite Astralkörper weiblich;
beim Weibe ist der zweite Astralkörper männlich.
d.h. der Astral Körper ist hermaphroditisch.
Das Kundalinifeuer ist nun die im <u>zweiten</u>
Astralkörper erregte Thätigkeit, die zunächst
Wärme und Licht ist.

So lange das Kundf. nicht erregt wird,
<u>tastet</u> man zwischen den Gegenständen
und Wesen der höheren Welt; wie in
der Nacht zwischen den physischen Gegenständ.
Ist das Kundf. da, so beleuchtet man
sich selbst die Gegenstände.

[Transcription: see p. 453.]

Archive no. 672

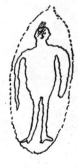

Transcription:
Chakras

    Vision: light affects the
    rhodopsin in the eye, this
    chemical stimulus implants itself
    in the brain and reproduces there   Kundalini fire
    The astral center causes
    <u>it</u> (the stimulus) to surface in the soul
        as color
                <u>blue</u>
What causes the astral center to adjust to the physical
        is the
                Kundalini fire

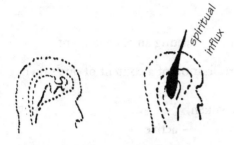

A kind of mental chamber is produced; the chamber is created through the content of meditation. When the content of meditation is then allowed to fade, it can be replaced by a content entering from the spiritual sphere. Retaining the functions of thinking without the content of thinking.

Samadhi.

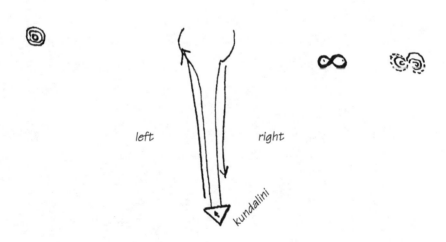

> Activity: will
> Passivity: thinking

Passive thinking is *observing*; that is, reflecting an alien content.

The active will is action; that is, realization of a content of one's own.

At the moment the kundalini is awoken,
> passive thinking becomes ~ active
and the active will becomes ~ passive

The moment of awakening can be characterized by saying that the *being* acquires an active (that is, productive) thinking, and a passive (that is, receiving) will.

Conceive the outcome of productive thinking as a sum of thought forms:

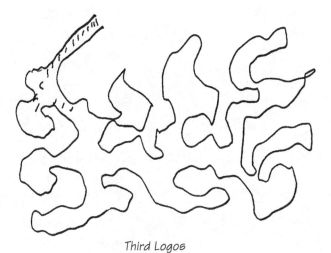

Third Logos

Second Logos

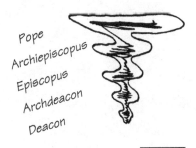

Pope
Archiepiscopus
Episcopus
Archdeacon
Deacon

PART THREE

EXPLANATIONS RELATING
TO THE EXERCISES

There are only very few explanations in Rudolf Steiner's handwriting relating to the main exercises, since these explanations were repeatedly given in lectures and esoteric lessons. Familiarity with them was presumed among esoteric pupils. For this reason, relevant texts have here been compiled from the Collected Works to elucidate various instructions contained in the exercises.

For detailed elucidations in the esoteric lessons, see: *Esoteric Lessons— From the Esoteric School*, CW 266 I–III.

The value of symbolic ideas on the path of inner schooling

Excerpt from a lecture, Bologna, April 8, 1911, CW 35

We can describe the exercises to be undertaken as a "schooling of the soul." We embark on this by seeing from a different perspective contents of the soul usually appraised as images or reflections of an external reality. In the concepts and ideas that we form, we initially seek something that will provide a reflection or at least a sign or symbol of something lying outside these concepts and ideas. In the sense intended here, spiritual researchers seek inner contents that are similar to the concepts and ideas of ordinary life or scientific research; however, they initially consider these, not in relation to their objective cognitive value, but instead allows them to live in his soul as active powers. You can say that they plant them as spiritual seeds in the soil of the soul, and waits in complete inner tranquility and quiet for them to reveal their effect on soul life. They can then observe that in *repeated* use of such an exercise, the soul's condition changes. However, it must be firmly emphasized that the repetition is what counts. You see, it is not a matter of the content of concepts making something occur in the soul in the usual way, in the manner of a process of cognition; but rather of a real inner process in which concepts do not act as cognitive elements but as actual powers. Their effect is due, in fact, to these powers frequently taking repeated hold of our life of soul. Everything depends primarily on the effect within the soul, invoked by experiencing a concept, being repeatedly activated by the same power. This is why the most will be achieved by meditations on the same content over longer periods, and repeated at particular intervals. The length of such a meditation is therefore of less importance; it can last for a very short time, as long as it is accomplished in absolute inner tranquility and complete inner seclusion from all external impressions and all ordinary mental activity.

The key thing is to sequester soul life with the content indicated. This has to be said, because it must be clear that no one must disrupt their ordinary life in order to practice these exercises. The time needed to engage in them is usually available to everyone. And the change the exercises bring about in the psyche, when properly undertaken, does not in the least affect the ordinary awareness we need in daily life. (Our view of intrinsic aspects of these things is not altered by the fact that people's nature inevitably leads them to unhelpful exaggerations and peculiarities.)

Most of our ordinary concepts are of very little use when engaging in this activity of the psyche. All contents of the soul that expressly relate to an objective reality lying outside them have little effect in the exercises described here. Instead, *ideas and mental images* are needed that we can regard as *emblems* or *symbols*. The most useful are ones relating to a multiple content in a living, encompassing way. Experience has shown that Goethe's idea of the "archetypal plant" is a good example. You remember that in a conversation with Schiller, Goethe once drew a symbolic image of this "archetypal plant" in a few quick strokes. He also said that whoever invokes this as a living picture in the soul will have something from which all possible forms can be conceived through lawful modifications of the original image, and that these multiple forms *can exist*. However you initially regard the objective cognitive value of such a "symbolic archetypal plant," bringing it to life in the soul in the way indicated, and then calmly awaiting its inner effect, will lead to something we can call an altered condition of soul. The ideas or images that spiritual researchers say are useful in this respect may sometimes seem very unusual.

We can come to terms with this peculiarity if we consider that such ideas should not be seen in terms of their truthfulness in the usual sense; they are truthful insofar as they act in the soul as real powers. The spiritual researcher places no value on what the images used to school the soul *signify*, but instead on what the soul experiences when engaging with them. Here, of course, only a few isolated examples of effective symbolic pictures or ideas can be given. One can conceive the human being in an image in which our lower, more animal-like human nature relates to our spirit being in the symbolic coherence of an animal form with a superimposed human form (somewhat like a centaur). The more vivid and pictorial, and the more charged with content the symbol appears, the better it will be. Under the conditions described here, this symbol will work upon the soul so that after some time (in fact, quite a lengthy period) the soul will sense inner life processes as inwardly strengthened, mobile, and mutually illumining. An ancient, very useful symbol is the so-called staff of Mercury, or caduceus; in other words, the image of a straight vertical line around which a curving line runs in a spiral. However, we will need to picture such a form as a system of forces; one force system runs along the vertical line, and another forms a spiral around it at a correspondingly slower speed. (To make this more tangible, we can picture the growth of a plant's stalk with the corresponding emergence of leaves along its length; or also the image of an electromagnet. By such means, as we pursue this image, we can also explore the picture of human development, with increasing human capacities symbolized by the vertical, and the wide diversity of impressions corresponding to the spiral, and so forth.) Mathematical forms can be especially resonant if we see in them symbols of universal processes. A good example is the so-called cassini curve with its three shapes: an ellipsoid form, a lemniscate, and the form consisting of two connected branches. In such an instance it is a matter of experiencing the idea or image so that the transition from one curved form into the other, in accordance with mathematical laws, corresponds to certain specific feelings in the soul.

Other exercises can then be added to these, also consisting of symbols, but now corresponding to ideas that can be expressed in words. Light can be seen as symbolizing the wisdom that orders phenomena in the world in a living, vital way. The wisdom that appears in self-sacrificing love can be symbolized as warmth arising in the presence of light. One can conceive of phrases coined from such images, *which are therefore solely symbolic in character*. Our life of soul can give itself up to such phrases in meditation. Success depends largely on the extent to which we achieve inner tranquility and seclusion of the psyche within such symbols. This success will give the soul a sense of being lifted out of the corporeal organism. Something like a change in the way the psyche experiences existence occurs. If we accept that in ordinary life we feel our consciousness issuing from a unity differentiated into mental pictures that originate in perceptions of the various senses; then, as a result of such exercises the soul feels itself imbued by an experience of its own nature, whose various aspects show less abrupt transitions than, for example, colors and tones in our ordinary awareness. Due to the success of the exercises, the soul experiences its capacity to withdraw into a sphere of inner being that was empty—was something that could not be perceived—before embarking on the exercises.

Before this kind of inner experience is achieved, a whole range of transitions occur in the pupil's state of soul. One such becomes noticeable, through practice, in attentive awareness of the moment when we waken from sleep. Here we can clearly sense forces taking hold of the configuration of the bodily organism as though emanating from a Something we were previously unaware of. We feel, as though in a memory picture, an *echo* of effects upon the bodily organism proceeding from this Something during sleep. And if, in addition, we have acquired the capacity to experience this Something within the bodily organization, we will become aware of the difference in the relationship of this Something to our bodies during waking life as opposed to sleep. We will be unable to express this in any other way than by saying that this Something is within our bodies when we are awake, but outside them during sleep; except that these expressions, "within" and "outside," are not ordinary spatial ideas, but a description of specific experiences which souls have after undergoing these exercises.

The exercises are of an intimate, inner kind, configured in individual form for each person. Once a beginning has been made with them, the individual aspect arises from a certain inner practice that emerges in ongoing schooling. But what becomes apparent as absolute necessity is positive awareness of living in a reality that is autonomous and of suprasensory nature in relation to our outward bodily organization. For the sake of simplicity, let us call a person who seeks such soul experiences a "spiritual researcher." In carefully self-monitoring awareness, such a spiritual researcher knows that the sense-perceptible bodily organization is founded on a suprasensory one; and that it is possible to experience oneself within this in the same way that normal consciousness experiences itself within the physical body. (Here it is possible to refer to the exercises only in principle. A detailed account can be found in my book *How to Know Higher Worlds*.)

The Rose Cross meditation

Those who wish to attain higher knowledge must first do something to create their higher organs…. This can happen, for instance, by learning to have inner experiences that do not belong to those of normal awareness. A more or less typical inner experience of this kind is described in my book *Esoteric Science*, which details the way to build up the idea and image of the Rose Cross…. There are many symbols, but the Rose Cross is the most important because it is a symbol of human development itself. (Vienna, March 28, 1910, CW 119.)

*

The Rose Cross meditation is incorporated into many exercises, and mostly desig-nated by the sign ♁ *. The account of the Rose Cross meditation given in* Esoteric Science, *first published in 1910, describes how this meditation can become inner experience.*

I

The Rose Cross Meditation from *Esoteric Science*, CW 13

I will illustrate inner contemplation of a symbolic idea with just one example. First an idea of this kind must be built up inwardly, and this can be done in the following way: picture a plant, rooted in the soil, putting forth leaf after leaf as it unfolds toward flowering. And now picture a human being standing next to the plant. Vividly call to mind that this person has qualities and capacities we can consider more perfect than the plant. This person can act upon feelings to move here or there at will, whereas the plant is rooted to the spot, to the soil. But now consider also that a person has characteristics that I do not perceive in the plant, but whose very lack renders the plant in some ways more perfect than the human being. A person is full of desires and passions that govern conduct. I might say that one is led astray by these impulses and passions. The plant, as I can see, follows the pure laws of growth from leaf to leaf, opening its blossom passionlessly to the chaste rays of the sun. While a person has a certain perfection lacking in the plant, he has purchased this at the price of allowing drives, desires, and passions to inform his being, in addition to what I see as the purity of the plant's powers. Now I picture the green sap flowing through the plant as the expression of pure, passionless laws of growth. And then I likewise picture the red blood flowing through human veins as the expression of impulses, desires, and passions. All this I bring vividly to mind. Then I continue by considering the human being's capacity to develop, to use higher powers of soul to cleanse and purify the drives and passions, eradicating the baser nature of these passions and impulses so that they are reborn at a higher level. I can picture the blood as expression of purged and purified drives and passions. Beholding the rose, for instance, in my mind's eye, I can see the green color of plant sap transformed into the red sap in the rose flower, which still, like the green leaf, obeys the pure, passionless laws of growth. The red of the rose can now become for me the symbol of blood whose impulses and passions have been cleansed, dispelling their baser nature so that their purity now resembles the powers at work in the red rose. I now try to entertain such thoughts not only in my mind, but also to bring them alive in my feelings. When I picture the purity and tranquil nature of the growing plant, this can give me a sense of bliss. I can engender a sense, a feeling, of how higher states of perfection must be bought at the cost of acquiring desires and appetites. This can transform the bliss I previously felt into a sense of earnestness; but then into a feeling of liberating joy stirring in me when I fill myself with the thought of the red blood as the potential bearer of experiences, as inwardly pure as the red sap of the rose blossom. It is important that such thoughts, serving as development toward and preparation for a symbolic idea, should not be devoid of feeling. Having immersed yourself in such thoughts and feelings, transform them now into the following symbolic image. Picture a black cross and let this be the *symbol* of the impulses and passions whose base nature has been eradicated. Where the beams of the cross intersect, picture seven resplendent red roses in a circle. Let these roses be a symbol of the blood that expresses cleansed, purified passions and impulses.[175] The aim here is to invoke a symbolic picture in the same way as exemplified earlier for a memory picture. An image of this kind has a soul-awakening power if you give yourself to it in inner contemplation. During contemplation you must try to exclude all other images and thoughts. Your soul should behold only the symbolic image described here, and should do so as vividly as possible. There is good reason for first elaborating certain ideas relating to the plant and the human being rather than merely presenting this symbol here for meditation. You see, the effect of such a symbol depends on first cultivating and composing it in the way described, before using it for inner contemplation. If you picture it without first undergoing this inner elaboration, it will remain cold and far less effective. These preparatory thoughts endow it with a soul-illumining power. During contemplation itself, however, all these preparatory thoughts should be laid aside, leaving you beholding only the vivid image itself, but allowing the *feeling* that has been invoked by these preparatory thoughts to resonate with it. The feeling experience is complemented by the symbolic image, and the effective thing here is for the soul to dwell in this experience. The longer we can dwell in this, without any other idea intruding, the more effective the whole process will be. It is good, however, if apart from the time given to the contemplation itself, we also frequently build up the picture again in thoughts and feelings as described, so that the feeling experience does not fade. The more patience one has for renewing the accompanying feelings in this way, the more important will the image be for the soul. (My book *How to Know Higher Worlds* suggests other ways to approach inner contemplation. Particularly effective are the meditations described there relating to the growth and wilting of a

---

175. Whether any particular scientific discipline considers the above thoughts to be justified or not is really beside the point. What counts here is the elaboration of ideas relating to the plant and the human being, drawing on simple, direct observation without any theorizing. Such ideas do have intrinsic meaning alongside theoretical views about natural phenomena, which of course have their own place, no less important. Here, though, the thoughts described do not aim to present facts scientifically, but to build up a *symbolic* image that has a real effect on the psyche, irrespective of the objections anyone may raise in relation to its composition.

plant; the growth forces slumbering in a seed; the forms of crystals, and so forth. In this present volume I wished only to give a single example of the nature of meditation.)

A symbol such as that described here does not invoke any outward thing or entity existing in nature; but this is precisely what gives it the power to awaken certain purely inner capacities of soul. Someone might object that while the "whole symbol" as such does not exist in nature, all its parts are borrowed from the natural world: the black color, the roses, and so forth. All such things are perceived by our senses. If you feel troubled by this you should remember that higher soul capacities are awakened not by mental images that reflect the sensory world, but instead only by *the way* in which these various parts are *brought together*. And this whole, formed from different parts and details, is not in fact an image of anything that exists in the world of the senses.

I wanted to illustrate here one example of the process involved in effective meditative contemplation. In spiritual schooling, very diverse images of this kind can be used, and can be prepared and developed in the most varied ways. Certain phrases, verses and single words can also be given as the subject of contemplation. In every instance these means of inner contemplation aim to detach the soul from sensory perception and to stimulate it to activity in which physical sense impressions are of no significance; but where, instead, the key thing is the unfolding of slumbering soul capacities. One can also just contemplate particular feelings, which can prove especially effective.

———

II

Transforming the colors of the cross from black into white,
and the roses from red into green

Human development presents itself to us in the symbol belonging to the deeply significant Rose Cross verse:[176] in the black cross with the red roses. We experience this symbol as something alive, in which the spiritual powers that have developed us live and act as we are born out of the godhead. But then we also know that the further development of our soul is possible by exerting our own powers. We know that not only our blood should be pure like the red sap of the roses, but also that the black cross must also be transformed through our cleansing of the nature of our sheaths or bodies, and growing beyond what is merely personal, giving ourselves up to something infinitely greater. Then we die in Christ, and inwardly the dark, black cross is transformed into a shining, luminous cross. The red roses widen into an infinite circle when the soul increasingly lives its way into the macrocosm, until it experiences itself as this circle. In the all-encompassing macrocosm we experience ourselves in a new existence.

Then, mysteriously, the colors of the symbol change: the roses appear green and the cross white. The soul can sense the full significance of this only by feeling the power that streams toward it. As though shining toward it from higher spheres of spirit, the soul perceives and recognizes this sacred symbol. Rigorous and powerful, it reveals itself to be a prompting to continual work to attain the great ideal that each individual human being can realize when one is reborn in the Holy Spirit.

---

176. The words: *Ex Deo nascimur* ("From God we are born"); *In Christo morimur* ("In Christ we die"); *Per spiritum sanctum reviviscimus* ("Through the Holy Spirit we are reborn").

The verse, "More radiant than the sun..."

Rudolf Steiner's own account of the esoteric lesson
in Berlin on October 24, 1905, CW 266/I

The verse: More radiant than the sun
               purer than snow
               finer than the ether
               is the self
               the spirit in my heart
               this self am I
               I am this self.

This verse raises us to our higher self each morning. Such verses are
not arbitrary, but are drawn from the world of spirit. They contain
much more, therefore, than we usually think. We regard them in the
right way by realizing that we can never fully fathom their content;
but the more we immerse ourselves in them, the more we can keep
finding in them. The Esoteric School can, therefore, give only isolated
suggestions for ways of exploring their content. A few such suggestions
are given below.

More radiant than the sun

We see the objects around us only when the sun shines upon them.
What makes them visible are the sunrays they reflect back into the
observer's eye. If no light existed, things would not be visible. But this
external light renders visible only the objects of the physical world. A
light that is "more radiant than the sun" must illumine things for us if
we are to see beings and things of soul and spirit. This light does not
emanate from an external sun, but comes from a light source that we
ourselves kindle within us when we seek in ourselves for the higher,

eternal self. This higher self is different in origin from the lower self. The latter senses our ordinary, everyday surroundings. But what lives in these daily surroundings has once arisen and will fade, and what we feel in relation to it therefore only has a transient value. Our transient self, too, is built up from such feelings and the thoughts we have about them. All things that become visible through the sun did not always exist, and one day will no longer do so. Even the sun once formed and will one day pass away. But the soul exists precisely to perceive the eternal of things. When the whole earth eventually passes away, the souls who inhabited it will still exist. And what they have experienced on earth they will bear with them elsewhere as a memory. It is like this: when someone does me a good service, the deed passes; but what the person has implanted in my soul endures and does not fade. Whatever we experience is always the origin of something that endures in us. Thus we ourselves draw what is permanent from things and bear it into eternity. And when, one day, human beings are transplanted to a quite different arena of evolution, they will bring with them what they have gathered here. And their deeds in the new world will be woven from their memory of the old. You see, there is no seed that does not bear fruit. When we are bound to another person in love, this love is a seed, and we will harvest the fruit in the future, belonging with this person through all time. Thus something lives in us that is one with the divine power that unites all things in an eternal tapestry. This "something" is our higher self. And it is *this* that is "more radiant than the sun." The light of the sun illumines us only from without. My soul sun illumines from within, and therefore it is more radiant than the sun.

Purer than snow

Everything is intrinsically pure. It can be rendered impure only by combining with something else that should not be combined with it. Water is intrinsically pure. But what is contained as dirt or impurity in water would also be pure in itself, if it had not wrongly combined with water. Coal is pure in itself, and becomes dirty only when it combines in the wrong way with water. When water assumes its own shape in the snow crystal, it eliminates everything that has wrongly combined with it. In the same way, the human soul becomes pure by eliminating everything that has wrongly combined with it. What belongs to it is the divine, the eternal, and imperishable. Every ideal, every thought of something great and beautiful, belongs to the inner contour of the soul. And when it contemplates such ideals, such thoughts, it purifies itself as water is purified when it becomes a snow crystal. And because the spirit is finer than all substance, so the "higher self," that is, the soul living in the heights, is "purer than snow."

Finer than the ether

Ether is the finest level of substance. But *all* substance remains dense compared with the soul. It is not *density* that endures, but whatever is "fine." The stone we conceive as substance passes away as substance. But the *thought* about the stone that lives in the soul endures. God made this thought, and from it he formed the dense stone. Just as ice is only consolidated water, so the stone is only a condensed thought of God. In the same way, all things are condensed thoughts of God. But "the higher self" dissolves all things, and in it then live the thoughts of God. And when the self is woven of these thoughts of God, it is "finer than the ether."

The spirit in my heart

We understand something only by encompassing it with the heart. Rationality and reason are merely mediators of the heart's understanding. We reach the idea of God through reason and rationality; but once we possess the thought in this way, we still have to learn to *love* it. We slowly and gradually learn to love all things. This does not mean that we should give our hearts away to everything we encounter without exercising our judgment, for our experience can initially deceive us. But when we seek to enquire into a being or a thing to discover its inherent divinity, we also begin to love it. If I have a deeply flawed person in front of me, I ought not to love his flaws; this would be a mistake and would be of no service to him. But if I ponder on how he became so flawed or corrupt, and when I support him in overcoming his flaws, then I help him; and I myself struggle my way through to the truth. I must continually be alert to *how* I can love. God is in all things, but I must first seek out what is divine in a being or thing. I should not simply love the external aspect of a being or thing, for this is deceptive, and I might easily love what is flawed or mistaken. But behind *all* illusion lies the truth, and that is something we can always love. When the heart seeks love of truth in all beings, then the spirit lives "in the heart." Such love is the garment that the soul should always wear, for then it weaves the divine into the things around it.

———

Single meditative phrases from "Light on the Path" by Mabel Collins

I

The first four phrases
From an enclosure to a letter dated December 28, 1903,
to M. Scholl CW 264, Appendix

If understood, the first four teachings open the portal to esotericism. What do we bring toward the objects of our cognition? If we examine ourselves we find that joy and pain are *our own* response to impressions of the sensory and suprasensory worlds. We so easily believe that we have shed likes and dislikes. But we must climb down into the most hidden corners of our souls and bring up *our own pleasure and displeasure*. You see, it is only when all such pleasure and displeasure is consumed by the bliss of the higher self that knowledge is possible. You might think this would make one a colder and more prosaic person, but this is not true. A piece of gold remains the same piece of gold, retains color and weight, even when it is reshaped into a piece of jewelry. Thus kama[177] remains what it is, retaining the same content and intensity even when spiritually formed. The kama power should not be rooted out, but incorporated into the content of the *divine fire*. Thus the eye's delicate sensibility should not discharge itself in tears but instead gild the impressions it receives. Resolve every tear to lend its pearl-like shimmer to the rays of light that enter the eye. *Your* pleasure and *your* pain is wasted energy—wasted as a power of knowledge. The power that flows out into this pleasure and this pain should stream into the subject of cognition.

---

177. Theosophical name for the astral body.

Before the eye can see it must shed the habit of tears

If we despise the criminal in the usual sense, and revere the saint, we have not yet taught our eyes to relinquish the habit of tears. Burn up all your tears in the will to help. Do not weep over the poor but *perceive* their situation and help them! Do not grumble about evil, but understand it and transform it into good. Your tears merely dull the pure clarity of light. You will feel all the more *sensitively* the less *self-regardingly sensitive* you are. A sound strikes the ear clearly if this clarity is not disturbed by the rapture, the sympathy, that meet it as it enters the ear.

Before the ear can hear it must lose its sensitiveness

In other words, allow the heartbeats of the other to resound within you and do not disturb them by the pulse of your own heart. You should open your ear and not your nerve endings, for the latter will tell you whether you find a tone *agreeable* or not; but your open ear will say what the *nature* of the tone is. When you attend patients, allow every fiber of their body to speak to you, and do not quell the impression they make on you.

Together, the first two phrases mean: reverse your will, allowing it to become as powerful as possible, but not letting it stream into things as *yours*; instead inquire into the real nature of things, and endow them with your will. Allow you and your will to stream out of things. Allow the luminosity of your eyes to flow from every flower or star, holding back yourself and your tears. Give your words to things that are dumb, so that they speak through you. These unspeaking things, you see, do not prompt your pleasure but your activity. Present for you is not what they have *become* without you; instead, what they should become must exist through you.

And as long as you impose your wish upon anything at all, without this wish of yours being born from the thing itself, you injure it. And as long as you injure anything, no master can hearken to you. The master hearkens only to those who need him; but those who wish to impose themselves on things do not need the master. The human being's lower self is like a sharp needle that wants to bury itself in everything. As long as it desires this, no master will wish to hear its voice.

*Before the voice can speak in the presence of the masters it must have relin-
quished the power to wound.*

As long as the sharp needles of "*I* want" stick out of one's words, the
words remain the messengers of one's lower self. When these needles
are removed so that the voice becomes soft and accommodating, wrap-
ping itself like veils around the mysteries of all things, it weaves itself
into a spirit garment (*Mayavirupa*) in which the master's delicate utterance clothes itself. With every thought that we truly dedicate to the
inner truth of things, we weave a thread in the garment that clothes the
master, allowing him to appear to us. If we make ourselves an emissary
of the world, an organ through which the depths of world riddles speak,
then we "pour the life of our soul into the world"; our heart's blood
washes our feet so that they may swiftly bear us to wherever action is
needed. And when the *soul* is present, in the *absence* of the lower "I,"
not where we *stand* in enjoyment but where our active feet have carried
us, then the master will also appear.

*Before the soul can stand in their presence, the feet must be washed in its
heart's blood.*

Those who remain *standing* within themselves cannot find the master;
whoever wishes to find him must let the power of their soul, their heart's
blood, flow into their actions—their active feet.

This is the *initial* meaning of the four basic teachings. When we live
with this initial truth, the second can be revealed to us, and then subsequent ones. These teachings are esoteric truths, and every esoteric truth
has at least seven meanings.

———

II

Three further teachings from "Light on the Path"

From a letter to A. Kolbe, dated October 4, 1905, CW 264

Seek the way

Seek the way in inner contemplation

Seek the way by boldly striding out of yourself

The two last sentences are only apparently contradictory. In fact they express two extraordinarily true realities.

Inner contemplation is the first half of a schooling path. Initially, at our current stage of development, we live *in* sensory perceptions of the outer world. Even when processing these sense impressions with the rational mind, we still remain in the "outer world."

When we free ourselves from sensory impressions, withdrawing into ourselves, the power of thinking remains available to us. This thinking is then emptied of its outer content. This is "inner contemplation." But precisely because thinking is "emptied," new content can now flow to it from within.

And *this* content is spiritual in nature, as the previous content was sensory in nature. Precisely by this means, though, we step out of ourselves. We step out of the sphere of the lower I into the "outer spiritual world." And this is indicated in the sentence, *"Seek the way by boldly striding out of yourself."*

———

The meditation
"I am – It thinks – She feels – He wills"

I

Transcript dated 1905

If you engage in a path of esoteric development, you must be clear, above all, that a power is contained in certain extremely simple phrases, and this power takes effect if you allow such a phrase to live in your soul. You do not grasp this properly if you try to understand such phrases only intellectually, for then they will tell you very little to begin with. You have to allow the phrase to fill you inwardly, surrendering to it all your powers of soul. Such a phrase is: "I am."

This phrase in fact contains the whole secret of contemporary humanity. Only a being who has the outward form of a human being at the present stage of evolution can think, feel, and will such a phrase inwardly. A being of this kind must have a form shaped in such a way that all the powers active in the body culminate in the forward arch of the forehead. This arching brow and the "I am" belong together. In former evolutionary periods of the human form, there was a stage at which this form had not yet pushed forward into this kind of brow. The "I am" could not yet be inwardly thought, felt, and willed at that stage. It would be quite wrong, however, to think that this form of the body produces the "I am." The "I am" was already present beforehand, but was as yet unable to express itself in a corresponding form. Before coming to expression in the human bodily form, it expressed itself in a world of soul. In fact, it is the power of the "I am" that united in the far distant past with the human physical body (that did not yet have an arching brow); and this power of the "I am'" urged this earlier form forward into the modern form of the forehead. This is why, by contemplating the "I am," we can sense in us the power that endowed us with our present form itself. And this power is a higher one than the powers that exist in us in ordinary life; it is the creative power of soul that forms the body from the soul realm. For this reason, esoteric pupils must live their way fully into the "I am" for a short while. In other words, they must think this "I am," at the same time inwardly experiencing something like this: "I want and will my existence; I want to place myself into the whole context of the world." If we compress all this into a single inner act of consciousness, at the same time placing our whole power of awareness in the region of the brow and the inner parts of the brain that lie beneath it, we do in fact transpose ourselves into a higher world out of which the form of the brow arose. But we should not imagine that we can conquer these higher worlds from one moment to the next. Instead we must have the patience to repeatedly engage in this contemplation daily over a long period. If we have this patience, we will notice after a while that the thought surfacing within is no longer something we merely think, but instead is a living, power-imbued thought. Pupils will be able to say to themselves, roughly, that the power in this thought is as inwardly alive as the power in the seed of a plant that raises and forms it into the plant's different parts. And soon this thought will appear as if light were streaming out from it. In this inner emanation of light, we feel joy in existence. A feeling pervades us that we can only call "loving delight in creative existence." And a power imbues the will as if this thought were suffusing it with a warmth that gives it energy. We can imbibe all this from proper contemplation of the "I am" as described. We can gradually recognize that intellectual, psychological, and moral power of the highest kind are born within us in this way, so that we enter into an ever more conscious relationship with a higher world.

A second such phrase is, "It thinks." In a way similar to that described in relation to the "I am," this "It thinks" embodies the power through which the form of the human speech organs have been formed out of higher worlds. When thinking did not yet unfold within a human body, but still existed in a higher world of soul, it caused the speech organs not yet present in the human form to be incorporated into it. Therefore, if esoteric pupils contemplate the "It thinks" in the same way as the first phrase, concentrating awareness on the region of the larynx, they will experience the creative power of soul that announced itself from higher worlds in the creation of the speech organs. If, once again, we have the necessary patience, we will experience rays streaming from the "It thinks" like the point from which a spiritual, musical harmony emanates, filling us with a feeling of sacred piety; and at the same time, with a power which tells us that we as human beings will gradually grow ever wiser. We will gain an intimation of the power that pours through the universe as divine-spiritual power, ordering all things by measure, number, and weight.

A third phrase is, "She feels." At a still earlier time the power of this phrase, likewise, did not yet indwell human beings. It resided in a higher world of soul, working down from there and transforming the shape that the human body previously had. Until that point, this human body's hands were not yet different from the feet. Today's hands and feet were, at that time, identically formed organs of movement, and we therefore did not yet have an upright stance. A great step forward in human development occurred when our front movement limbs were reconfigured into limbs for working. We acquired our upright stance in consequence, allowing us to overcome our lower nature by direct-ing our gaze upward and outward into heavenly worlds of spirit. But this was also what first endowed us with the capacity to create karma, for only the deeds of beings so configured fall under the sway of their own responsibility. Spiritual beings thus transformed the human being by streaming into the human body the "She feels" that previously had resided only within them. When esoteric pupils contemplate this "She feels" in a way similar to that described above, they elevate themselves to corresponding creative powers of higher worlds. In the "She feels," we must concentrate our whole awareness on both arms and hands. The thought of "She feels" will then stream out an inner life of indescribable bliss, which we can call that of love within active existence. We thereby acquire an awareness of how creative love pours through universal space, giving the breath of life to everything by its deed.

A fourth phrase is "He wills." The power of this phrase was what allowed the human body to first emerge from its surroundings as an autonomous entity in the very ancient past. Before this power worked upon it from higher worlds of soul, the human body was not yet enclosed in an outer skin; instead, streams of substance flowed into and out of it from all sides. It had as yet no separate life, but was part of the whole life of its surroundings. Of course these surroundings were quite different then from our present earthly environment. If esoteric pupils contemplate this "He wills" with their whole thinking, feeling, and will, focusing awareness on the whole surface of the outer skin, they gradually transpose themselves into the high creative powers of the "He wills." These are the powers of the suprasensory world that endow sensory things with their form and shape. If we have enough persistence, inner experience of this thought will enable us to feel as if elevated above all sensory and corporeal existence, gazing down upon the field of sensory creation in a way that allows us to work upon it in correspondence with divine-spiritual thoughts acquired in the world of spirit. The power that emanates from this thought is that of blissful transport into pure spirituality, and a sense that one can endow this sensory world with what it needs from higher realms.

As they contemplates these dynamic thoughts, esotericists must simultaneously direct attention to the breathing process, and reconfigure it for a short while from unconscious activity to an intentionally regulated one. Whereas the described influx of forces from higher worlds brought about the transformations we have indicated in the human form, the very same powers within this form engendered our present breathing system, which is necessary for a being such as we are, with bodily autonomy, hands that engage in self-directed work, and speech organs that turn inner soul experience into externally audible tones. By directing our attention to the breathing process, we support our elevation into higher creative realms.

When esoteric pupils thus gradually learn to consciously experience the higher universal powers always slumbering within, of which previously they were unaware, the things they have so far learned in their studies will assume vibrant, tangible, resonant life. Pupils will need to acquaint themselves with the fact that the human being has passed through various stages of metamorphosis throughout earthly evolution before reaching our present condition. These metamorphic stages are called the conditions of Saturn, Sun, and Moon. The esotericist must also be aware that in later epochs certain earlier states will, in a sense, be recapitulated. During Earth evolution, therefore, the Saturn, Sun, and

Moon stages were repeated. Saturn recapitulation corresponds to the creative labor of the "He wills" upon our external bodily sheath; Sun recapitulation corresponds to the creative labor of the "She feels" on the arms and hands; and Moon recapitulation corresponds to the labor of the "It thinks" on the speech organs. In this way, clearly, we move on from a view of the body as an entity created merely in the sensory world, and live our way into a view of higher worlds where powers work creatively upon the human being. And in this way the mere concepts we have acquired of things such as Saturn, Sun, and Moon become living vision and experience. The path leading increasingly from the exoteric to the esoteric depends upon this. The exercises given here, though, must be seen as only a beginning. One first has to work through what is presented here with a great deal of energy and persistence, and then one can receive further exercises for wakening still higher powers slumbering within. It is necessary to gain an intimation of the spiritual realities contained in the words "I am," "It thinks," "She feels," and "He wills," and to feel their connection with the diverse limbs of the body—a configuration that has emerged from a world of spirit.

It must also be said, by way of information, that in the powerful phrases above, the three forms

IT – SHE – HE

are firmly grounded in the nature of the higher worlds.

"It" signifies universal thinking, or the beings in the higher world in whom creative thinking is as inherent as sensory perception in the human being, who stands at a lower level than they.

"She" signifies the universal soul whose feeling streams from her, whereas human feeling streams in through external stimulus. All feeling of the world soul is creative world love, through which things enter into existence.

"He" signifies universal will, the universal spirit whose will works out of itself, whereas the working of human will is invoked by the external world. This "He" is the primal creative power of the world.

———

Archive no. 5329

II

Notebook Page

Interpretation

Originally the human being was not yet delimited from the surroundings. With this delimiting came *separateness*; this separateness is the effect of the *God willing* within him: *He wills*

When the human being stood upright, and began to use arms and hands, personal karma arose. Feeling becomes deed through the hands: *She feels*

With the larynx, which can produce articulated voice only in an upright being, speech comes as the expression of thinking. This thinking creates its expression in language: *It thinks*

No later than development of the forebrain appears

I consciousness: *I am*

———

Archive no. 3205

III

Notebook Page

Interpretation

I am: with concentration on the *forehead*: becoming aware
of what the human being actually is *now*.

It thinks: with concentration on the *larynx*: becoming aware
of what the human being had to become in order to
reveal the inner nature (spirit) outwardly (speaking).

She feels: with concentration on the *two arms*: becoming aware
of what the human being had to become in order to
bring inner nature into mutual interplay with outer
reality (standing upright, grasping).

He wills: with concentration on the *body's outer boundary*:
Becoming aware of what the human being had to
become to reflect within what is outside (to perceive).
(perceiving, opening to outer surroundings).

— the human being becoming objective. —

———

Facsimile of archive no. 3205

Ich bin : mit Concentration auf das
Vorderhaupt. Bewußtwerden dessen,
was der Mensch eigentlich jetzt ist.

Es denkt : mit Concentration auf den
Kehlkopf : Bewußtwerden dessen,
was der Mensch werden müßte, um
sein Inneres (Geist) nach außen zu
offenbaren (sprechen).

Sie fühlt : mit Concentration auf die beiden
Arme : Bewußtwerden dessen,
was der Mensch werden müßte, um
sein Inneres mit dem Äußeren
in Wechselwirkung zu bringen
(aufrichten, grüßen).

Er will : mit Concentration auf die Körpergrenze,
Bewußtwerden dessen, was der
Mensch werden müßte, um das Äußere
im Innern zu spiegeln (wahrzunehmen).
(Wahrnehmen, sich öffnen nach außen).

Gliederung des Menschen: —

The verse "In the pure rays of the light..."[178]

From the esoteric class in Munich, December 5, 1907, CW 266/I

Meditative words and phrases are spells that open the portals of the soul so that divine life can enter. This is why it is not enough to speculate rationally about such words. We need to open the soul to powers higher than merely rational ones. If we speculate intellectually about such phrases, we only activate the powers we already possess. But we need to awaken higher powers. Meditative words and phrases are not riddles we are trying to solve; they themselves enable us to solve riddles, for they are far wiser than reason can ever be. This is why we should let them work upon us fully, absorbing what flows into the soul from them; we must let them come to full life in our souls.

Meditative phrases have not been speculatively devised, but are born from the laws of the world of spirit. Something particular lives in every vowel. The vowels have a distinctive sound quality, each one different. Just as the soul experiences the effect of tones, so it should give itself up to the images that the words convey. In meditation we should be as far removed as possible from abstract thinking, trying instead to think as tangibly as we can.

Let us take a meditative verse that almost all of you know: "In the pure rays of the light..."

In the first line:

In the pure rays of the light

we can, for instance, picture the quiet gleaming of moonlight as representation of the gentle light of the godhead, which pervades all Creation.

---

178. Translator's note: See the translator's foreword for discussion of translating this verse.

This picture should live very clearly and inwardly in the soul to accompany the words:

> *In the pure rays of the light*
> *gleams out the godhood of the world*

Then follow the lines:

> *in pure love for every being*
> *shines out the godliness of my soul*

Now try to fully penetrate the gentle moonlight with your love, to pour it into you so that through the warmth of your own love the gentle light begins to shine with radiance, and so that you feel in this flooding luminosity the godhood radiant within your own soul. With the following words:

> *I rest in the godhood of the world*

try to picture being encompassed by and immersed in the divine spirit. You can feel as though you were in a warm bath, entirely embedded in divine substance that surrounds you with its gentle warmth.

> *I will find myself*
> *in the godhood of the world.*

With these words you could picture a distant lighthouse shining toward you, and imbue yourself with the feeling that you will find your own self in the divine.

However, it is not just the images that live in the soul that draw us upward toward the divine and open the portal of the soul. Profound wisdom and divine life have also been implanted in the vowels. It is not a matter of indifference which vowels resound in the soul. Let us take the vowel *i* [ee]. This always expresses a centralizing, a reaching for the center or middle point. The *a* [ah] signifies something quite different: it is the expression of inner worship of the divine. The *i* [ee] strives toward the center of the universe while the *a* [ah] remains at a distance and inclines in worship before what is most sacred.

So if we now take a look at our verse again, we find in line 1

> *In den reinen Strahlen des Lichts*
> In the pure rays of the light

that in the first *i* [ee] the soul strives toward the divine center, while in the *a* [ah] of "Strahlen"[179] the soul steps back in worship. In the second *i* [ee] she rushes onward again toward the divine.[180]

In line two we have the *ä* [ae]:

> *Erglänzt die Gottheit der Welt*
> gleams out the godhood of the world

The *ä* [ae] is a weakened form of *a* [ah].[181] Devotional worship of the "ah" changes in the "ae" into bashful reverence. In sacred, humble reverence, we do not dare approach God. In the following "o" the soul, however, hurries to embrace the divine entirely in sacred love and inwardness. In the next line:

> *In der reinen Liebe zu allen Wesen*
> in pure love for every being

The *i* [ee] leads the soul back again to the divine center.[182] Then in the *a* [ah] in the following line:

> *Erstrahlt die Göttlichkeit meiner Seele*
> shines out the godliness of my soul

---

179. We can almost hear this vowel sound in the English by imagining a slightly darkened "a" in rays.

180. Translator's note: Here too, perhaps, we can get a glimpse of this *ee* quality in the "I" of "light," whose sound is roughly "ai."

181. Translator's note: Here the vowel sound has been sacrificed to meaning and the consonantal quality of the "gl."

182. Translator's note: The "ee" quality here has been given to the preceding word "pure" where the "u" comes very close to it.

the soul is again imbued entirely with a worshipping quality.[183] And as the humble reverence of the *ä* [ae] transforms in the second line to inward encompassing of the divine, so in line four, full, warm, reverent worship of the *a* [ah] changes to a bashful desire to be encompassed, that scarcely dares touch the hem of godhood: *ö* [oe].[184]

In line five:

> *Ich ruhe in der Gottheit der Welt*
> I rest in the godhood of the world

the *u* [oo] is dominant, and expresses resting and embeddedness.[185] The soul is now merged as one with the divine.

In the two last lines, the *i* keeps repeating:

> *Ich werde mich selbst finden*
> *In der Gottheit der Welt.*
> I will find myself
> in the godhood of the world.

Thus at the end the soul is led ever deeper into the divine center of the world.

This is just *one* way of understanding this verse, and a small part of the wisdom that it embodies. It would be confusing if I were to elaborate on the further profound secrets that it conceals. No letter or sign here is without very deep significance.[186] The divine Word of Creation resounded thus when it first gave rise to the universe. You yourselves once heard it resound, but as yet your souls were not aware of it. At that time you were descending out of the spirit, and you will return to it again in full awareness. Born from the spirit, living in an earthly body,

---

183. Translator's note: The "ah" quality can be glimpsed in English in the "I" (ai) of "shines."
184. Translator's note: Clearly this is not possible here, though the last two syllables of "godliness" have a narrowing quality, and the final vowel approaches the "oe."
185. Translator's note: The sound was here again sacrificed to the sense!
186. Translator's note: This being so, even readers with no knowledge of German might prefer to meditate on this verse in the original language.

you will return through the power of the spirit to the divine spirit of the world.

i [ee]	striving toward the center
a [ah]	worship
ä [ae]	bashful reverence
o	encompassing
ö [oe]	bashful touching
u [oo]	resting in God

The review (or "rückschau") exercise

I

From the esoteric lesson in Munich on June 6, 1907, CW 266/I

The review must be undertaken in reverse, from the evening back to the morning, since we should accustom ourselves to the mode of perception of the astral plane.[187]

II

From: *Esoteric Science*, 1910, CW 13

It is of great value to free ourselves entirely from personal thoughts at such moments (of inner stillness and peace), raising ourselves beyond personal concerns to those affecting human beings in general. If we can fill our souls with communications from the higher world of spirit, and these hold our interest to the same degree as personal matters or concerns, our souls will reap special fruits. By seeking to work upon our life of soul in this way, and regulate it, we will also become able to observe our own concerns with the same composure we might have if they belonged to someone else. Regarding our own experiences, our own joys and sufferings, as if they belonged to another, is a very good preparation for spiritual schooling. You can gradually accomplish this to the necessary degree if you allow images of the day's experiences to pass before your mind's eye each evening. In doing so, try to see yourself within the experiences; in other words, observing yourself from without. A certain facility in this kind of self-observation develops if

---

187. On the astral plane everything appears in mirror image to the earthly plane.

we start by picturing small sections of the day. Gradually we become increasingly skilled and versatile in handling this *rückschau*, so that eventually, after longer practice, we can look back on the whole day in a short span of time. Looking back at the day's events in reverse order has particular value for spiritual schooling because it induces the soul to free its thinking from habitual adherence to the course of sensory occurrences. Thinking backward is still correct thinking, but no longer governed by the sensory course of events. We need to do this if we are to live our way into the suprasensory world; and it properly strengthens our thinking, picturing activity. Apart from reflecting on our daily life in this way, therefore, it is also good to picture other things in reverse; for example, the action of a play, story, melody, and so forth. The ideal for the spiritual pupil will be to increasingly meet events in life with inner certainty and tranquility, not judging them by *our own* state of soul, but according to their own inner meaning and value. Attending to this ideal will enable us to create an inner foundation for immersing ourselves fully in contemplation of the symbolic, and the other thoughts and feelings described above.

III

From a lecture given in Oxford, August 20 1922, CW 214

Now I'd like to describe a simple will exercise as a specific example, so you can study the principle involved here. In ordinary life we are used to thinking in a way that corresponds to how the world itself unfolds. We allow whatever happens to approach us in the way it happens. What happened earlier to us we think of as earlier, and what happened later, as later. And even if we do not necessarily think chronologically in more logical thought, nevertheless the effort is there in the background to adhere to the course of outward reality. But to become more practiced in handling soul-spiritual forces, we need to free ourselves from the external course of events. There is a good exercise for this, which is at the same time a will exercise: we can try to re-experience our day (which in outward reality proceeds from the morning to the evening) in reverse, from the evening back to the morning, and as we do so we can try as far as possible to enter into small details.... When we are able (and this is what counts) to free our thinking entirely from the way in which reality unfolds in three dimensions, then we will see how this enormously strengthens our will. We will also achieve this if we become able to feel a melody in reverse, or to picture a play of five acts backward from the fifth to the fourth act, and so on, back to the beginning of the play. All these things strengthen the will by inwardly consolidating it and freeing it from sensory attachment to outward events.

IV

From a lecture in Penmaenmawr, August 20, 1923, GA 227

We have to make a purely inner exertion to think backward, and this effort is significant. By doing so we free our souls from the reins that otherwise continually pull on us; and thus we bring our inner, soul-spiritual experience gradually to the point where it can really release itself from the corporeal and also from the etheric.

A good way to prepare for this release is to try to picture our experiences of the day's events in reverse each evening: first, what we experienced last of all, then working back through the day; but if possible, also thinking through the details of each smaller sequence in reverse; for instance, picturing backward how we climbed the stairs; thinking ourselves first at the top of the stairs then on the penultimate step, the third from the top, and so on, conceiving in reverse what we actually accomplished forward.

You may say that so many things happen each day that this will take a long time. Well, try first taking a very short sequence, going up and downstairs in reverse: just up and down. By doing this you acquire an inner flexibility so that after a while you will really be able to picture the whole sequence of the day in reverse, in three or four minutes.

Thoughts on "study"

I

Letter dated July 14, 1904, CW 264

Every pupil of the Esoteric School is obliged to undertake study.

II

From *The Stages of Higher Knowledge*
(first German edition 1905), CW 12

Many people still underestimate the power of what lies concealed and implicit in these messages from a higher world. And in connection with this they accord too much importance to all kinds of other exercises and practices. "What use is it to me," they say, "if others tell me how things appear in higher worlds: I want to see for myself." People often lack the patience to repeatedly engage with such accounts of higher worlds. If they did this they would find that these "mere accounts" carry a kindling power within them, and that one's own inspiration awakens in response to the inspirations of others. Of course, additional exercises are needed, besides "learning," if the pupil wishes to make rapid progress in experiencing higher worlds. But no one should underestimate the endless importance of study in particular. And no one can expect to gain rapid mastery in higher worlds who does not at the same time humble the self to engage tirelessly with the accounts and reports by capable researchers, which one only initially *hears*, of processes and beings of higher worlds.

III

From a lecture in Stuttgart, September 4, 1906, CW 95

The domains involved in Rosicrucian schooling are the following, and they need to go hand-in-hand with training of the six qualities already referred to: control of thinking, initiative of will, composure, open-mindedness or positivity, faith, and inner balance.[188]

Schooling itself involves the following:

1. Study. Without study the modern European cannot achieve self-knowledge. We must first try to unfold the thoughts of all humanity within ourselves, and learn to think *with* the system of the cosmos. We must say, "If others have thought this, it must be integral to human-ity, and I will try out what it's like to live with it." There's no need to hammer on it like a dogma, but we need to acquaint ourselves with such things through study. The pupil must come to know about the evolution of the suns and planets, the earth and humanity. These thoughts, as the subject of our study, purify our minds. Their strict trajectories of thought help us enhance our strictly logical thoughts, purifying them so that we learn to think in a rigorous, logical way. If we study a very difficult book, for instance, it is less important to grasp its content than to enter into the author's trains of thought and learn to think as he does. For this reason, no book should seem too difficult to us; that would mean we don't feel like exerting ourselves to think. The best books are those we have to study time and time again; those which we do not immediately understand, but must think through sentence by sentence. When studying, it is less a matter of "what" than of "how." The great truths, such as planetary laws, allow us to acquire

---

188. Translator's note: Steiner sometimes gave the order and names of the six "balancing" exercises in slightly varied ways, as here. In most of his accounts, "composure" is followed by "positivity" and then "open-mindedness"; whereas here, open-mindedness and positiv-ity appear to be synonymous; and a seemingly new quality, "faith" is included as the fifth exercise. See *Six Steps in Self-Development*, Rudolf Steiner Press, 2010, for a compilation of these variations.

broad trajectories of thought, and this is the key thing. There is also a great deal of egotism in saying, "I prefer studying moral teachings rather than ones about planetary systems."

IV

From a lecture in Munich, June 6, 1907, CW 99

Study in a Rosicrucian sense is the ability to immerse oneself in a thought content originating not in physical reality but in higher worlds, also called living in pure thought. Most philosophers today deny this is possible; they say that all thinking inevitably has a certain residue of sensory perception. In fact this is not the case; no one, for example, can see a true circle. A circle can be seen only in spirit, in the mind's eye; on the blackboard it is only a collection of small particles of chalk. You get a true circle only by looking beyond all instances in external reality. Thus in mathematics, thinking is something suprasensory. But in other realms, too, we have to learn to think in a suprasensory way; and initiates have always practiced this mode of thinking in relation to human nature. Rosicrucian theosophy is suprasensory knowledge of this kind; and studying it, as we have been doing, is the first stage of Rosicrucian schooling itself. I do not present Rosicrucian theosophy for some kind of external reason, but because it is the first stage of Rosicrucian initiation.

People often think there is no need to speak of the different aspects of human nature, or of humanity's development, or of the diverse stages of planetary evolution. They would prefer to acquire fine feelings rather than engaging in serious study. But however many fine feelings you collect in your soul, this alone will not enable you to rise to higher worlds. Rosicrucian theosophy does not seek to engender feelings as such, but instead wishes feelings to resonate in response to the mighty realities of the spiritual worlds.

...

Those who seek to work their way up into higher worlds must accustom themselves to a form of thinking that allows one thought to emerge from another. I elaborated such a mode of thinking in my books

Philosophy of Freedom (CW 4) and *Truth and Science* (CW 3). These are not written so that you could take one thought contained in them and place it elsewhere in the book; but are, rather, written in the same way as an organism develops. One thought emerges from the other. These books have absolutely nothing to do with the person who wrote them, for he gave himself up to what the thoughts themselves elaborated in him, and the way they structured and organized themselves.

Thus for anyone who seeks to accomplish this in a certain primary way, study is a way of acquainting oneself with elementary facts of spiritual science; and, when one is ready to ascend to a higher level, it becomes an immersion in structures of thought that allows one thought to arise and emerge from another.

———

Contemplation of one's own divine ideal

Here it is not a matter of entertaining this or that idea of the divine, but of pondering one that is really intimate to us in a subjective sense. For the Christian this can be Christ; for the Hindu, "the Master," for the Muslim, Mohammed. A modern scientist may even engage in devotional contemplation of "divine nature." What matters here is the *devotional feeling* rather than the idea we form of the "divine."

From a letter to an esoteric pupil
Berlin, August 12, 1904, CW 264

What counts is not the particular nature of the ideal, but engendering the right inner mood. Whether we think of "the Master" or the starry heavens does not matter. There have been atheists who said they had no divine ideal whatsoever; yet when their attention was drawn to the starry heavens, they recognized that they too could sense a feeling of reverence and devotion in response to it.

From an esoteric lesson
Munich June 6, 1907, CW 266/I

No alcohol at all.
Vegetarian diet is not absolutely essential
but is recommended where possible.
No lentils, beans or peas.

Meditation and concentration exercises will be the prime thing, but the way the seeker eats will also be of some importance once starting to transform the astral body.

The most important thing is to avoid alcohol in all forms; even alcohol-filled sweets and puddings are very harmful. Alcohol and spiritual exercises lead astray in the worst possible way. From a scientific perspective, the deleterious effect of alcohol on brain function has been proven. Those who focus their whole endeavor on seeking the spirit should refrain from partaking of something that entirely precludes perceiving the spirit. Eating meat and fish is not advisable. In meat a person ingests all animal passion, and in fish all of universal kama. Mushrooms and fungi are extremely harmful: they contain inhibiting moon power; and everything that arose on Old Moon embodies rigidity. Likewise, pulses [dry beans such as pinto, kidney, and navy beans; dry peas; and lentils] are not recommended because of their high nitrogen content. Nitrogen renders the ether body impure.[189]

---

189. According to notes of a question and answer session following the lecture in Leipzig on April 25, 1906, in CW 97 ("The Christian Mystery"), Steiner remarked that "All this relates to the development of esoteric powers, but not to the more intellectual study and acquisition of spiritual truths."

Meditations with or without indications
of the time they should take

From a lecture (questions and answers)
in Dornach, April 22, 1924, CW 316

A participant: A question that concerns us all is how to cope with all the meditations we have received. At what time of day should we do them? Should we practice them in a proper rhythm? And how should we do this? So far it seems that most of us feel at least somewhat pressured by all the meditative content and do not yet know how to live with it properly.

Well, you see, strict instructions really ought not to be given in relation to such matters, for this intervenes too much in individual freedom. A proper view of these things will not allow any sense of pressure or burden to arise. When I gave those meditations at Christmas I always explained the direction in which they lead the soul; and the same has been said of all meditations such as these. They of course include meditations such as those now being given in the First Class.[190]

All these meditations are different in nature from those given to individuals seeking an effect suited to them individually. Those who want a personal meditation should naturally know whether they ought to practice it in the morning or evening, and how they should conduct themselves in other ways in accordance with it, and so on. These are meditations that aim to intervene in an individual's esoteric life, depending on capacities and karma. They lead quite naturally to one not remaining isolated, but seeking to acknowledge others who share one's strivings. We must regard these meditations as intended for personal meditative

---

190. CW 270.

practice. For meditations like those included in the esoteric instruction at Christmas, the intended effect is the important thing and should be given most attention; except where I say (which so far I have not) that it would be good to practice such a meditation at a particular time, or under particular circumstances, or to accompany a particular situation. And then it is a matter of using one's own circumstances (one's particular situation in life) to undertake such meditations. Such meditations are made simple, aren't they, if one finds the time for them? The more often the better. They will always have their effect. These meditations ought really to involve the quest for personal development. What dawns on us through them should lead us to seek connection with others, and find it too. And really the most burdensome thing would be to issue specific rules and dictates about these meditations, such as that they ought to be done all at once, whether individually or in a group. All such measures will also mean the meditation loses something it should have. You see, every meditation is impaired if we start from a *duty or obligation* to do it. You should take careful note of this. Starting from a sense of having to do a meditation detracts from it. In the case of personal meditations, it is therefore very necessary for our practice to develop them gradually into something that we feel a thirst for in our souls. And those who thirst for meditation will accomplish their morning and evening meditation in the best way, just as we eat when we're hungry. We have the right feeling about meditation if it becomes something we cannot do without, which we experience as belonging intrinsically to the whole life of our psyche.

———

APPENDIX

EDITORS' COMMENTARIES

A

The breathing exercises

The European must be very careful with breathing exercises and embark on only them at a late stage, after appropriate instructions. (Leipzig, July 10, 1906, in CW 94)

Those familiar with Rudolf Steiner's works and his frequent warnings about breathing exercises may wonder how this accords with the relatively numerous exercises accompanied by directions for rhythmic breathing.

It would be wrong to conclude from such warnings, relating primarily to certain potential dangers involved in breathing exercises, that Rudolf Steiner absolutely rejected them. In *Esoteric Science* (CW 13) first published at the beginning of 1910, Steiner stated that the "ideal" of personal development is not to undertake any exercises involving the physical body at all, including breathing exercises. Instead, he said, everything that needs to occur in the physical body should emerge as a consequence *only* of pure intuition exercises. But immediately preceding these comments he also wrote that at a certain stage in the practice the spiritual pupil will "briefly experience the need to bring the breathing (or suchlike) into a kind of harmony with what the soul accomplishes in the exercises or in inner contemplation." A similar formulation appears in the lecture given in Dornach on April 24, 1924 (in CW 316).

Rudolf Steiner's view of the indispensible preconditions for breathing exercises was expressed in the lecture series *Macrocosm and Microcosm* (Vienna, March 1910, CW 119), which he gave a few months after publishing *Esoteric Science*. Sufficient preparation is absolutely necessary, he said, before one starts doing breathing exercises; and by this he meant careful study of spiritual-scientific literature. His actual words are as follows:

In this domain, unfortunately, many unconsidered instructions are given. Those who know anything of such matters are horrified that numerous people engage in breathing exercises today without due preparation. To the spiritual researcher they appear like children playing with matches. ... Those who wish to work on their breathing should do this only in the knowledge that for spiritual pupils, insight becomes prayer; and that they must be filled with deep reverence. Without this, no instructions whatever should be given in relation to these matters of profound significance, which require the greatest responsibility.[191]

At the time this was a general kind of warning. But in the years following the World War I, when Indian yoga breathing exercises became increasingly popular in the West, Steiner warned very specifically against them. In various ways he pointed out that in copying such exercises, the modern Europeans could risk destroying their physical body, because their soul life was no longer oriented to sensibility, as it was in the ancient Indians, but instead to intellectual activity. In a life unfolding intellectually, therefore, he recommended using exercises that stay in a purely soul-spiritual realm. This is why exercises such as those contained in *How to Know Higher Worlds* "touched very slightly at most" on the physical breathing process, as he said in a public lecture in Stuttgart on September 3, 1921 (in CW 78). Likewise, in reports on his own lectures in 1922 (CW 25) he stated that modern people ought not to copy eastern yoga breathing because, "in the course of humanity's evolution they have entered into an organization that precludes *such* yoga exercises.'" The word "such" was emphasized by Rudolf Steiner himself, and presumably relates primarily to very specific breathing exercises, described as part of the classic eightfold yoga path in the Patanjali Sutras (second century AD). Rudolf Steiner's library contained a book inscribed with his name entitled *Yoga Aphorisms by Patanjali, with notes by W. Q.* (German translation of the fourth English edition, Berlin 1904). Aphorism II/51 in this volume states that besides exercises regulating the inbreath, holding of breath, and outbreath to enhance concentration, there "is another kind" of regulation of the breathing

---

191. Vienna, March 31 1910, CW 119.

oriented to the breathing's "inner sphere." W. Q. Judge's note explains that this statement refers to a regulation of breathing involving "closely observing a directing of the breath to certain nerve centers in the human body and its consequent influence on these centers in order to produce physiological and subsequently physical effects."

Why Rudolf Steiner gave his esoteric pupils any breathing exercises at all is a question answered in principle in his accounts of the three main types of spiritual schooling methods appropriate in our time. Here the rhythmic ordering of life, including breathing, is not just a stage of ancient eastern schooling, but also forms part of the Christian-Rosicrucian method, albeit to a lesser degree and in modified form (CW 95).

A lecture of 1922 offers a clear explanation of the difference between the exercises he gives to make breathing rhythmic, and those of the ancient eastern yoga path. In contrast to the exertions of the ancient yogi, who sought to fuse the thinking process with the breathing process, this connection must be entirely separated today. Whereas the ancient yogis returned to their own intrinsic rhythm, modern people must return to the rhythm of the outer world:

> Read the very first exercises I gave in *How to Know Higher Worlds*, where I show how, say, we should observe a plant's germination and growth. Meditation here focuses on detaching picturing and thinking from the breathing, and allowing it to immerse itself in the growth forces of the plant itself. Thinking should go out into the rhythm that pervades the outer world. The moment that thinking really frees itself from bodily functions in this way, sundering itself from the breath and gradually merging with the outer rhythm, it does not however immerse itself in sensory perceptions, in the sensory properties of things, but in each thing's spiritual nature.... All modern meditation exercises are focused on detaching thinking from the breathing process.... That is the difference between modern meditation and the yoga exercises of very ancient times.[192]

---

192. Dornach, May 27, 1922, CW 212.

These explanations show the key importance of exercises by Rudolf Steiner that contain directions for rhythmic breathing in association with particular phrases or meditations. Such phrases, always oriented to relationships between the inner and outer world, are clearly intended to help us detach thinking from the breathing process, and lead thinking into the rhythm of the outer world.[193]

Important references to this issue can be found in the following lectures, among others: Leipzig, July 10, 1906, CW 94; Stuttgart, September 2, 3, 4, 1906, CW 95; Munich, June 6, 1907, CW 99; Kassel, June 29, 1907, CW 100; Munich, June 1, 1907, January 16, 1908, January 26 1908, CW 266; Dornach, November 30, 1919, CW 194. See also the esoteric lessons: Berlin, April 13, May 6, and October 2, 1906, Munich June 1, 1907, Berlin January 16 and 26, 1908, all in CW 266/I.[194]

---

193. For instance, exercise Archive no. NB 86, p. 388.
194. In *Esoteric Lessons* 1904–1909, SteinerBooks 2007.

B

References to "lotus flowers and chakras" and "kundalini"

Although only a few exercises specifically mention this, a great many different accounts of the path of spiritual-scientific schooling show that all exercises serve primarily to nurture development of the astral organs of perception, the so-called lotus flowers, and to awaken the "kundalini fire." In a lecture given in Leipzig on July 9, 1906 (in CW 94), Steiner said:

The first stage ... is connected with development of the so-called lotus flowers, the sacred wheels or (in Sanskrit terminology) *chakras*, situated at quite specific places in the body. We can distinguish seven such astral organs. The first, the two-petalled lotus, lies close to the root of the nose; the second, the sixteen-petalled, lies at the level of the larynx; the third, the twelve-petalled, at the level of the heart; the fourth, the eight- to ten-petalled,[195] close to the navel; the fifth, the six-petalled, somewhat lower down; the sixth, the four-petalled (in Sanskrit terminology) *svastika* lies still lower down and is connected with the whole realm of fertilization; and the seventh cannot be spoken of without further explanation. These six organs have the same kind of significance for the soul world as the physical senses have for perception of the sensory world. Through the exercises I have described, they first become brighter, and then start moving. In modern people they are immobile. In Atlanteans they still moved, and in Lemurians they were very active and dynamic. But in those days they revolved in the opposite direction from the clockwise way they turn in an esoterically developed person today. Analogous to the dreamlike clairvoyant state of the Lemurians is the fact that in mediums today possessing an atavistic clairvoyance, the lotus flowers still

---

195. In notes of the same lecture by a different participant, an additional phrase here states: "two of them are less evolved."

turn in an anti-clockwise direction, as they did once in Atlantean and Lemurian times. Mediumistic clairvoyance is unconscious, without control of thinking, while that of the true clairvoyant is conscious and carefully monitored by his thinking. Mediumism is very dangerous, whereas healthy esoteric schooling not in the least so.

Detailed accounts of the exercises for developing the lotus flowers are contained in the two books *How to Know Higher Worlds* and *Esoteric Science*; and, among many relevant lectures, those given in Vienna, March 28, 1910 (CW 119) and London, May 1, 1913 (CW 152). From these sources we can assume that the so-called supplementary or balancing exercises serve specifically to develop the twelve-petalled lotus, while the exercises "For the Days of the Week," corresponding to the eightfold path of the Buddha and the eight Beatitudes of Christ, serve development of the sixteen-petalled lotus.[196] We know that the seven-week exercise (Archive no. A 5351, p. 386) was given in response to a request for an exercise to develop the lotus flowers.

The meditative verses also have this aim. This is clear particularly from the lecture of May 1, 1913 (CW 152), since the example of meditation given there in connection with the lotus flowers involves the most frequently given meditative verse, "In the pure rays of the light… / in pure love for every being…" Just as this verse is entirely founded on the light-love polarity, so is that contained in the first Mystery Play, *The Portal of Initiation*: "The weaving being of light shines out through breadths of space…the blessing of love warms through the cycles of all time…." The words of this verse, according to Steiner, give us the "key" to the heights, and will accompany the pupil even when there is nothing left to guide him that "sensory eyes can perceive" (*The Portal of Initiation*, Scene III).

From this is it is clear that light and love (which belong together at higher levels of human life as the two major principles of earthly

---

196. See the lectures given in Berlin on March 16, 1905 (CW 53); Paris, June 6, 1906 (CW 94); and Stuttgart, September 2, 1906 (CW 95).

human existence, in the same way that positive and negative electricity or positive and negative magnetism are [Berlin, February 22 1906, CW 54]) must be of fundamental importance for inner development. The following notes recorded in a notebook (Archive no. 105, facsimile page 394/395) show the tangible connection between these principles and development of the lotus flowers and the kundalini light. The text beneath the sketch of the human body states:

This physical body is built up by the powers of the astral body; it brings this as far as the sense organs. These—eyes—see objects through sunlight from without.

––––––––

In the astral body itself we have to distinguish a
second half: *[drawing]*
like the other pole in a magnet.

In the man the second astral body is feminine;
in the woman the second astral body is masculine;
in other words, the astral body is hermaphrodite.

The kundalini fire is the activity stimulated
in the *second* astral body, which is initially warmth and light.

As long as the kundalini fire is not stimulated,
we feel our way between objects
and beings of the higher world, as in the
night between physical objects.
Once the kundalini fire is present, we ourselves illumine these objects.

––––––––

Light as symbol of wisdom, and warmth as symbol of love are, accordingly, the polarity of the "kundalini"; in Rudolf Steiner's characterization in *How to Know Higher Worlds* they are the spiritual "power of perception" whose proper awakening, alongside development of the astral organs of perception (lotus flowers), is the precondition for spiritual vision. This is why, as long as he used the term, Steiner spoke of the "kundalini" in relation to kundalini "fire" and kundalini "light."

"Kundalini" or also *"kundali"* (meaning roughly "wound, rolled up," and therefore also called "snake fire" or "snake power") is one of various Indian names for this esoteric power, which H. P. Blavatsky introduced into theosophical literature. According to Arthur Avalon, kundalini is seen as "the foundation of all yoga practice," the "mightiest manifestation of creative power in the human body"; "it sustains the life of all earthly beings" and is the " 'Word' (not originating in the human being) immanent in the body." And because it is the primal fount of all language, "the mantras are invariably" its manifestations, for it embodies "all letters," and "this is why one uses mantras when awakening the kundalini." But it should not be superstitiously assumed "that just speaking a mantram will produce a result, or that *japa* [recitation] of the mantra can be accomplished by mere repetition." A mantram too must first be awakened from sleep.[197]

In *How to Know Higher Worlds* (in the chapter "Changes in the Dream Life of the Eoteric Student"), Rudolf Steiner described how the kundalini can be awakened for western consciousness on the path of spiritual-scientific schooling, once the astral organs, the lotus flowers, have been properly developed. This account and the notebook entry Archive no. 105, transcribed above, complement each other. It is possible that the notebook entry was directly related to the writing of that whole chapter in *How to Know Higher Worlds*, since they both date from the same year, 1905. In later revised editions he replaced the term "kundalini"; first with "spiritual organ of perception," and then with "spiritual power of perception." However, it is always described in the same words as "element of higher substantiality"; as "spiritual light" radiating from the developed higher organs, which renders objects and beings of the higher world visible in the same way that outer sunlight makes physical objects visible.

H.W.

---

197. Arthur Avalon, *The Serpent Power*, Dover Publications Inc. 1974; also S. J. Woodruffe, *The Garland of Letters,* Ganesh & Co. 2001.

EDITORIAL NOTES

Title of the volume:

The title of this book was provided by the editors. The term "Soul Exercises" was often used by Rudolf Steiner for the instructions he gave in meditation. See page 403 of this book, for instance.

Part One

Text sources:

"General Conditions…"

From as early as 1903, Rudolf Steiner referred in his lectures to the "preparatory or supplementary exercises" (often called "balancing exercises" in this translation) as the prerequisite for all meditation practice. (See, for instance, the detailed account in *Founding a Science of the Spirit* (CW 95), Rudolf Steiner Press 1999, first German edition 1906.) Under the heading "General Conditions…" they were transcribed and duplicated for Rudolf Steiner's esoteric pupils in October 1906. The original transcription has been lost, and the wording follows that of the copied version.

The Persian legend about Jesus Christ mentioned on page 3 comes from Goethe's "Notes and Treatises for Better Understanding the West-East Divan – General Aspects."

After publication of the book *Esoteric Science* at the beginning of 1910, mention in the main exercises of the balancing or supplementary exercises usually referred to the relevant pages of that book.

"Additional Rules Following on from the 'General Conditions'…"

Rudolf Steiner likewise transcribed these for duplicating in around 1907, but again the original has been lost. The text corresponds to the duplicated version. At the time the heading was "Rules for those who have made efforts to fulfill the requirements in the first circular (lessons)."

"For the Days of the Week"

These exercises must likewise have first been given around 1907. See the chapter, "'Some Effects of Initiation" in *How to Know Higher Worlds* (CW 10) as well as Chapter 3 in The Gospel of St. Luke (CW 114).

"The Twelve Virtues as a Subject of Meditation"

No original source for this has been preserved, nor is precise dating possible. In the book recording her experiences of Rudolf Steiner and Marie Steiner,[198] Ilona Schubert reports the following in relation to this exercise:

> In a private conversation Rudolf Steiner had in relation to the zodiac and the corresponding months, he said that it was H.P. Blavatsky who assigned the virtues to each month, in the following sequence and with these designations:

Aries	April	Devotion
Taurus	May	Equilibrium
Gemini	June	Perseverance
Cancer	July	Selflessness
Leo	August	Compassion
Virgo	September	Courtesy
Libra	October	Contentment
Scorpio	November	Patience
Sagittarius	December	Control of thoughts
Capricorn	January	Courage
Aquarius	February	Discretion
Pisces	March	Magnanimity

Dr. Steiner confirmed these, but added to them the explanation, "If one conscientiously practices these virtues, new powers and capacities will emerge from them." And then he wrote down the following list:

---

198. *Selbsterlebtes im Zusdammensein mit Rudolf Steiner und Marie Steiner*, 2nd edition, Basel 1977.

Devotion becomes the power of sacrifice
Equilibrium becomes progress
Endurance becomes faithfulness
Selflessness becomes catharsis
Compassion becomes freedom
Courtesy becomes tactfulness of heart
Happiness becomes composure
Patience becomes insight
Control of thoughts becomes a sense of truth
Courage becomes redemptive power
Discretion becomes meditative power
Magnanimity becomes love

Finally Dr. Steiner said, "Always start practicing a virtue on the twenty-first of the preceding month, and practice it until the first of the following month. Thus one should practice as follows: Devotion from March 21 to May 1, and so forth. The dates at which the zodiac signs traditionally change should not be considered. One simply practices devotion in April, and always starts, as stated, on the twenty-first of the previous month."

The words in parentheses on page 16 indicate slight variations arising in the process of translation from English to German.

Part Two

Original sources and reproducing of texts:"

Most of these meditative texts are to be found in the Archive of Rudolf Steiner's literary estate (*Nachlassverwaltung*), usually in handwritten manuscripts, some as photocopies or only as transcripts (that is, recorded by someone else). Transcripts are marked in this volume with an "A" preceding the archive number. Of the exercises available only as transcript, we have included only those we are certain are authentic. A number of the originals are to be found in the Goetheanum Archive, to which thanks are due for making them available for this volume.

The exercises compiled in section A–2b are those available in duplicated or cyclostyled form as follows:

Exercises A, B, and D: as duplicated manuscript handwritten by Rudolf Steiner; also in duplicated manuscript handwritten by someone else; and typewritten manuscript.

Exercise C: only as duplicated manuscript handwritten by someone else.

Exercise E: only as duplicated typescript.

For exercises C and E, handwritten originals by Rudolf Steiner certainly did exist, but have been lost.

When issuing exercises A to D of these duplicated meditation texts, Rudolf Steiner initially wrote out in his own hand the verse "More radiant than the sun..." then later increasingly "In the pure rays of the light..." along with an individually given phrase for meditation. Sometimes the heading "Main Exercise" was written at the top. The meditative phrase "All above as below..." forms a set constituent of the fifth exercise, and was therefore included for all recipients of the exercise.

Printed reproduction:

The printed wording of the exercises corresponds precisely to the original manuscripts, as does, largely, the layout. In complex instances one has to compare the printed text with the printed facsimile. Underlining of words or phrases in the original is reproduced as italic. Spelling has been adapted to current usage. Abbreviations are sometimes written out in full for clarity. Punctuation corresponds exactly to the originals.[199] In order to reproduce the texts exactly as they were given, occasional grammatical unevenness has not been corrected.[200] According to Rudolf Steiner,

---

199. Translator's note: This is not always the case in the translations. See Translator's Foreword.

200. Translator's note: Again, such "unevenness" or infelicity cannot always easily be reproduced in translation.

the character of mantric verses "is always such that it sometimes renders grammatical structure difficult" (Berlin, January 19, 1915 in CW 157). However, such oddities might also sometimes be due to a slip of the pen. For example, in relation to the exercise Archive no. 6613 (on page 323) dated May 1919, the recipient, Hans Erhard Lauer, added a note in his own hand as follows: "The fourth line of the first part of the meditation (morning) ought to read (in line with Steiner's oral communication) 'And then you enter into spirit day,' whereas the manuscript states: 'He you enter....'."

Supplementary remarks in Rudolf Steiner's handwriting on a few of the originals, which do not form part of the exercise itself (that is, name of the recipient, starting date for the exercise, and so forth) were mostly not included in the main text, but have been recorded in the index. Wherever Steiner himself wrote the name of the recipient on the exercise sheet, we can assume that the exercise was not written down in the latter's presence but was later given or sent to him. We have always omitted remarks in a different hand, but noted them in the index.

The exercises in English:

Foreign pupils familiar with German received their meditations in that language. For those with little or no German, Marie Steiner translated the verses into English, French, Italian, or Russian. However, Rudolf Steiner himself also himself wrote down a few exercises in either English or French, such as Archive no. 7157, page 343.[201]

The verses:

All the verses were original mantric formulations by Rudolf Steiner, except for the verse "More radiant than the sun...," which originated in the Esoteric School of Theosophy of the Theosophical Society.

---

201. Translator's note: As stated elsewhere, and in the Translator's Foreword, I slightly adapted some of the original English versions where necessary because of grammatical errors or infelicities in the original.

Verses that "reverse the sequence of ideas":

In the earliest exercises, the meditative verse appears just once, or also twice, but always in the same form. From around 1906, increasingly, the first sequence of ideas is "pictured in reverse" (see Archive no. 3098, p. 170) in the second verse of two. This reversal is a distinctive aspect of exercises given by Rudolf Steiner. Clearly, it aims to serve to cultivate inner strengthening of the will, as does the evening review exercise. This reversal can already be seen in the verse "More radiant than the sun..." as given on page 40 (Archive no. 3103), where the Rose Cross symbol is also added to it.

Starting dates for meditations:

In various exercises, dates are given for the start of esoteric schooling, but usually without reference to the year. Since these dates are obviously no longer relevant, they have been left out to avoid misunderstanding, but are included in the index. Regarding such a date indication, Rudolf Steiner wrote in a letter to an esoteric pupil (August 2, 1904, in CW 264): "For reasons known only to the esotericist, one must embark on schooling at very particular times. Later all this will become clear to you." The dates given all involve the period between new moon and full moon, and this is explicit in exercise Archive no. 3046 on page 162. It is not known that any explanation for this was later offered, but this fact sometimes enables us to date particular exercises more precisely.

Dating of the exercises:

Occasionally a recipient noted on a sheet the date an exercise was given. Marie Steiner and Anna Wagner Gunnarson transcribed many exercises, and noted dates and relevant circumstances. For other exercises, dates could be deduced from letters to the recipient. Dates thus determined from such archive material are given in the index *and* on the relevant page in this volume. If a rough dating is derived only from the content of an exercise (for instance, reference to *Esoteric Science*, 1910) this is *not* included in the index but only on the relevant page.

Part Three

Originals of some texts:

"Transformation of the color of the cross…":

This text is an extract from a passage drawn from the "cultic knowledge" section of Rudolf Steiner's esoteric school. A handwritten manuscript relating to this probably existed but is no longer extant, although there are several transcripts. The text comes from an original in an unknown hand, bearing the initials "F.M.," published in full in CW 265.

Explanatory comments about the verse "More radiant than the sun…":

Text reproduced from a handwritten summary of the esoteric lesson in Berlin on October 24, 1905, for Anna Wagner, who was unable to attend because of illness. Rudolf Steiner's handwritten original is not extant. The text comes from a handwritten transcript by Guenther Wagner in the Archive.

Explanatory comments about the phrases "I am – It thinks – She feels – He wills":

Only a single page of the handwritten original of these comments is still extant. The text was reproduced from handwritten and typescript transcripts in the Archive, which were clearly passed around in this form. These transcripts diverge from each other in minor respects.

Early publications:

General Rules

Of these, the "General Conditions…" first appeared in 1947 in volume 1 of the three small volumes "From the Contents of the Esoteric School"; the part "For the Days of the Week" was published in volume 3, Dornach 1951. All of them together were first published as "General Rules" in a German edition in 1968, and in English in the volume *Esoteric Development* (SteinerBooks 2003), CW 245.

Main exercises for morning and evening:

A few of these were first published in 1947 and 1948 in volume 1 of "From the Contents of the Esoteric School"; the edition was expanded with several more verses in 1968 and published as "Instructions for Esoteric Schooling." Several more appeared in 1984 in CW 264, *From the History and Contents of the First Section of the Esoteric School 1904 – 1914*, SteinerBooks 2007. All these exercises are included in the present volume, except those contained in the letters in CW 264.

In 1968 when "Instructions for Esoteric Schooling" [CW 245, *Esoteric Development*] was published, there were as yet no plans to publish all of Steiner's esoteric teaching material as part of his collected works. This only came about later, and led to the development of the new series of CW 264–270, relating to the history and content of Rudolf Steiner's esoteric teaching activity. For this reason, the 1968 compilation entitled "Instructions…" [*Anweisungen für eine esoterische Schulung*] was divided between the volumes of this series, and no longer figures as such within the collected works. It is, however, still available as a separate edition.

LIST OF EXERCISES

with additional information
in the same sequence as in the volume

Every exercise is listed below with the initial words of the meditation verses it contains. The sub-line cites circumstances associated with each, insofar as these are known, in the following order:

- Name and location of the recipient
- Date and place where the exercise was given
- Archive number.

The Archive code shows the kind of original contained in the Archive:

    NB   designates an excerpt from one of Steiner's notebooks.
    A   designates a transcript of a text, where no original is extant

Where neither code precedes the Archive no., this means the exercise is a single sheet in Rudolf Steiner's handwriting (or a photocopy of the original).

Text that is present on the original but does not appear here in print is indicated either

        as *addition*:   text in Rudolf Steiner's handwriting
or   as *note*:   text in someone else's handwriting

A – 1

A – 2c

A – 3

A – 4

A – 7

A – 9

B – 2

Archive no. A 0068. Contained in a letter which the recipient wrote to
Steiner dated January 28, 1913.

For Herr W.B. Paton, England, around January 1, 1913, Cologne,
Archive no. 6803
Addition top left: "Paton"

I in me and I in all
For Alexander Schubert, Klagenfurt and Vienna, January 1913,
possibly February 1912, Archive no. 7037
Note: "A meditation given by Dr. Steiner to Al. Schubert, January 1912 or 13"

God creating my spirit
Around Easter 1913, Archive no. NB 186

I feel myself within my being's core
For Frau Ilse or Ernst Aisenpreis, Munich or Dornach, circa 1913, Archive no. 7034
Note: "From the estate of Ernst Aisenpreis † 1950 / B. Aisenpreis"

Turn my soul toward
For Frau Ilse or Ernst Aisenpreis, Munich or Dornach, circa 1913, Archive no. 7033
Note: "From the estate of Ernst Aisenpreis † 1950 / B. Aisenpreis"

Mothering spirit of worlds
For Robert Kaempfer, Archive no. 7101
Addition alongside "Morning," far right: "(20 mins." This may mean: 5 mins.
for the Rose Cross meditation

For Frau Elise Selin, Viborg, circa June 1, 1913, Helsinki, Archive no. A 0116

Within my heart
For Frl. (Miss) G.B., June 3, 1913, Helsinki, Archive no. 7102
Note on the reverse: "H:fors June 3 1913 Frl, G. B-m." in the handwriting
of Olga von Freymann

For Frl. (Miss) Astrid Juel, Lund, June 1913, Stockholm, Archive no. A 0094
In the handwriting of Anna Wagner Gunnarsson

As child my body raised
For Herr C.F. Dahl, Stockholm, probably June, Archive no. 5842
Note: "C.F. Dahl 1913"

Notes: "Meditation by Dr. Steiner received in Torquay, 1924"; next to the verses: "complete tranquility" and next to the drawing: "Picture something radiant yellow." It is not known how this drawing relates to the exercise.

C – 1

C – 2

C – 3

ALPHABETIC INDEX OF FIRST LINES

RUDOLF STEINER'S COLLECTED WORKS

The German Edition of Rudolf Steiner's Collected Works (the Gesamtausgabe [GA] published by Rudolf Steiner Verlag, Dornach, Switzerland) presently runs to over 354 titles, organized either by type of work (written or spoken), chronology, audience (public or other), or subject (education, art, etc.). For ease of comparison, the Collected Works in English [CW] follows the German organization exactly. A complete listing of the CWs follows with literal translations of the German titles. Other than in the case of the books published in his lifetime, titles were rarely given by Rudolf Steiner himself, and were often provided by the editors of the German editions. The titles in English are not necessarily the same as the German; and, indeed, over the past seventy-five years have frequently been different, with the same book sometimes appearing under different titles.

For ease of identification and to avoid confusion, we suggest that readers looking for a title should do so by CW number. Because the work of creating the Collected Works of Rudolf Steiner is an ongoing process, with new titles being published every year, we have not indicated in this listing which books are presently available. To find out what titles in the Collected Works are currently in print, please check our website at www.steinerbooks.org, or write to SteinerBooks 610 Main Street, Great Barrington, MA 01230 :

Written Work

CW 1	Goethe: Natural-Scientific Writings, Introduction, with Footnotes and Explanations in the text by Rudolf Steiner
CW 2	Outlines of an Epistemology of the Goethean World View, with Special Consideration of Schiller
CW 3	Truth and Science
CW 4	The Philosophy of Freedom
CW 4a	Documents to "The Philosophy of Freedom"
CW 5	Friedrich Nietzsche, A Fighter against His Own Time
CW 6	Goethe's Worldview
CW 6a	Now in CW 30
CW 7	Mysticism at the Dawn of Modern Spiritual Life and Its Relationship with Modern Worldviews
CW 8	Christianity as Mystical Fact and the Mysteries of Antiquity
CW 9	Theosophy: An Introduction into Supersensible World Knowledge and Human Purpose
CW 10	How Does One Attain Knowledge of Higher Worlds?
CW 11	From the Akasha-Chronicle
CW 12	Levels of Higher Knowledge

CW 13	Occult Science in Outline
CW 14	Four Mystery Dramas
CW 15	The Spiritual Guidance of the Individual and Humanity
CW 16	A Way to Human Self-Knowledge: Eight Meditations
CW 17	The Threshold of the Spiritual World. Aphoristic Comments
CW 18	The Riddles of Philosophy in Their History, Presented as an Outline
CW 19	Contained in CW 24
CW 20	The Riddles of the Human Being: Articulated and Unarticulated in the Thinking, Views and Opinions of a Series of German and Austrian Personalities
CW 21	The Riddles of the Soul
CW 22	Goethe's Spiritual Nature And Its Revelation In "Faust" and through the "Fairy Tale of the Snake and the Lily"
CW 23	The Central Points of the Social Question in the Necessities of Life in the Present and the Future
CW 24	Essays Concerning the Threefold Division of the Social Organism and the Period 1915-1921
CW 25	Cosmology, Religion and Philosophy
CW 26	Anthroposophical Leading Thoughts
CW 27	Fundamentals for Expansion of the Art of Healing according to Spiritual-Scientific Insights
CW 28	The Course of My Life
CW 29	Collected Essays on Dramaturgy, 1889-1900
CW 30	Methodical Foundations of Anthroposophy: Collected Essays on Philosophy, Natural Science, Aesthetics and Psychology, 1884-1901
CW 31	Collected Essays on Culture and Current Events, 1887-1901
CW 32	Collected Essays on Literature, 1884-1902
CW 33	Biographies and Biographical Sketches, 1894-1905
CW 34	Lucifer-Gnosis: Foundational Essays on Anthroposophy and Reports from the Periodicals "Lucifer" and "Lucifer-Gnosis," 1903-1908
CW 35	Philosophy and Anthroposophy: Collected Essays, 1904-1923
CW 36	The Goetheanum-Idea in the Middle of the Cultural Crisis of the Present: Collected Essays from the Periodical "Das Goetheanum," 1921-1925
CW 37	Now in CWs 260a and 251
CW 38	Letters, Vol. 1: 1881-1890
CW 39	Letters, Vol. 2: 1890-1925
CW 40	Truth-Wrought Words
CW 40a	Sayings, Poems and Mantras; Supplementary Volume
CW 42	Now in CWs 264-266

CW 78   Anthroposophy, Its Roots of Knowledge and Fruits for Life
CW 79   The Reality of the Higher Worlds
CW 80   Public lectures in various cities, 1922
CW 81   Renewal-Impulses for Culture and Science–Berlin College Course
CW 82   So that the Human Being Can Become a Complete Human Being
CW 83   Western and Eastern World-Contrast. Paths to Understanding It
         through Anthroposophy
CW 84   What Did the Goetheanum Intend and What Should
         Anthroposophy Do?

Lectures to the Members of the Anthroposophical Society

CW 88   Concerning the Astral World and Devachan
CW 89   Consciousness–Life–Form. Fundamental Principles of a Spiritual-
         Scientific Cosmology
CW 90   Participant Notes from the Lectures during the Years 1903-1905
CW 91   Participant Notes from the Lectures during the Years 1903-1905
CW 92   The Occult Truths of Ancient Myths and Sagas
CW 93   The Temple Legend and the Golden Legend
CW 93a   Fundamentals of Esotericism
CW 94   Cosmogony. Popular Occultism. The Gospel of John.
         The Theosophy in the Gospel of John
CW 95   At the Gates of Theosophy
CW 96   Origin-Impulses of Spiritual Science. Christian Esotericism in the
         Light of New Spirit-Knowledge
CW 97   The Christian Mystery
CW 98   Nature Beings and Spirit Beings – Their Effects in Our Visible
         World
CW 99   The Theosophy of the Rosicrucians
CW 100   Human Development and Christ-Knowledge
CW 101   Myths and Legends. Occult Signs and Symbols
CW 102   The Working into Human Beings by Spiritual Beings
CW 103   The Gospel of John
CW 104   The Apocalypse of John
CW 104a From the Picture-Script of the Apocalypse of John
CW 105   Universe, Earth, the Human Being: Their Being and
         Development, as well as Their Reflection in the Connection
         between Egyptian Mythology and Modern Culture
CW 106   Egyptian Myths and Mysteries in Relation to the Active Spiritual
         Forces of the Present
CW 107   Spiritual-Scientific Knowledge of the Human Being
CW 108   Answering the Questions of Life and the World through
         Anthroposophy

CW 267   Soul-Exercises: Vol. 1: Exercises with Word and Image Meditations for the Methodological Development of Higher Powers of Knowledge, 1904-1924

CW 268   Soul-Exercises: Vol. 2: Mantric Verses, 1903-1925

CW 269   Ritual Texts for the Celebration of the Free Christian Religious Instruction. The Collected Verses for Teachers and Students of the Waldorf School

CW 270   Esoteric Instructions for the First Class of the School for Spiritual Science at the Goetheanum 1924, 4 Volumes

CW 271   Art and Knowledge of Art. Foundations of a New Aesthetic

CW 272   Spiritual-Scientific Commentary on Goethe's "Faust" in Two Volumes. Vol. 1: Faust, the Striving Human Being

CW 273   Spiritual-Scientific Commentary on Goethe's "Faust" in Two Volumes. Vol. 2: The Faust-Problem

CW 274   Addresses for the Christmas Plays from the Old Folk Traditions

CW 275   Art in the Light of Mystery-Wisdom

CW 276   The Artistic in Its Mission in the World. The Genius of Language. The World of the Self-Revealing Radiant Appearances – Anthroposophy and Art. Anthroposophy and Poetry

CW 277   Eurythmy. The Revelation of the Speaking Soul

CW 277a   The Origin and Development of Eurythmy

CW 278   Eurythmy as Visible Song

CW 279   Eurythmy as Visible Speech

CW 280   The Method and Nature of Speech Formation

CW 281   The Art of Recitation and Declamation

CW 282   Speech Formation and Dramatic Art

CW 283   The Nature of Things Musical and the Experience of Tone in the Human Being

CW284/285 Images of Occult Seals and Pillars. The Munich Congress of Whitsun 1907 and Its Consequences

CW 286   Paths to a New Style of Architecture. "And the Building Becomes Human"

CW 287   The Building at Dornach as a Symbol of Historical Becoming and an Artistic Transformation Impulse

CW 288   Style-Forms in the Living Organic

CW 289   The Building-Idea of the Goetheanum: Lectures with Slides from the Years 1920-1921

CW 290   The Building-Idea of the Goetheanum: Lectures with Slides from the Years 1920-1921

CW 291   The Nature of Colors

CW 291a   Knowledge of Colors. Supplementary Volume to "The Nature of Colors"

CW 292   Art History as Image of Inner Spiritual Impulses

SIGNIFICANT EVENTS
IN THE LIFE OF RUDOLF STEINER

1829: June 23: birth of Johann Steiner (1829-1910)—Rudolf Steiner's father—in Geras, Lower Austria.

1834: May 8: birth of Franciska Blie (1834-1918)—Rudolf Steiner's mother—in Horn, Lower Austria. "My father and mother were both children of the glorious Lower Austrian forest district north of the Danube."

1860: May 16: marriage of Johann Steiner and Franciska Blie.

1861: February 25: birth of *Rudolf Joseph Lorenz Steiner* in Kraljevec, Croatia, near the border with Hungary, where Johann Steiner works as a telegrapher for the South Austria Railroad. Rudolf Steiner is baptized two days later, February 27, the date usually given as his birthday.

1862: Summer: the family moves to Mödling, Lower Austria.

1863: The family moves to Pottschach, Lower Austria, near the Styrian border, where Johann Steiner becomes stationmaster. "The view stretched to the mountains...majestic peaks in the distance and the sweet charm of nature in the immediate surroundings."

1864: November 15: birth of Rudolf Steiner's sister, Leopoldine (d. November 1, 1927). She will become a seamstress and live with her parents for the rest of her life.

1866: July 28: birth of Rudolf Steiner's deaf-mute brother, Gustav (d. May 1, 1941).

1867: Rudolf Steiner enters the village school. Following a disagreement between his father and the schoolmaster, whose wife falsely accused the boy of causing a commotion, Rudolf Steiner is taken out of school and taught at home.

1868: A critical experience. Unknown to the family, an aunt dies in a distant town. Sitting in the station waiting room, Rudolf Steiner sees her "form," which speaks to him, asking for help. "Beginning with this experience, a new soul life began in the boy, one in which not only the outer trees and mountains spoke to him, but also the worlds that lay behind them. From this moment on, the boy began to live with the spirits of nature...."

1869: The family moves to the peaceful, rural village of Neudorfl, near Wiener-Neustadt in present-day Austria. Rudolf Steiner attends the village school. Because of the "unorthodoxy" of his writing and spelling, he has to do "extra lessons."

1870: Through a book lent to him by his tutor, he discovers geometry: "To grasp something purely in the spirit brought me inner happiness. I know that I first learned happiness through geometry." The same tutor allows him to draw, while other students still struggle with their reading and writing. "An artistic element" thus enters his education.

1871: Though his parents are not religious, Rudolf Steiner becomes a "church child," a favorite of the priest, who was "an exceptional character." "Up to the age of ten or eleven, among those I came to know, he was far and away the most significant." Among other things, he introduces Steiner to Copernican, heliocentric cosmology. As an altar boy, Rudolf Steiner serves at Masses, funerals, and Corpus Christi processions. At year's end, after an incident in which he escapes a thrashing, his father forbids him to go to church.

1872: Rudolf Steiner transfers to grammar school in Wiener-Neustadt, a five-mile walk from home, which must be done in all weathers.

1873-75: Through his teachers and on his own, Rudolf Steiner has many wonderful experiences with science and mathematics. Outside school, he teaches himself analytic geometry, trigonometry, differential equations, and calculus.

1876: Rudolf Steiner begins tutoring other students. He learns bookbinding from his father. He also teaches himself stenography.

1877: Rudolf Steiner discovers Kant's *Critique of Pure Reason*, which he reads and rereads. He also discovers and reads von Rotteck's *World History*.

1878: He studies extensively in contemporary psychology and philosophy.

1879: Rudolf Steiner graduates from high school with honors. His father is transferred to Inzersdorf, near Vienna. He uses his first visit to Vienna "to purchase a great number of philosophy books"—Kant, Fichte, Schelling, and Hegel, as well as numerous histories of philosophy. His aim: to find a path from the "I" to nature.

October 1879-1883: Rudolf Steiner attends the Technical College in Vienna—to study mathematics, chemistry, physics, mineralogy, botany, zoology, biology, geology, and mechanics—with a scholarship. He also attends lectures in history and literature, while avidly reading philosophy on his own. His two favorite professors are Karl Julius Schröer (German language and literature) and Edmund Reitlinger (physics). He also audits lectures by Robert Zimmerman on aesthetics and Franz Brentano on philosophy. During this year he begins his friendship with Moritz Zitter (1861-1921), who will help support him financially when he is in Berlin.

1880: Rudolf Steiner attends lectures on Schiller and Goethe by Karl Julius Schröer, who becomes his mentor. Also "through a remarkable combination of circumstances," he meets Felix Koguzki, an "herb gatherer" and healer, who could "see deeply into the secrets of nature." Rudolf Steiner will meet and study with this "emissary of the Master" throughout his time in Vienna.

1881: January: "... I didn't sleep a wink. I was busy with philosophical problems until about 12:30 a.m. Then, finally, I threw myself down on my couch. All my striving during the previous year had been to research whether the following statement by Schelling was true or not: *Within everyone dwells a secret, marvelous capacity to draw back from the stream of time—out of the self clothed in all that comes to us from outside—into our innermost being and there, in the immutable form of the Eternal, to look into ourselves.* I believe, and I am still quite certain of it, that I discovered this capacity in myself; I had long had an inkling of it. Now the whole of idealist philosophy stood before me in modified form. What's a sleepless night compared to that!"

Rudolf Steiner begins communicating with leading thinkers of the day, who send him books in return, which he reads eagerly.

July: "I am not one of those who dives into the day like an animal in human form. I pursue a quite specific goal, an idealistic aim—knowledge of the truth! This cannot be done offhandedly. It requires the greatest striving in the world, free of all egotism, and equally of all resignation."

August: Steiner puts down on paper for the first time thoughts for a "Philosophy of Freedom." "The striving for the absolute: this human yearning is freedom." He also seeks to outline a "peasant philosophy," describing what the worldview of a "peasant"—one who lives close to the earth and the old ways—really is.

1881-1882: Felix Koguzki, the herb gatherer, reveals himself to be the envoy of another, higher initiatory personality, who instructs Rudolf Steiner to penetrate Fichte's philosophy and to master modern scientific thinking as a preparation for right entry into the spirit. This "Master" also teaches him the double (evolutionary and involutionary) nature of time.

1882: Through the offices of Karl Julius Schröer, Rudolf Steiner is asked by Joseph Kurschner to edit Goethe's scientific works for the *Deutschen National-Literatur* edition. He writes "A Possible Critique of Atomistic Concepts" and sends it to Friedrich Theodore Vischer.

1883: Rudolf Steiner completes his college studies and begins work on the Goethe project.

1884: First volume of Goethe's *Scientific Writings* (CW 1) appears (March). He lectures on Goethe and Lessing, and Goethe's approach to science. In July, he enters the household of Ladislaus and Pauline Specht as tutor to the four Specht boys. He will live there until 1890. At this time, he meets Josef Breuer (1842-1925), the coauthor with Sigmund Freud of *Studies in Hysteria*, who is the Specht family doctor.

1885: While continuing to edit Goethe's writings, Rudolf Steiner reads deeply in contemporary philosophy (Edouard von Hartmann, Johannes Volkelt, and Richard Wahle, among others).

1886: May: Rudolf Steiner sends Kurschner the manuscript of *Outlines of Goethe's Theory of Knowledge* (CW 2), which appears in October, and which he sends out widely. He also meets the poet Marie Eugenie Delle Grazie and writes "Nature and Our Ideals" for her. He attends her salon, where he meets many priests, theologians, and philosophers, who will become his friends. Meanwhile, the director of the Goethe Archive in Weimar requests his collaboration with the *Sophien* edition of Goethe's works, particularly the writings on color.

1887: At the beginning of the year, Rudolf Steiner is very sick. As the year progresses and his health improves, he becomes increasingly "a man of letters," lecturing, writing essays, and taking part in Austrian cultural life. In August-September, the second volume of Goethe's *Scientific Writings* appears.

1888: January-July: Rudolf Steiner assumes editorship of the "German Weekly" (*Deutsche Wochenschrift*). He begins lecturing more intensively, giving, for example, a lecture titled "Goethe as Father of a New Aesthetics." He meets and becomes soul friends with Friedrich Eckstein (1861-1939), a vegetarian, philosopher of symbolism, alchemist, and musician, who will introduce him to various spiritual currents (including theosophy) and with whom he will meditate and interpret esoteric and alchemical texts.

1889: Rudolf Steiner first reads Nietzsche (*Beyond Good and Evil*). He encounters Theosophy again and learns of Madame Blavatsky in the Theosophical circle around Marie Lang (1858-1934). Here he also meets well-known figures of Austrian life, as well as esoteric figures like the occultist Franz Hartman and Karl Leinigen-Billigen (translator of C.G. Harrison's *The Transcendental Universe*.) During this period, Steiner first reads A.P. Sinnett's *Esoteric Buddhism* and Mabel Collins's *Light on the Path*. He also begins traveling, visiting Budapest, Weimar, and Berlin (where he meets philosopher Edouard von Hartman).

1890: Rudolf Steiner finishes volume 3 of Goethe's scientific writings. He begins his doctoral dissertation, which will become *Truth and Science* (CW 3). He also meets the poet and feminist Rosa Mayreder (1858-1938), with whom he can exchange his most intimate thoughts. In September, Rudolf Steiner moves to Weimar to work in the Goethe-Schiller Archive.

1891: Volume 3 of the Kurschner edition of Goethe appears. Meanwhile, Rudolf Steiner edits Goethe's studies in mineralogy and scientific writings for the *Sophien* edition. He meets Ludwig Laistner of the Cotta Publishing Company, who asks for a book on the basic question of metaphysics. From this will result, ultimately, *The Philosophy of Freedom* (CW 4), which will be published not by Cotta but by Emil Felber. In October, Rudolf Steiner takes the oral exam for a doctorate in philosophy, mathematics, and mechanics at Rostock University, receiving his doctorate on the twenty-sixth. In November, he gives his first lecture on Goethe's "Fairy Tale" in Vienna.

1892: Rudolf Steiner continues work at the Goethe-Schiller Archive and on his *Philosophy of Freedom*. *Truth and Science*, his doctoral dissertation, is published. Steiner undertakes to write introductions to books on Schopenhauer and Jean Paul for Cotta. At year's end, he finds lodging with Anna Eunike, née Schulz (1853-1911), a widow with four daughters and a son. He also develops a friendship with Otto Erich Hartleben (1864-1905) with whom he shares literary interests.

1893: Rudolf Steiner begins his habit of producing many reviews and articles. In March, he gives a lecture titled "Hypnotism, with Reference to Spiritism." In September, volume 4 of the Kurschner edition is completed. In November, *The Philosophy of Freedom* appears. This year, too, he meets John Henry Mackay (1864-1933), the anarchist, and Max Stirner, a scholar and biographer.

1894: Rudolf Steiner meets Elisabeth Förster Nietzsche, the philosopher's sister, and begins to read Nietzsche in earnest, beginning with the as yet unpublished *Antichrist*. He also meets Ernst Haeckel (1834-1919). In the fall, he begins to write *Nietzsche, A Fighter against His Time* (CW 5).

1895: May, *Nietzsche, A Fighter against His Time* appears.

1896: January 22: Rudolf Steiner sees Friedrich Nietzsche for the first and only time. Moves between the Nietzsche and the Goethe-Schiller Archives, where he completes his work before year's end. He falls out with Elisabeth Förster Nietzsche, thus ending his association with the Nietzsche Archive.

1897: Rudolf Steiner finishes the manuscript of *Goethe's Worldview* (CW 6). He moves to Berlin with Anna Eunike and begins editorship of the *Magazin fur Literatur*. From now on, Steiner will write countless reviews, literary and philosophical articles, and so on. He begins lecturing at the "Free Literary Society." In September, he attends the Zionist Congress in Basel. He sides with Dreyfus in the Dreyfus affair.

1898: Rudolf Steiner is very active as an editor in the political, artistic, and theatrical life of Berlin. He becomes friendly with John Henry Mackay and poet Ludwig Jacobowski (1868-1900). He joins Jacobowski's circle of writers, artists, and scientists—"The Coming Ones" (*Die Kommenden*)—and contributes lectures to the group until 1903. He also lectures at the "League for College Pedagogy." He writes an article for Goethe's sesquicentennial, "Goethe's Secret Revelation," on the "Fairy Tale of the Green Snake and the Beautiful Lily."

1898-99: "This was a trying time for my soul as I looked at Christianity.... I was able to progress only by contemplating, by means of spiritual perception, the evolution of Christianity . . . . Conscious knowledge of real Christianity began to dawn in me around the turn of the century. This seed continued to develop. My soul trial occurred shortly before the beginning of the twentieth century. It was decisive for my soul's development that I stood spiritually before the Mystery of Golgotha in a deep and solemn celebration of knowledge."

1899: Rudolf Steiner begins teaching and giving lectures and lecture cycles at the Workers' College, founded by Wilhelm Liebknecht (1826-1900). He will continue to do so until 1904. Writes: *Literature and Spiritual Life in the Nineteenth Century; Individualism in Philosophy; Haeckel and His Opponents; Poetry in the Present;* and begins what will become (fifteen years later) *The Riddles of Philosophy* (CW 18). He also meets many artists and writers, including Käthe Kollwitz, Stefan

Zweig, and Rainer Maria Rilke. On October 31, he marries Anna Eunike.

1900: "I thought that the turn of the century must bring humanity a new light. It seemed to me that the separation of human thinking and willing from the spirit had peaked. A turn or reversal of direction in human evolution seemed to me a necessity." Rudolf Steiner finishes *World and Life Views in the Nineteenth Century* (the second part of what will become *The Riddles of Philosophy*) and dedicates it to Ernst Haeckel. It is published in March. He continues lecturing at *Die Kommenden*, whose leadership he assumes after the death of Jacobowski. Also, he gives the Gutenberg Jubilee lecture before 7,000 typesetters and printers. In September, Rudolf Steiner is invited by Count and Countess Brockdorff to lecture in the Theosophical Library. His first lecture is on Nietzsche. His second lecture is titled "Goethe's Secret Revelation." October 6, he begins a lecture cycle on the mystics that will become *Mystics after Modernism* (CW 7). November-December: "Marie von Sivers appears in the audience...." Also in November, Steiner gives his first lecture at the Giordano Bruno Bund (where he will continue to lecture until May, 1905). He speaks on Bruno and modern Rome, focusing on the importance of the philosophy of Thomas Aquinas as monism.

1901: In continual financial straits, Rudolf Steiner's early friends Moritz Zitter and Rosa Mayreder help support him. In October, he begins the lecture cycle *Christianity as Mystical Fact* (CW 8) at the Theosophical Library. In November, he gives his first "Theosophical lecture" on Goethe's "Fairy Tale" in Hamburg at the invitation of Wilhelm Hubbe-Schleiden. He also attends a tea to celebrate the founding of the Theosophical Society at Count and Countess Brockdorff's. He gives a lecture cycle, "From Buddha to Christ," for the circle of the *Kommenden*. November 17, Marie von Sivers asks Rudolf Steiner if Theosophy does not need a Western-Christian spiritual movement (to complement Theosophy's Eastern emphasis). "The question was posed. Now, following spiritual laws, I could begin to give an answer...." In December, Rudolf Steiner writes his first article for a Theosophical publication. At year's end, the Brockdorffs and possibly Wilhelm Hubbe-Schleiden ask Rudolf Steiner to join the Theosophical Society and undertake the leadership of the German Section. Rudolf Steiner agrees, on the condition that Marie von Sivers (then in Italy) work with him.

1902: Beginning in January, Rudolf Steiner attends the opening of the Workers' School in Spandau with Rosa Luxemburg (1870-1919). January 17, Rudolf Steiner joins the Theosophical Society. In April, he is asked to become general secretary of the German Section of the Theosophical Society, and works on preparations for its founding. In July, he visits London for a Theosophical congress. He meets Bertram

Keightly, G.R.S. Mead, A.P. Sinnett, and Annie Besant, among others. In September, *Christianity as Mystical Fact* appears. In October, Rudolf Steiner gives his first public lecture on theosophy ("Monism and Theosophy") to about three hundred people at the Giordano Bruno Bund. On October 19-21, the German Section of the Theosophical Society has its first meeting; Rudolf Steiner is the general secretary, and Annie Besant attends. Steiner lectures on practical karma studies. On October 23, Annie Besant inducts Rudolf Steiner into the Esoteric School of the Theosophical Society. On October 25, Steiner begins a weekly series of lectures: "The Field of Theosophy." During this year, Rudolf Steiner also first meets Ita Wegman (1876-1943), who will become his close collaborator in his final years.

1903: Rudolf Steiner holds about 300 lectures and seminars. In May, the first issue of the periodical *Luzifer* appears. In June, Rudolf Steiner visits London for the first meeting of the Federation of the European Sections of the Theosophical Society, where he meets Colonel Olcott. He begins to write *Theosophy* (CW 9).

1904: Rudolf Steiner continues lecturing at the Workers' College and elsewhere (about 90 lectures), while lecturing intensively all over Germany among Theosophists (about a 140 lectures). In February, he meets Carl Unger (1878-1929), who will become a member of the board of the Anthroposophical Society (1913). In March, he meets Michael Bauer (1871-1929), a Christian mystic, who will also be on the board. In May, *Theosophy* appears, with the dedication: "To the spirit of Giordano Bruno." Rudolf Steiner and Marie von Sivers visit London for meetings with Annie Besant. June: Rudolf Steiner and Marie von Sivers attend the meeting of the Federation of European Sections of the Theosophical Society in Amsterdam. In July, Steiner begins the articles in *Luzifer-Gnosis* that will become *How to Know Higher Worlds* (CW 10) and *Cosmic Memory* (CW 11). In September, Annie Besant visits Germany. In December, Steiner lectures on Freemasonry. He mentions the High Grade Masonry derived from John Yarker and represented by Theodore Reuss and Karl Kellner as a blank slate "into which a good image could be placed."

1905: This year, Steiner ends his non-Theosophical lecturing activity. Supported by Marie von Sivers, his Theosophical lecturing—both in public and in the Theosophical Society—increases significantly: "The German Theosophical Movement is of exceptional importance." Steiner recommends reading, among others, Fichte, Jacob Boehme, and Angelus Silesius. He begins to introduce Christian themes into Theosophy. He also begins to work with doctors (Felix Peipers and Ludwig Noll). In July, he is in London for the Federation of European Sections, where he attends a lecture by Annie Besant: "I have seldom seen Mrs. Besant speak in so inward and heartfelt a manner...." "Through Mrs. Besant I have found the way to H.P. Blavatsky."

September to October, he gives a course of thirty-one lectures for a small group of esoteric students. In October, the annual meeting of the German Section of the Theosophical Society, which still remains very small, takes place. Rudolf Steiner reports membership has risen from 121 to 377 members. In November, seeking to establish esoteric "continuity," Rudolf Steiner and Marie von Sivers participate in a "Memphis-Misraim" Masonic ceremony. They pay forty-five marks for membership. "Yesterday, you saw how little remains of former esoteric institutions." "We are dealing only with a 'framework'… for the present, nothing lies behind it. The occult powers have completely withdrawn."

1906: Expansion of Theosophical work. Rudolf Steiner gives about 245 lectures, only 44 of which take place in Berlin. Cycles are given in Paris, Leipzig, Stuttgart, and Munich. Esoteric work also intensifies. Rudolf Steiner begins writing *An Outline of Esoteric Science* (CW 13). In January, Rudolf Steiner receives permission (a patent) from the Great Orient of the Scottish A & A Thirty-Three Degree Rite of the Order of the Ancient Freemasons of the Memphis-Misraim Rite to direct a chapter under the name "Mystica Aeterna." This will become the "Cognitive Cultic Section" (also called "Misraim Service") of the Esoteric School. (See: *From the History and Contents of the Cognitive Cultic Section* (CW 264). During this time, Steiner also meets Albert Schweitzer. In May, he is in Paris, where he visits Edouard Schuré. Many Russians attend his lectures (including Konstantin Balmont, Dimitri Mereszkovski, Zinaida Hippius, and Maximilian Woloshin). He attends the General Meeting of the European Federation of the Theosophical Society, at which Col. Olcott is present for the last time. He spends the year's end in Venice and Rome, where he writes and works on his translation of H.P. Blavatsky's *Key to Theosophy*.

1907: Further expansion of the German Theosophical Movement according to the Rosicrucian directive to "introduce spirit into the world"—in education, in social questions, in art, and in science. In February, Col. Olcott dies in Adyar. Before he dies, Olcott indicates that "the Masters" wish Annie Besant to succeed him: much politicking ensues. Rudolf Steiner supports Besant's candidacy. April-May: preparations for the Congress of the Federation of European Sections of the Theosophical Society—the great, watershed Whitsun "Munich Congress," attended by Annie Besant and others. Steiner decides to separate Eastern and Western (Christian-Rosicrucian) esoteric schools. He takes his esoteric school out of the Theosophical Society (Besant and Rudolf Steiner are "in harmony" on this). Steiner makes his first lecture tours to Austria and Hungary. That summer, he is in Italy. In September, he visits Edouard Schuré, who will write the introduction to the French edition of *Christianity as Mystical Fact* in Barr, Alsace. Rudolf Steiner writes the autobiographical statement known as the "Barr Document." In *Luzifer–Gnosis*, "The Education of the Child" appears.

1908: The movement grows (membership: 1150). Lecturing expands. Steiner makes his first extended lecture tour to Holland and Scandinavia, as well as visits to Naples and Sicily. Themes: St. John's Gospel, the Apocalypse, Egypt, science, philosophy, and logic. *Luzifer-Gnosis* ceases publication. In Berlin, Marie von Sivers (with Johanna Mücke (1864-1949) forms the *Philosophisch-Theosophisch* (after 1915 *Philosophisch-Anthroposophisch*) *Verlag* to publish Steiner's work. Steiner gives lecture cycles titled *The Gospel of St. John* (CW 103) and *The Apocalypse* (104).

1909: *An Outline of Esoteric Science* appears. Lecturing and travel continues. Rudolf Steiner's spiritual research expands to include the polarity of Lucifer and Ahriman; the work of great individualities in history; the Maitreya Buddha and the Bodhisattvas; spiritual economy (CW 109); the work of the spiritual hierarchies in heaven and on Earth (CW 110). He also deepens and intensifies his research into the Gospels, giving lectures on the Gospel of St. Luke (CW 114) with the first mention of two Jesus children. Meets and becomes friends with Christian Morgenstern (1871-1914). In April, he lays the foundation stone for the Malsch model—the building that will lead to the first Goetheanum. In May, the International Congress of the Federation of European Sections of the Theosophical Society takes place in Budapest. Rudolf Steiner receives the Subba Row medal for *How to Know Higher Worlds*. During this time, Charles W. Leadbeater discovers Jiddu Krishnamurti (1895-1986) and proclaims him the future "world teacher," the bearer of the Maitreya Buddha and the "reappearing Christ." In October, Steiner delivers seminal lectures on "anthroposophy," which he will try, unsuccessfully, to rework over the next years into the unfinished work, *Anthroposophy (A Fragment)* (CW 45).

1910: New themes: *The Reappearance of Christ in the Etheric* (CW 118); *The Fifth Gospel; The Mission of Folk Souls* (CW 121); *Occult History* (CW 126); the evolving development of etheric cognitive capacities. Rudolf Steiner continues his Gospel research with *The Gospel of St. Matthew* (CW 123). In January, his father dies. In April, he takes a month-long trip to Italy, including Rome, Monte Cassino, and Sicily. He also visits Scandinavia again. July-August, he writes the first mystery drama, *The Portal of Initiation* (CW 14). In November, he gives "psychosophy" lectures. In December, he submits "On the Psychological Foundations and Epistemological Framework of Theosophy" to the International Philosophical Congress in Bologna.

1911: The crisis in the Theosophical Society deepens. In January, "The Order of the Rising Sun," which will soon become "The Order of the Star in the East," is founded for the coming world teacher, Krishnamurti. At the same time, Marie von Sivers, Rudolf Steiner's coworker, falls ill. Fewer lectures are given, but important new ground is broken. In Prague, in March, Steiner meets Franz Kafka (1883-1924) and Hugo Bergmann (1883-1975). In April, he delivers his paper to the

Philosophical Congress. He writes the second mystery drama, *The Soul's Probation* (CW 14). Also, while Marie von Sivers is convalescing, Rudolf Steiner begins work on *Calendar 1912/1913*, which will contain the "Calendar of the Soul" meditations. On March 19, Anna (Eunike) Steiner dies. In September, Rudolf Steiner visits Einsiedeln, birthplace of Paracelsus. In December, Friedrich Rittelmeyer, future founder of the Christian Community, meets Rudolf Steiner. The *Johannes-Bauverein*, the "building committee," which would lead to the first Goetheanum (first planned for Munich), is also founded, and a preliminary committee for the founding of an independent association is created that, in the following year, will become the Anthroposophical Society. Important lecture cycles include *Occult Physiology* (CW 128); *Wonders of the World* (CW 129); *From Jesus to Christ* (CW 131). Other themes: esoteric Christianity; Christian Rosenkreutz; the spiritual guidance of humanity; the sense world and the world of the spirit.

1912:   Despite the ongoing, now increasing crisis in the Theosophical Society, much is accomplished: *Calendar 1912/1913* is published; eurythmy is created; both the third mystery drama, *The Guardian of the Threshold* (CW 14) and *A Way of Self-Knowledge* (CW 16) are written. New (or renewed) themes included life between death and rebirth and karma and reincarnation. Other lecture cycles: *Spiritual Beings in the Heavenly Bodies and the Kingdoms of Nature* (CW 136); *The Human Being in the Light of Occultism, Theosophy, and Philosophy* (CW 137); *The Gospel of St. Mark* (CW 139); and *The Bhagavad Gita and the Epistles of Paul* (CW 142). On May 8, Rudolf Steiner celebrates White Lotus Day, H.P. Blavatsky's death day, which he had faithfully observed for the past decade, for the last time. In August, Rudolf Steiner suggests the "independent association" be called the "Anthroposophical Society." In September, the first eurythmy course takes place. In October, Rudolf Steiner declines recognition of a Theosophical Society lodge dedicated to the Star of the East and decides to expel all Theosophical Society members belonging to the order. Also, with Marie von Sivers, he first visits Dornach, near Basel, Switzerland, and they stand on the hill where the Goetheanum will be. In November, a Theosophical Society lodge is opened by direct mandate from Adyar (Annie Besant). In December, a meeting of the German section occurs at which it is decided that belonging to the Order of the Star of the East is incompatible with membership in the Theosophical Society. December 28: informal founding of the Anthroposophical Society in Berlin.

1913:   Expulsion of the German section from the Theosophical Society. February 2-3: Foundation meeting of the Anthroposophical Society. Board members include: Marie von Sivers, Michael Bauer, and Carl Unger. September 20: Laying of the foundation stone for the *Johannes Bau* (Goetheanum) in Dornach. Building begins immediately. The third mystery drama, *The Soul's Awakening* (CW 14), is completed.

Also: *The Threshold of the Spiritual World* (CW 147). Lecture cycles include: *The Bhagavad Gita and the Epistles of Paul* and *The Esoteric Meaning of the Bhagavad Gita* (CW 146), which the Russian philosopher Nikolai Berdyaev attends; *The Mysteries of the East and of Christianity* (CW 144); *The Effects of Esoteric Development* (CW 145); and *The Fifth Gospel* (CW 148). In May, Rudolf Steiner is in London and Paris, where anthroposophical work continues.

1914: Building continues on the *Johannes Bau* (Goetheanum) in Dornach, with artists and coworkers from seventeen nations. The general assembly of the Anthroposophical Society takes place. In May, Rudolf Steiner visits Paris, as well as Chartres Cathedral. June 28: assassination in Sarajevo ("Now the catastrophe has happened!"). August 1: War is declared. Rudolf Steiner returns to Germany from Dornach—he will travel back and forth. He writes the last chapter of *The Riddles of Philosophy*. Lecture cycles include: *Human and Cosmic Thought* (CW 151); *Inner Being of Humanity between Death and a New Birth* (CW 153); *Occult Reading and Occult Hearing* (CW 156). December 24: marriage of Rudolf Steiner and Marie von Sivers.

1915: Building continues. Life after death becomes a major theme, also art. Writes: *Thoughts during a Time of War* (CW 24). Lectures include: *The Secret of Death* (CW 159); *The Uniting of Humanity through the Christ Impulse* (CW 165).

1916: Rudolf Steiner begins work with Edith Maryon (1872-1924) on the sculpture "The Representative of Humanity" ("The Group"—Christ, Lucifer, and Ahriman). He also works with the alchemist Alexander von Bernus on the quarterly *Das Reich*. He writes *The Riddle of Humanity* (CW 20). Lectures include: *Necessity and Freedom in World History and Human Action* (CW 166); *Past and Present in the Human Spirit* (CW 167); *The Karma of Vocation* (CW 172); *The Karma of Untruthfulness* (CW 173).

1917: Russian Revolution. The U.S. enters the war. Building continues. Rudolf Steiner delineates the idea of the "threefold nature of the human being" (in a public lecture March 15) and the "threefold nature of the social organism" (hammered out in May-June with the help of Otto von Lerchenfeld and Ludwig Polzer-Hoditz in the form of two documents titled *Memoranda*, which were distributed in high places). August-September: Rudolf Steiner writes *The Riddles of the Soul* (CW 20). Also: commentary on "The Chemical Wedding of Christian Rosenkreutz" for Alexander Bernus (*Das Reich*). Lectures include: *The Karma of Materialism* (CW 176); *The Spiritual Background of the Outer World: The Fall of the Spirits of Darkness* (CW 177).

1918: March 18: peace treaty of Brest-Litovsk—"Now everything will truly enter chaos! What is needed is cultural renewal." June: Rudolf Steiner visits Karlstein (Grail) Castle outside Prague. Lecture cycle: *From Symptom to Reality in Modern History* (CW 185). In mid-November,

Emil Molt, of the Waldorf-Astoria Cigarette Company, has the idea of founding a school for his workers' children.

1919: Focus on the threefold social organism: tireless travel, countless lectures, meetings, and publications. At the same time, a new public stage of Anthroposophy emerges as cultural renewal begins. The coming years will see initiatives in pedagogy, medicine, pharmacology, and agriculture. January 27: threefold meeting: " We must first of all, with the money we have, found free schools that can bring people what they need." February: first public eurythmy performance in Zurich. Also: "Appeal to the German People" (CW 24), circulated March 6 as a newspaper insert. In April, *Toward Social Renewal* (CW 23)—"perhaps the most widely read of all books on politics appearing since the war"—appears. Rudolf Steiner is asked to undertake the "direction and leadership" of the school founded by the Waldorf-Astoria Company. Rudolf Steiner begins to talk about the "renewal" of education. May 30: a building is selected and purchased for the future Waldorf School. August-September, Rudolf Steiner gives a lecture course for Waldorf teachers, *The Foundations of Human Experience (Study of Man)* (CW 293). September 7: Opening of the first Waldorf School. December (into January): first science course, the *Light Course* (CW 320).

1920: The Waldorf School flourishes. New threefold initiatives. Founding of limited companies *Der Kommenden Tag* and *Futurum A.G.* to infuse spiritual values into the economic realm. Rudolf Steiner also focuses on the sciences. Lectures: *Introducing Anthroposophical Medicine* (CW 312); *The Warmth Course* (CW 321); *The Boundaries of Natural Science* (CW 322); *The Redemption of Thinking* (CW 74). February: Johannes Werner Klein—later a cofounder of the Christian Community—asks Rudolf Steiner about the possibility of a "religious renewal," a "Johannine church." In March, Rudolf Steiner gives the first course for doctors and medical students. In April, a divinity student asks Rudolf Steiner a second time about the possibility of religious renewal. September 27-October 16: anthroposophical "university course." December: lectures titled *The Search for the New Isis* (CW 202).

1921: Rudolf Steiner continues his intensive work on cultural renewal, including the uphill battle for the threefold social order. "University" arts, scientific, theological, and medical courses include: *The Astronomy Course* (CW 323); *Observation, Mathematics, and Scientific Experiment* (CW 324); the *Second Medical Course* (CW 313); *Color.* In June and September-October, Rudolf Steiner also gives the first two "priests' courses" (CW 342 and 343). The "youth movement" gains momentum. Magazines are founded: *Die Drei* (January), and—under the editorship of Albert Steffen (1884-1963)—the weekly, *Das Goetheanum* (August). In February-March, Rudolf Steiner takes his first trip outside Germany since the war (Holland). On April 7, Steiner receives a letter regarding "religious renewal," and May 22-23, he agrees to address the question in a practical way. In June, the Klinical-Therapeutic Institute opens in Arlesheim under the direction of Dr. Ita Wegman. In August, the Chemical-Pharmaceutical Laboratory opens in Arlesheim (Oskar Schmiedel and Ita Wegman, directors). The Clinical Therapeutic Institute is inaugurated in Stuttgart (Dr. Ludwig Noll, director); also the Research Laboratory in Dornach (Ehrenfried Pfeiffer and Gunther Wachsmuth, directors). In November-December, Rudolf Steiner visits Norway.

1922: The first half of the year involves very active public lecturing (thousands attend); in the second half, Rudolf Steiner begins to withdraw and turn toward the Society—"The Society is asleep." It is "too weak" to do what is asked of it. The businesses—*Die Kommenden Tag* and *Futura A.G.*—fail. In January, with the help of an agent, Steiner undertakes a twelve-city German tour, accompanied by eurythmy performances. In two weeks he speaks to more than 2,000 people. In April, he gives a "university course" in The Hague. He also visits England. In June, he is in Vienna for the East-West Congress. In August-September, he is back in England for the Oxford Conference on Education. Returning to Dornach, he gives the lectures *Philosophy, Cosmology, and Religion* (CW 215), and gives the third priest's course (CW 344). On September 16, The Christian Community is founded. In October-November, Steiner is in Holland and England. He also speaks to the youth: *The Youth Course* (CW 217). In December, Steiner gives lectures titled *The Origins of Natural Science* (CW 326), and *Humanity and the World of Stars: The Spiritual Communion of Humanity* (CW 219). December 31: Fire at the Goetheanum, which is destroyed.

1923: Despite the fire, Rudolf Steiner continues his work unabated. A very hard year. Internal dispersion, dissension, and apathy abound. There is conflict—between old and new visions—within the society. A wake-up call is needed, and Rudolf Steiner responds with renewed lecturing vitality. His focus: the spiritual context of human life; initiation science; the course of the year; and community building. As a foundation for an artistic school, he creates a series of pastel sketches. Lecture cycles: *The Anthroposophical Movement; Initiation Science* (CW 227) (in England at the Penmaenmawr Summer School); *The Four Seasons and the Archangels* (CW 229); *Harmony of the Creative Word* (CW 230); *The Supersensible Human* (CW 231), given in Holland for the founding of the Dutch society. On November 10, in response to the failed Hitler-Ludendorf putsch in Munich, Steiner closes his Berlin residence and moves the *Philosophisch-Anthroposophisch Verlag* (Press) to Dornach. On December 9, Steiner begins the serialization of his *Autobiography: The Course of My Life* (CW 28) in *Das Goetheanum*. It will continue to appear weekly, without a break, until his death. Late December-early January: Rudolf Steiner refounds the Anthroposophical Society (about 12,000 members internationally) and takes over its leadership. The new board members are: Marie Steiner, Ita Wegman, Albert Steffen, Elizabeth Vreede, and Guenther Wachsmuth. (See *The Christmas Meeting for the Founding of the General Anthroposophical Society* (CW 260). Accompanying lectures: *Mystery Knowledge and Mystery Centers* (CW 232); *World History in the Light of Anthroposophy* (CW 233). December 25: the Foundation Stone is laid (in the hearts of members) in the form of the "Foundation Stone Meditation."

1924:   January 1: having founded the Anthroposophical Society and taken over its leadership, Rudolf Steiner has the task of "reforming" it. The process begins with a weekly newssheet ("What's Happening in the Anthroposophical Society") in which Rudolf Steiner's "Letters to Members" and "Anthroposophical Leading Thoughts" appear (CW 26). The next step is the creation of a new esoteric class, the "first class" of the "University of Spiritual Science" (which was to have been followed, had Rudolf Steiner lived longer, by two more advanced classes). Then comes a new language for Anthroposophy—practical, phenomenological, and direct; and Rudolf Steiner creates the model for the second Goetheanum. He begins the series of extensive "karma" lectures (CW 235-40); and finally, responding to needs, he creates two new initiatives: biodynamic agriculture and curative education. After the middle of the year, rumors begin to circulate regarding Steiner's health. Lectures: January-February, *Anthroposophy* (CW 234); February: *Tone Eurythmy* (CW 278); June: *The Agriculture Course* (CW 327); June-July: Speech [?] Eurythmy (CW 279); *Curative Education* (CW 317); August: (England, "Second International Summer School"), *Initiation Consciousness: True and False Paths in Spiritual Investigation* (CW 243); September: *Pastoral Medicine* (CW 318). On September 26, for the first time, Rudolf Steiner cancels a lecture. On September 28, he gives his last lecture. On September 29, he withdraws to his studio in the carpenter's shop; now he is definitively ill. Cared for by Ita Wegman, he continues working, however, and writing the weekly installments of his *Autobiography* and *Letters to the Members/Leading Thoughts* (CW 26).

1925:   Rudolf Steiner, while continuing to work, continues to weaken. He finishes *Extending Practical Medicine* (CW 27) with Ita Wegman. On March 30, around ten in the morning, Rudolf Steiner dies.